THE PILGRIM COLONY

The Saint Sebald Colony, the Two Wartburgs, and the Synods of Iowa and Missouri

by

Albert Llewellyn Hock

Lutheran University Press
Minneapolis, Minnesota

THE PILGRIM COLONY

A History of
Saint Sebald Evangelical Lutheran Church
Wartburg College and Wartburg Theological Seminary 1852-1930
the Evangelical Lutheran Synod of Iowa and Other States
and Their Relationships to
the German Evangelical Lutheran Synod of Missouri, Ohio
and Other States
1840 to 1940

by

Albert Llewellyn Hock

The Pilgrim Colony
The Saint Sebald Colony, the Two Wartburgs, and the Synods of Iowa and Missouri

by Albert Llewellyn Hock

Copyright 2004 Lutheran University Press. All rights reserved.All rights reserved. Except for brief quotations in critical articles or reviews, no part of this book may be reproduced in any manner without prior permission of the publisher.

Library of Congress Cataloging-in-Publication data

Hock, Albert Llewellyn, 1918-
    The pilgrim colony : the Saint Sebald Colony, the two Wartburgs, and the synods of Iowa and Missouri / by Albert Llewellyn Hock.
        p.cm.
    Includes bibliographic references
    ISBN-10: 1-932688-06-4 (alk. paper)
    ISBN-13: 1-978-932688-06-7
        1. Saint Sebald Evangelical Lutheran Church (Strawberry Point, Iowa) 2. Strawberry Point (Iowa)—Church history. 3. Lutheran Church-Missouri Synod—History. 4. Evangelical Lutheran Synod of Iowa and Other states—History. 5. Wartburg College—History. 6. Wartburg Seminary—History. I. titles.

BX8076.S795H63 2005
284.1'7736—dc22

                                                        200504770

Lutheran University Press, PO Box 390759, Minneapolis, Minnesota 55439
Manufactured in the United States of America

CONTENTS

FOREWORD

I began this study at the request of the church council of Saint Sebald Lutheran Church of rural Strawberry Point, Iowa, contemplating a mere pamphlet, but hoping for a more complete history of the congregation than had been accomplished before. It soon became clear that the full story of Saint Sebald's life and ministry could not be told in isolation. Saint Sebald's involvement with Wartburg Seminary, Wartburg College, the Evangelical Synod of Iowa and Other States, and the Evangelical Lutheran Synod of Missouri, Ohio, and Other States was too significant to ignore. Furthermore, it is important to history that the story of Saint Sebald's role in the development of the Lutheran church in the Midwest not be forgotten.

I have told the story of the two Wartburgs and of the synods they and the Saint Sebald colony were involved with from the 1840s to the 1930s. In 1930 the histories of the Iowa, Ohio, and Buffalo synods closed when they merged into the American Lutheran Church. By 1935 all the college roots at Waverly and Clinton, Iowa, Saint Paul, Minnesota, Hebron, Nebraska, and Eureka, South Dakota, had merged into the single stalk that is Wartburg College. At about the same time all the second generation of Wartburg Seminary's Fritschels except Max had died and the great Dr. J. Michael Reu was serving his last years. I leave it to other historians to pursue the stories of these synodical and educational institutions through the years that followed.

However, I have taken the unique story of Saint Sebald Lutheran Church, the pilgrim colony with which so much of the other histories begin, to the present day for readers who would like to know what God is still doing with that little flock.

The Saint Sebald colony, the two Wartburgs, and the synods of Iowa and Missouri all grew out of the German awakening of the middle

1800s, the longing for assurance of salvation through Christ and among Lutherans a return to the teachings of Martin Luther. In the early 1800s the preaching of the gospel had disappeared from most of Germany's Protestant pulpits. The teachings of the Lutheran Reformation were treated as obsolete. Human reason had supplanted the Bible and the Confessions as the source of faith.

Johann Konrad Wilhem Loehe's leadership in the German awakening and the return to the Lutheran Confessions brought about the birth of the Missouri and Iowa synods, the two Wartburgs, and the Saint Sebald colony. The constituencies of all these entities looked to Loehe as the founding father of their respective institutions. In their founding, their common goal and their reason for being was to bring the gospel to bear upon the American scene via confessional Lutheranism. One purpose of this history is to help successors of these pioneers listen again to the faith that their fathers struggled to anchor in America and to support its preaching and teaching in our own time.

Loehe hoped that, given a choice, German immigrants would turn from watered down Lutheran teachings frequently offered in early America in favor of pure Lutheran doctrine. He also hoped that his American planters of the gospel vine would be able to reach American Indians with the message of God's love and grace.

All of these institutions were in glad agreement in the gospel and the Lutheran Confessions. But disputes arose over how to organize church structures in America's democratic society. Coming out of German provinces where bishops and pastors operated under both benevolence and hostility from despotic governments, Loehe's missioners had difficulty discerning their role in the land where American citizens expected those governing to work under the consent of the governed.

This story includes an account of how this struggle affected the gestation and life of the Iowa and Missouri synods.

The Saint Sebald colony developed out of separation from the Frankenhilf colony, which today is Saint Michael Lutheran Church, Richville, Michigan. The separation was caused by broken relationships with the Missouri Synod. The pioneers of this colony and of the Missouri Synod had complete confessional agreement except on one point: the location of the Church's pastoral authority, the doctrine of the Church and the Ministry. Was pastoral authority a sacramental power of the Church transmitted through the laying on of hands at ordination, or was it a call extended by a congregation transmitting pastoral authority from its universal priesthood of all believers? The struggles over this question originated among the Saxon Lutheran immigrants in Saint Louis and Perry County, Missouri. It spread through all the Lutheran synods.

The question of the source of pastoral authority remains unresolved among Lutheran churches of the world to this day. Many Lutherans profess a high doctrine of the pastoral office conferred by the Church through its bishops. Others emphasize the baptismal ordinations of the priesthood of believers and see God's commission exercised through democratic procedures in church assemblies. Lacking a settled doctrine of how the Apostolic Church's teaching authority is to be transmitted, some church members express fear that there is again little to prevent the loss of confessional integrity among Lutherans.

"[T]he Constitution of the ELCA explicitly states that the highest norm for the Church is Scripture, together with the Lutheran Confessions which provide a hermaneutical framework for interpreting and proclaiming the Scriptural witness. It therefore behooves the ELCA carefully to consider the Joint Declaration [with the Roman Catholic Church on justification] in relation to Scripture and the Lutheran Confessions. Without such careful study and discussion, any vote in the Churchwide Assembly would suggest that the highest norm in the Church is simply majority rule." (Six members of the faculty of Luther Seminary, Saint Paul, Minnesota, Gerhard O. Forde, Patrick R. Keifert, Mary Knutsen, Marc Kolden, James Nestingten, and Gary M. Simpson in *dialog* 36, (summer 1997), p. 225., prior to the ELCA Assembly's vote on the Joint Declaration.)

Presiding Bishop Robert J. Marshall at the 1977 convention of the Lutheran Church in America during its debate on a Statement on Communion Practices ruled that the Church does not adopt theology; for that it has the Confessions and the article on faith in the church constitution.

In September 1996, eighteen pastors of the Evangelical Lutheran Church in America and of the Lutheran Church—Missouri Synod included in their *Founding Statement* of the Society of the Holy Trinity: "Concerning the Magisterium in the Church: When the teaching office in the Church is suppressed in the name of democratic participation or in the spirit of a North American anti-elitism, when the dynamic discernment of the gifts of the Spirit for the building up of Christ's body is supplanted by the rigorous application of proportional representation and a false understanding of the priesthood of all believers, then church assemblies become a battle ground in the 'culture wars,' and competition between ideologies of the left and the right replace the quest for truth based Scriptures, Creeds and Confessions. We affirm Article 14 of the Augsburg Confession which states that no one should publicly teach the Word of God in the churches without a regular call. We believe this call is from God through the Church, properly exercised by bishops, pastors and theologians. We believe that pronouncements on the faith and practice of the Church adopted by assemblies that are dominated by those who have no public teaching office undermine the right use of teaching authority in the Church."

Some church historians say that the Lutheran Church has never fit well into the American democratic mindset because of its strong doctrinal emphasis. *The Pilgrim Colony* documents some Lutheran attempts to fit a confessional church into a culture where individualism and diversity rule.

Concerning attempts to base teaching authority on the priesthood of believers, J. K. Wilhelm Loehe, founder of the Iowa Synod and mentor to many of the fathers of the Missouri Synod, wrote, "That there are divinely appointed physicians of the soul is easy to prove. It is the express will of God, that man through men not only be instructed in the way to eternal life, but also be led along that way, and the office of shepherd and that of teacher belong together (read Ephesians 4:11). Just as it is great presumption for one, disdaining the Church, to seek the way of the Lord from the Holy Scripture for himself alone; just as he undertakes, through his own efforts, to find what fifteen, yes eighteen centuries have not without manifold error and struggle of the whole Church been able to find and maintain: even so it is also great haughtiness to withdraw oneself from the physician of souls appointed by God, as though one could walk the way to the eternal home alone, which the Lord certainly did not consider advisable and therefore ordained shepherds (read Acts 20:28; Ephesians 4:11)." [1]

In presenting the argument as it went on within the Frankenhilf congregation and among all the Saginaw colonies, I borrowed, condensed, and edited much of the lively discussion George John Fritschel reconstructed in his *Aus den Tagen der Vaeter,* translated by Herbert M. Prottengeier. Obviously, no transcripts were made of these conversations. But Loehe advised those he sent to America to keep day books (diaries) and to inform him of events important to him. Many sent Loehe copies of their day book entries. These copies in the Loehe Museum in Neuendettelsau are a rich source of American church history. George Fritschel appears to have drawn from these reports to Loehe for his history.

In addition, because Fritschel no doubt often heard in person Deindoerfer and Grossmann rehearsing to his father Gottfried Fritschel the arguments presented by them and their opponents, he could report fairly both the theology of the participants and the hearty conviction with which it was debated. Even though the conversations that George Fritschel recounted were reconstructed from fallible memories, they no doubt faithfully exhibit the thinking, feelings, and tension of the conversations that continued for decades between the Iowa and Missouri synods. After 150 years, one can still sense from Fritschel's material why fellowship foundered over the doctrine of the Church and Ministry.

Fritschel also used as references *Quellen und Documente* (Sources and Documents) located in the archives of the Iowa Synod at Wartburg Theological Seminary, Dubuque, Iowa.

Appreciation

In addition to historians such as Gerhard Ottersberg, G. J. Zeilinger, George J. Fritschel, William H. Weiblen, and W. H.T. Dau, whose labors were the chief sources for this book, the writer is grateful to Robert C. Wiederaenders for his counsel and access to the archives of the Evangelical Lutheran Church in America, to Dr. Ronald Matthias for his counsel on the history of Wartburg College, to Vera Rahmiller for manuscript corrections, and most of all to C. Umhau Wolf, Ph.D., for his patient service as manuscript editor.

"Mission is never at home;
it is a pilgrim.
When it has wrought its blessing in one spot,
it moves on
and carries its blessing to other places.
When we were done in Fort Wayne
we went on to Saginaw County.
Now we are through in Saginaw County,
so we are going farther." [2]

CHAPTER ONE

THE APOSTLE TO AMERICA

This is a story about people of faith; pilgrims who heard the call of God saying, "Who will go for us? Whom shall I send?" One by one they answered, "Here am I. Send me." Like Abraham, having been called and sent, they went out, not knowing where they were to go. They "sojourned in the land of promise, as in a foreign land...having acknowledged that they were strangers and exiles on the earth." Hebrews 11:9,13.

They came to a foreign land a generation before the Statue of Liberty was erected there to welcome newcomers. They came with all their warts, two generations before medical screenings of immigrants on Ellis Island. Those who came were survivors of life's hardships, of accidents, of epidemics. None were turned away.

The origins of Saint Sebald Evangelical Lutheran Church rest in a Michigan colony founded in 1853 by pilgrims and pioneers inspired by J. K. Wilhelm Loehe. Loehe was pastor of a Lutheran congregation in the little village of Neuendettelsau (New Dettelsau), a few miles southeast of Nuremberg (also spelled Nuernberg) in Bavaria.

Loehe was born February 21, 1808, the fifth of six children, in the small city of Fuerth, five miles west of Nuremberg, in the province of Franconia in the kingdom of Bavaria. Loehe was left fatherless at the age of eight. The storms caused by the French Revolution were dying out as he studied first at Fuerth and then at Nuremberg. In 1826 he enrolled at the University of Erlangen, ten miles north of his home, where he began his life-long study of theology. One of his teachers was Professor Christian Krafft, a Reformed leader of the spiritual awakening that was stirring Loehe's Franconia. Krafft instilled in Loehe a strong spiritual consciousness moved by a pietistic spirit.

The theology that Loehe came to believe emphasized that the Christian is a sinner in need of grace, who by Word and Sacrament has come to faith. By faith Christians have devoted their lives to God's purposes. This requires discipline and struggle against sin and readiness to accept counsel and reproof from fellow Christians in the Church. Faith also involves being a channel of God's love to others, being open to God's calls, and being ready to serve where God leads.

As a student Loehe organized a missionary society, a harbinger of what he was yet to do. Loehe did all of his theological study at Erlangen except for one semester at the University of Berlin. He passed his theological examinations in 1830. On July 25, 1831, he was ordained a Lutheran pastor at Ansbach in its cathedral.

"On the day of his ordination he prayed that he would receive a sign, a word, from the mouth of God. He opened his Bible and three times he was confronted with the commissioning text in Isaiah 6:8-10 which speaks of going out to the people with a message that they will not hear. Loehe responded, 'Here I am, Lord, send me.' This sense of service in the work of mission and proclamation was a prominent motif in his own piety and in what he asked of others.

"Later that year he began his internship in Kirchenlamitz (not far from the present Czech border). Already he was an accomplished preacher who drew unusually large audiences, but his Biblical and confessional radicalism also found enemies. In 1834 he was recalled on account of his conflicts with more 'sober' parishioners, colleagues and overseers. In its report the Consistory said that Loehe was a very captivating man, but his understanding of worldly matters, his social skills, were lacking. Loehe must have recognized that the force of his personality and the severity of his theology would always be a source of conflict. He wrote, 'So it goes and so it will go with me. I am a knife and one who gladly permits himself to be cut?'" [3]

He began his ministry serving as assistant pastor successively in nine communities, including Kirchenlamitz. There he enthusiastically addressed social problems from the pulpit, which caused such consternation in the congregation and among the village authorities that after two years he was dismissed. In Nuremberg he served several churches in succession as administrator.

In Behringersdorf he met and confirmed his future wife, Helene Andreae-Hebenstreit.

Loehe did his ministries in the Unionist Protestant State Church of Bavaria under a Catholic king. The church life he observed around him was at an all-time low. The Enlightenment of the 1700s with its rejection of tradition, its look to reason for the final answer on every question, and its appeal to what is "natural" had undermined the gospel. The Church was strongly influenced by this rationalism, a movement away from spirituality to intellectuality.

Rationalism may have been scholarly, but it was short on the gospel. Wilhelm Loehe was a Lutheran who confessed the faith of the Augsburg Confession and of the fathers of the early church. He soon became known throughout Germany for powerful, spirit-filled preaching. The Sacraments also reclaimed their place along side the Word in Loehe's ministry. This won joyful attention from humble Christians. Over the years, Loehe's influence had much to do with bringing the churches

Wilhelm Loehe

of Germany back to an appreciation of biblical and confessional preaching.

But Loehe was also widely rejected—often by the well-to-do who did not want their way of life disturbed by Loehe's gospel. Church authorities began to look upon Loehe as a backwoods troublemaker who offended the intelligent.

The Church of Bavaria was managed by consistories made up of Lutherans and Calvinists (or Reformed). Most of them cared little about differences between Lutheran and Calvinist teachings. Often a Lutheran pastor was assigned to a Calvinist congregation or vice versa.

Loehe remained in the state church, although at times a break seemed inevitable. In 1860 he was suspended for eight weeks because he refused to perform marriage for a man who he believed had been divorced for reasons contrary to Scriptures. "He fearlessly bore testimony against the rationalism of his time and against the lax position of the state church." [4]

Loehe was installed as pastor in Neuendettelsau in 1837. There one week before his installation, on the sixth anniversary of his ordination, he wed Helene. She bore him four children and died in the sixth year of their marriage. Loehe never married again. He raised his children with the assistance of his sister who came to live in the parsonage with him.

Neuendettelsau was the only parish Loehe would serve. When he arrived it was a village of forty to fifty homes—huts made of mud brick without windows—with two to four families living in each. Loehe looked at these huts and exclaimed, "I wouldn't even want my dog to be buried here." Thirty-five years later, *he* was buried there.

This was not the setting in which Loehe had hoped to minister. He had envisioned an urban scene where he might teach and preach the gospel to thousands. But this small village soon became a center from which Lutherans went forth carrying the message of salvation to nations all around the globe. "Here amidst unlovely surroundings and among uncultured and poor people he began his life's work.... At the time of his death, January 2, 1872, the insignificant village of Neuendettelsau had become world renowned," wrote Professor G. J. Zeilinger. [5]

In 1998 the village observed its seven-hundredth anniversary. It was at first only a nobleman's castle. The castle lord donated land for a monastery with the provision that the land be dedicated to the care of the needy. Today Neuendettelsau includes large hospitals, homes for the mentally retarded, hospices, workshops for making paraments and communion wafers, a deaconess motherhouse, and a publishing house—all of whose beginnings can be traced to Loehe.

Loehe's parishioners attended church by tradition but spiritually were nearly dead. His goal was to awaken this congregation through preaching and teaching. He created plenty of opportunity for this. Soon the congregation celebrated two weekday services besides the Sunday worship. Never seeking popularity, Loehe told his people the truth they needed to hear from the Law and the gospel. He counseled them day and night. He celebrated with them the real presence of Christ incarnate among them in the bread and wine. He taught them that the Sacrament of the Altar was the high point of Lutheran community and of the Christian life. He pushed for weekly, even daily communion. By these means of grace Loehe was able to blow the flickers of spiritual life among dead embers into flame. His congregation became glowingly alive.

"Loehe was involved in the rediscovery of the sacraments in Lutheranism.... part of the era called neo-

Lutheranism. As Loehe's emphasis on the sacraments can be called a rediscovery, so too neo-Lutheranism gets its name from the fact that it was marked by a conscious return to the work, the message, and the doctrinal shape of the Lutheran Reformation. One could say that it was a rediscovery of Lutheranism....

"(In) the Augsburg Confession, in Article Twenty-four `On the Mass,' it is stated in no uncertain terms that 'the mass is retained among us and is celebrated with greatest reverence.'...

"However the mass was done away with to some extent by later Lutheranism, beginning with Lutheran orthodoxy whose pedantic concern about doctrine meant that preaching became the center of Lutheran worship at the expense of the Sacrament." [6]

Loehe was a student of the historical liturgies of the Lutheran, Orthodox, and Catholic traditions. To him the true church was a fellowship gathered around the Lord's table, nourished by Word and Sacrament, and led by a bishop in the New Testament sense of the term. He reintroduced private confession in the Lutheran church, and in time most of the people in his congregation came to prefer this practice. Calvinists in the Bavarian church as well as some Lutherans accused him of tilting toward the Roman Catholic Church.

Loehe believed that the Church's spirituality is expressed foremost in its liturgy. For him the priesthood of believers was a holy people that was nurtured by and exercised its gifts in the sacramental liturgy that is the celebration of the whole redemptive work of Christ.

Toward the end of his life, he published *Agenda*, a liturgical book that was later used at Saint Sebald and throughout the Evangelical Lutheran Synod of Iowa and Other States. As Iowa pastors adopted some of Loehe's liturgical practices such as chanting the liturgy, they, too, met resistance. At historic St. John Lutheran Church in Dubuque, people became alarmed and asked, "Should we really do this? Isn't it Roman Catholic?" In some congregations such misgivings flared into conflict.

In 1874 Loehe produced a rite, *The Apostolic Visit to the Sick*. It included Confession and Absolution, anointing for the sick and dying, and prayers for healing. He also composed the first complete funeral liturgy for Lutherans.

So, Loehe was ahead of his time. Today's *Lutheran Book Of Worship* used by the Evangelical Lutheran Church in America includes much from these and from Loehe's *Agenda* that once seemed so unLutheran to German immigrants in Iowa.

Loehe's salary never varied much up or down. It was perhaps $3,500 a year in today's dollars. He started work at 5:00 A.M. and went to bed at midnight. He published articles, pamphlets, and books, including a number of sermon collections that were widely read and brought frequent visitors to Neuendettelsau. Many a working man walked all night to hear "Pfarrer Loehe" preach. Often a gilded carriage stopped at the humble village church.

Some of these later migrated to Saint Sebald. "There was the miller (Konrad) Prottengeier from the old mill valley, one of those who, with his entire family, arose in the middle of the night in order to be at Neuendettelsau where one could obtain the Bread of the Evangel which had become so scarce and precious," wrote Professor Georg J. Fritschel.[7]

Loehe founded in Neuendettelsau a number of Lutheran social service institutions: hospitals, schools, and homes for the handicapped and the outcast. This ministry was organized in 1849 as a "Society for Inner Missions" *(Gesellschaft fuer innere Mission im Sinne der Lutherischen Kirche)*. This ministry came to include fifteen specialized training centers.

Dr. Horst Becker, retired director of the Society for Inner Missions, addressed the Wartburg College convocation March 24, 1998, on Loehe's ministries. He described how Loehe came to renew in 1853 the historic women's diaconate by establishing in Neuendettelsau the Lutheran Society for Deaconesses *(Lutherischer Verein fuer Weiblische Diaconie)*, for the training of women for nursing, educational, and other forms of ministry.

Loehe was motivated, Becker said, out of concern for the sick, the orphaned, the aged, and the handicapped, whose poverty-stricken families hid them behind the walls of their homes. Loehe began by training five women to bring teaching and nursing skills into these homes. Loehe and a friend taught these women for two years. They used a "gasthaus" (a restaurant) for their classroom. But these first trainees could not function. When they came home, their brothers sent them to work in the fields.

So Loehe reinstated the diaconate into which he installed his trainees. Now they had a special profession as deaconesses with uniforms. Loehe begged the money to build their first motherhouse so that they had a place to go for refuge and a place to stay in old age. There came a time when the Society directed the work of 2,000 deaconesses.

Loehe had to become a builder, a bookkeeper, and a trainer of teachers, nurses, and missionaries in addition to his other duties. His theme was that you can do social service only when you are coming from the altar. His deaconess sisters received only pocket money. He taught them: What is it that I seek? I seek to serve. Whom? The Lord, through his afflicted and poor ones. What shall be my reward? That I serve. My necessity is that I do not stay by myself, but that I serve, anticipating neither pay nor gratitude, but out of a sense of gratitude and love. My reward is that I am privileged to serve.

Loehe's Mission Turns to America

Loehe's work with American missionary trainees developed in the 1840s. In 1841 Pastor Friedrich Konrad Dietrich Wyneken of Fort Wayne, Indiana, future president of the Missouri Synod, which was not yet in existence, came to Germany to beg Lutherans to send more missionaries to America. Lutheran immigrants from Germany were scattering through Ohio, Michigan, and Indiana, and for lack of Lutheran pastors were joining sects or becoming entirely lost to the church. Added to these were Lutherans from eastern congregations in the United States who were attracted by fertile land that could be acquired at $1.25 per acre.

Wyneken wrote and published his celebrated *Notruf* (distress call), a letter of appeal titled "The Distress of German Lutherans in North America." It said in part:

> "While you in Germany know nothing else than that your newborn children be implanted in the kingdom of God through the washing of regeneration, there (in America) the children of your brethren are growing up by the hundreds and are without that which is most essential, baptism. If years later a preacher who is passing through comes into a settlement, likely then the children are brought to him. I myself have had to baptize at one time twelve or more children of greatly varying ages, often ten to twelve years old. But who gives instruction to those who are baptized? How can the washing of regeneration continue its

action, grow, and become powerful when preaching or instruction is missing? Who will confirm the children? Who will administer Holy Communion to them afterward? Perhaps their parents of German extraction are themselves heathen, unbaptized; just imagine—German heathen!" [8]

At a pastors' conference in Fuerth, Loehe saw a copy of the letter and pledged his support. In the *Noerdlingen Sonntagsblatt* he made an earnest plea for workers. In 1843 he began publishing a special paper in behalf of America's need for missionaries, *Kirchliche Mitteilunger Aus und Ueber Nordamerika*. Wyneken's lectures in Nuremberg, Erlangen, Leipzig, Dresden and elsewhere stimulated young men to respond to his call.

Loehe volunteered to receive money to support missionaries to the scattered sheep of the Lutheran church in America. He was about to send a considerable amount to the Dresden Mission House for this purpose when a young man named Adam Ernst was sent to him sent by the mission house in the hope that Loehe might find a way to equip Ernst for missionary work. Shortly a second man, George Burger, appeared seeking to be trained for the same cause.

Loehe commenced to instruct them in theology. He thought it presumptuous to attempt to train them for the ministry. He intended them to become teachers of children and youths among the Lutheran immigrants in America. But God led his first students to become pastors instead.

The *Nothelfers*

Loehe knew there were many young men in Germany with gifted minds who had been excluded from or forced out of schools of higher learning by economic need. Some of these loved their church and might be willing to train as missionaries. Loehe issued an appeal of his own and developed in Germany a network of Lutheran Christians looking for volunteers for this work. Those who responded were directed to Loehe. He called them his *Nothelfers* (distress helpers), his emergency workers.

At first, Loehe himself did the teaching that gave these young *Nothelfers* the essentials of theology. He was assisted by a few neighboring pastors. Soon they founded a small school in Nuremberg. In a few years the school was enlarged and reestablished in Neuendettelsau. This work was the beginning of what later became the *Missionsanstalt*, or the Mission Institute, of Neuendettelsau. Friedrich Bauer became its head and made this task his life work. In time this seminary sent hundreds to carry the gospel to North America, Australia, Brazil, East Africa, and New Guinea. Today the institution no longer operates a seminary, but it is still active in foreign missions.

Loehe next had to create a fund-raising organization to provide money to train these young *Nothelfers* for their work and to equip them when they went to the United States. Wyneken had stirred the interest of Pastor Ludwig Petri of Hanover, who gave support to to Loehe's efforts. The result was that Hanover became a stopping point for the men from Neuendettelsau on their way to the port of Bremerhaven to embark for America.

Next, Loehe had to contact the American churches to secure help in placing his men. In 1842 his first two graduates, Adam Ernst and George Burger, were ready to teach in Lutheran parish schools. But when they arrived in New York, Professor Friedrich Winkler happened to meet them. He invited them to go with him to the Ohio Synod Evangelical Lutheran Theological Seminary at Columbus (now Trinity Lutheran Seminary of the Evangelical Lutheran Church in America). There they were induced to study more theology and to become ordained.

Soon others followed them and were united with the Ohio Synod. But this connection between Loehe and the Ohio Synod did not last long. Ohio's practice of teaching theology in English and dropping "Jesus says" from the distribution formula, "Take and eat, this is my body," was more than the Loehe men could endure.

Loehe had warned Ernst in a letter what to do if the Ohio Synod proved to be less than Lutheran:

> "In North America there are several parties which claim the name of the Lutheran Church. The first is in Buffalo and St. Louis and is composed exclusively of those who quite correctly will not recognize those as Lutheran who differ from the pure doctrine in the slightest. To it we are no doubt related. Against it is the Gettysburg or English Lutheran faction which preaches about the progress of the Lutheran Church, while all things it takes for progress can be termed nothing but regress. In between is the church which calls itself the German Lutheran.... To it you and the other friends now belong. We did not know this church at the time of

your departure as we now know it; otherwise we would have insisted you join it with all the means at your command....In the event you must separate, it would be simplest if you who were sent by us, along with other determined friends who have come from Germany, should create **one** synod, whether you are near or far from one another." [9]

After helping found the Missouri Synod, Ernst pioneered Lutheran work in Canada and became known as the father of Missouri Lutheranism in Canada. When the Canada District of the Missouri Synod was formed in 1879, Ernst became its first president.

Indian Missions—Loehe's Dream

Some of Loehe's disciples (W. G. C. Hattstaedt, Philipp Jakob Trautmann, and Friedrich Lochner) joined a little synod of congregations around Ann Arbor, founded by a missionary named Friedrich Schmid. Schmid was a Lutheran who had studied at the Basel Mission House, a Lutheran and Reformed institution. He had been called in 1833 to minister to former Wuertembergers in Washtenaw County, Michigan. He founded twenty congregations. In 1840 Schmid together with Pastor George Cronenwett, Pastor G. W. Metzger, and a layman formed the Michigan Synod. Today some of these congregations are part of the United Church of Christ. [10]

Loehe favored connecting his men with this group because Schmid and his people were also doing missionary work among the Native Americans of Michigan, partly supported by the Pennsylvania Ministerium and newly organized mission societies in both states. The Michigan Synod had also called Pastor Johann Auch to work with the Ojibways at Sebewaing. Enough Indians responded to form a congregation.

Schmid's work with the Ojibways gave Loehe the idea of founding German Christian colonies that would preach by their life and example to the Native Americans. While preaching at a mission festival, Loehe suggested that an Indian mission could begin by settling a colony of Lutherans near a tribal village. This stimulated people to declare themselves ready to go to America as a mission colony and to carry out this plan: Loehe's hired man Lorenz Loesel and his wife Margarethe Walther; four of Loehe's former students and their young wives: Mr. and Mrs. Martin Haspel and their two-year-old daughter,

Johann K. and Kunigunde Weber, Johann Adam and Maria List, Johann Georg and Margarethe Pickelmann; and two youths, Johann Leonhard Bernthal and Johann Bierlein.

This first colony was organized in February 1845 at Loehe's parsonage in Neuendettelsau. It adopted its first constitution and with Loehe's guidance called Pastor Friedrich August Craemer, a former University of Oxford professor, as the congregation's first pastor.

Craemer had a rich history. He had studied theology at Erlangen from 1830 to 1832. He was imprisoned following the Frankfort Insurrection of 1833 and was finally proved innocent in 1839. He had studied old and modern Greek, old and middle high German, French, and English. In 1841 he became tutor to the son of Count Karl von Einsiedel. After two years he tutored the children of Lord and Lady Lovelace in England, the latter a daughter of Lord Byron. He then became a tutor of German language and literature at Oxford.

It was Wyneken's *Notruf* that led Craemer to Wilhelm Loehe. Loehe asked him to lead the colony he was about to send to America. Craemer traveled through northern Germany to recruit more people and support for this work. He was ordained by Dr. Kliefoth in the cathedral of Schwerin on April 4, 1845.

Craemer led his group of fifteen Franconians to Bremerhaven, where their ship Caroline embarked on April 30. They arrived in Detroit on June 8. On July 10 a Great Lakes steamer dropped them on the navigable Cass River south of Saginaw on a tract that Schmid had purchased as Loehe's agent. In Saginaw they were greeted by missionary to the Indians Johann Auch, who had rented a large house for their temporary shelter.

These pioneers hewed their community out of virgin timberland southwest of Auch's mission at Sebewaing in the Thumb area of Michigan near the Ojibway (Chippewa) villages. The Cass River and Native American trails were their only connections with the outside world. They named the colony Frankenmuth (Franconian courage). They named their congregation Saint Lorenz after a third-century Christian martyr for whom a number of churches in Franconia had been named.

They built a log church 42 x 26 feet. In 1852 a frame church 74 x 40 feet was built under the direction of Johann Adam List, who had helped form the original colony in response to Loehe's call.

Craemer served as their pastor for five years. He temporarily joined the Michigan Synod. In 1847, on Loehe's advice, Craemer and other Loehe men helped found the Missouri Synod. In 1850, on the death of Professor A. Wolter, he left Frankenmuth to become president and professor of the Practical Seminary at Fort Wayne. Loehe had turned the seminary over to the Missouri Synod, and most of the students had been sent there by Loehe. When this seminary was combined with the Theoretical Seminary at Saint Louis in 1861, Craemer and Professor C. F. W. Walther constituted the whole faculty. For the sake of a number of Norwegian students enrolled, Craemer took up the study of their language. In 1875 he went with the Practical Seminary to Springfield, Illinois, as its president and chief instructor.

Craemer became friendly with the Indians and gained the confidence of Ojibway Chief Bemasikeh, who placed two boys in Craemer's care for education. Craemer and his wife served diligently and lovingly, often traveling on foot fifty to seventy miles to visit the Ojibways along the Kawkawlin, Swan, Chippewa, Pine and Bell rivers. In 1846, thirty Ojibway children came to the Frankenmuth school for instruction in Bible history and the Catechism. On the second day after Christmas 1846 Craemer baptized his first Ojibway. On Epiphany 1849 he baptized the nineteenth.

Because the Lutheran congregation was absorbing all of Craemer's time, the Dresden Mission Society, at Loehe's request, sent Pastor Eduard R. Baierlein to take over the Indian mission work and to settle among the Ojibways. He was installed as missionary September 6, 1849. Chief Bemasikeh received him into the tribe. He built a log church with a belfry for the Indians and a log cabin for his home, cleared land and set aside part of it as "God's Acre," and named the mission outpost Bethany.

Baierlein mastered the Ojibway language. A Roman Catholic missionary (later Bishop Baraga) shared with Baierlein his outlines of an Ojibway grammar and dictionary. In 1850 he had a book printed in Detroit containing a primer, reading lessons, Bible stories, hymns, and catechism selections. He translated the liturgy, the New Testament, some of the psalms, and parts of Isaiah into Ojibway.

The whole mission came under the control of the Missouri Synod in 1849. That year Baierlein baptized four Ojibway boys and a girl. The first Ojibway adult he baptized was the widowed daughter of Chief Bemasikeh. The old chief, dying unbaptized, admonished his people to follow Baierlein's counsel. By 1853 Bethany had grown to sixty Ojibway members.

Baierlein left in 1853, called by the Leipzig Mission Society to mission work in India. The work at Bethany continued under his assistant, Pastor Ernst Miessler and his wife Johanna.

But whiskey dealers, traders, and false prophets (both Ojibway and white) filled the native tribes with distrust and moved many to leave the missions. Sebewaing turned back to the native religious culture. Bethany also was abandoned. Only "God's Acre" with twenty graves, remains as a memorial of Loehe's dream to missionize Michigan's Native Americans. Johanna Miessler and a son, both of whom died at the child's birth, are buried in two of those graves

A Train of Loehe Men Respond to the *Notruf*

Back home in Germany the Frankenmuth beginnings aroused more interest in mission work. People who had decided to emigrate came to Loehe for advice, and he directed them to Frankenmuth. One hundred new colonists arrived there in 1846. The settlement soon counted eighty houses and cabins. Craemer conducted daily morning and evening worship services, Sunday Communions, Bible classes, and Sunday school. The log parsonage-church had two bells that the colonists had brought from Nuremberg.

In 1849 Craemer made twelve-mile trips from Frankenmuth to the saw-mill town of Saginaw and with six families started a preaching mission that became Saginaw's Holy Cross Lutheran Church. Johannes Deindoerfer, in his *Geschichte der Iowa-Synode (History of the Iowa Synod),* described the vicinity between Saginaw and Frankenmuth: "Imagine the great plain between Nuremberg and Fuerth covered with tall, green forest, a quite wide perfectly straight (strip) opening hewn through the middle. A heavy plank road lays in the middle of this clearing. One comes to a frame house or log cabin to the left or the right every ten or fifteen minutes with a twenty or twenty-five acre clearing. Sometimes several frame houses or log cabins are together. There is nothing but forest between these settlements. Thus you have a picture of Bridgeport which stretches about five miles along the plank road." When one came from Saginaw, Bridgeport was about a mile from Frankenmuth, whose forest and clearings stretched about five miles in diameter. It took about three-and-one-half hours to go from Frankenmuth to Saginaw.

The Frankenmuth (Saint Lorenz) colony founded by Friedrich August Craemer survives today as a strong congregation and one of the charter members of the Missouri Synod. It has sent more of its men into the preaching and teaching ministry than any other congregation of that synod. Frankenmuth, Michigan, is also a town of 3,250 that preserves the old Bavarian culture and cuisine with two huge restaurants, the Frankenmuth Historical Association with its museum, and an annual Bavarian festival.

After Ernst and Burger, two more Loehe-trained missionaries were sent to America in 1842, only a year after Wyneken's appeal. Loehe sent another one in 1843, five in 1844, seven in 1845, twenty-three in 1846, thirteen in 1847, nine in 1848, twelve in 1849, and seven in 1850, nearly all of whom helped found or joined the Missouri Synod.

In 1851 Loehe sent six men including Johnannes Deindoerfer, the first pastor at Frankenhilf-Saint Sebald. In 1852 he sent eight, including George Martin Grossmann, founder and president of Wartburg Seminary and Wartburg College and the yet-to-be-organized Iowa Synod. Eight more men followed in 1853. After that all the Loehe-trained men were sent to the Iowa Synod—eighty-one in all from 1854 to January 2, 1872, when Loehe died. From 1872 to 1925, forty-three more left the Mission Institute of Neuendettelsau for America.

CHAPTER 2

ESTABLISHING A SEMINARY AND A SYNOD IN AMERICA

L oehe soon became disappointed with the mission channels he had established with the Ohio Synod at Columbus and with the Michigan Synod at Ann Arbor. Loehe learned that some pastors of the Ohio synod and Michigan's Friedrich B. Schmid were indifferent toward the Lutheran confessions and willing to compromise their teachings in order to relate to Reformed Protestants. So Loehe looked elsewhere for a place where his men might study and work with comrades who were more faithful to the Lutheran Confessions.

One of the earliest and ablest of Loehe's men was Wilhelm Sihler, a former teacher in Dresden who had a Ph.D from the University of Berlin. He was highly esteemed by convinced Lutherans, and the Dresden Missionary Society had sent him to join the Loehe men in Ohio. He began working at Fort Wayne in 1844. He suggested to Loehe that a "practical" (as opposed to a theoretical) theological seminary be founded there to give the missionaries further training and to train more mature men for the ministry. Loehe and his friends agreed to send support. He called it his *Nothelferseminar* (emergency seminary).

So in October 1846, with Dr. Sihler as its head and professor, the Concordia Seminary began its work. Eleven students from Neuendettelsau lived and studied in a rented hall. Their classes met in the Fort Wayne parsonage. Soon Loehe and his friends furnished money to buy a piece of land and some buildings near the city. The seminary had a home.

Loehe also hoped for an organized Lutheran church body or synod in America that would stand firmly on the Scripture as proclaimed in the Lutheran Confessions. He suggested that his missioners get in touch with Saxon Lutherans in Perry County, Missouri, in the hope of founding a confessional synod.

This Missouri colony had come to America because it had fought a losing battle with the state church of Saxony similar to Loehe's struggles with the state church of Bavaria. In Saxony no orthodox pastor or candidate for ordination could expect to be appointed to a parish of one of the consistories of that kingdom or one of its duchies. Only by the plea of sincere Christians of a local parish might they hope for a call to minister. When they preached and administered the sacraments according to God's Word, they were often called to account by the civil magistrates and fined.

Led by Pastor Martin Stephan of Dresden and Pastor Carl Ferdinand Wilhelm Walther, about 750 Saxons left their homes in November 1838 and settled in Missouri. Stephan was a powerful preacher who greatly affected his hearers by stating in the plainest speech he could command the gospel of grace. In Germany, preaching Christ crucified in a culture of rationalism, Stephan had remarkable influence on all who heard him. Many had sought his counsel.

On the way to America, teaching that the Power of the Keys belonged only to the clergy, Stephan permitted the colonists to make him their bishop and to vow obedience to him in all religious matters and even in their business affairs. Already in Germany the emigrants had begun to address Stephan as "Bishop." A document called Stephan's *Investiture* was drawn up and signed on board ship by representatives of the emigrants. The pastors and lay leaders of the colony validated Stephan's authority and office in later documents. Stephan began to claim that he and his followers were the true Church, and that remaining with the Lutheran Church of Saxony meant choosing to be damned. In spite of this claim, Stephan had left his wife and seven children behind in Saxony.

The last of these immigrants arrived in Saint Louis on February 19, 1839. At Stephan's command, in early 1839 a majority of them moved from Saint Louis to Perry County, more than one hundred miles to the south. The pilgrims included six ministers, ten candidates of theology and four teachers. With the arrival of two later groups, the Saxons in Perry County and the Saint Louis area were nearly one thousand.

Mary Todd, assistant professor of history at Concordia University, River Forest, Illinois, wrote, "Once in St. Louis, the bishop appeared to revel in his office, ordering appropriate clerical vestments, including a miter, staff, cross and chain, and drawing up plans for his bishop's palace, the first structure to be built in the Saxon's permanent settlement." [11] In a few months he squandered the funds of the colony's treasury for his own household and personal comfort. Still, the pastors angrily defended their bishop when he was criticized in the local press.

Then trouble arose. Two girls in Trinity Congregation at Saint Louis made accusations against Stephan to their pastor, Otto Hermann Walther, C. F. W. Walther's brother. A council was held that publicly deposed Stephan and expelled him from the colony. Stephan maintained that he was innocent, calling the charges malicious slander. A civil court awarded him damages for the loss of his personal effects. After his expulsion, Stephan served a congregation at Horse Prairie in Randolph County, Illinois. He died there on February 22, 1846.

It was the younger clergy (average age 34) who had ousted Stephan, their 62-year-old father confessor, from leadership. Many of the flock felt they were without a shepherd. The lay leaders of the colony now demanded that secular authority be kept separate from the clerical leadership. They prepared a statement, *Protest,* accusing the Saxon pastors of complicity with Stephan in promoting the office of bishop. They drew support for their demands from the doctrine of the universal priesthood of all believers. The clergy maintained that the office of bishop had support from Scripture and from history. But they agreed that Stephan had abused their trust and had used them for his own greedy purposes.

What now? Pastors and lay people had been thrown into doubt. Were they still a Christian Church? Did they still possess the Power of the Keys? Were the calls they issued to pastors still valid? What about the ministry? Were their pastors truly ministers of Christ? Were the sacraments they administered valid? Some settlers felt that they had given Stephan too much authority. Others held with Stephan that ordained clergy were mediators between God and man and entitled to unconditional obedience in all things not in conflict with Scripture, that questions of doctrine were to be decided by the clergy alone, in whose hands alone rested the Office of the Keys. The clergy were divided over the question of whether it was the colonists alone as constituted congregations who had the authority to choose and call pastors to serve them. Walther led the group who felt that Stephan had abused his authority. He urged that the colony reorganize along strictly democratic lines.

In April 1841, a debate on these questions was conducted in Altenberg, Perry County, Missouri, between 29-year-old C. F.W. Walther and Dr. Adolf Marbach, a learned Lutheran lawyer. Dr. Marbach said that the colony, by separating itself from the Church in Germany, had ceased to be a Christian congregation. They had become a disorderly group of people with no authority to perform any church function whatever. The only proper solution, he said, was for the colonists to return to Germany and the Church there. Marbach had no suggestion as to how they might accomplish this.

Were the settlers not a Church? Walther answered this question with a resounding "Yes." They were indeed a Church. He presented eight theses to establish his doctrine of the Church. Through their faithfulness to Word and Sacrament and the Lutheran Confessions they were the Church visible.These theses were accepted by the colony and saved the Saxon Lutheran settlements in Missouri from disorganization.

On April 26, 1841, following the debate, Walther met with Trinity Church in Saint Louis to accept their call as their pastor. He had been considering this call since its arrival on February 8. Through his preparation for the debate and the argument itself, his scruples were removed. He came to full conviction that the local congregation could not be deprived of its identity as a Church and the privileges and authority that Christ gave his Church. Walther entered upon a ministry of almost fifty years during which Trinity Church became a blessing to thousands.

Walther went on to convince the other Saxon pastors and candidates and their congregations. Pastor Ernst Moritz Buerger at Seelitz had suspended himself from office. Pastor G. H. Loeber was considering either to resign and return to Germany or to stay in America as a lay person. The candidates for ordination had refused to preach and doubted if they could ever be lawfully called or even serve as vicars to the pastors. Earnest Christians had refused to attend public worship led by fany of the pastors.They had tried to content themselves with family worship at home. Walther was able to settle those doubts.These pastors and congregations entered trusting relationships that were needed for spiritual growth.

Walther's Trinity Congregation went on to test the theses he had presented at Altenberg. A person named Sproede led several who questioned these principles. This forced many congregational meetings for "examining the Scriptures...to see if these things were so" (Acts 17:11). Dr. D. H. Steffens described Marbach's and Sproede's opposition as serving a healthy purpose. "If, in the edifice Walther erected, there was danger of his misplacing a stone, the watchful eye of his opponent compelled him to stretch his line taut and build to it." [12]

Memory of the crisis under Stephan had left Sproede and many others at Trinity suspicious of and opposed to any hint of clerical authority. Walther was barred from the congregational meetings. The congregation insisted on self-rule in order to protect itself from falling once more under clerical control.

The outcome was the framing of a constitution for Trinity after two years of trying every paragraph by God's Word and the Church's traditions. This constitution established the form and model for the organization, government, and administration of the synod itself when it was organized four years later. It differed from the constitutions used by other Lutheran congregations of that time, in that it contained a confession of faith and stated the qualifications for membership. It was a model for administering all the congregations in the area. All Saxons in Saint Louis in their various congregations looked to Walther as their primary pastor or dean. The pastors and elders of the district made up the board of directors *(Generalvorstand)*, which administered the district and its treasury, exercised church discipline, and nominated candidates for the pastoral office. This organizational structure was kept until after Walther's death in 1887.

The Christians who ministered and worshiped together by means of this structure recognized themselves as "the visible Church." In a sermon at Trinity Church in 1842, lamenting the colony's sad experience under Stephan's tyranny, Walther said: "If Christian congregations do not want to come again under a human, an ungodly human domination, they must hold fast to the precious right of the spiritual priesthood, which all Christians possess. **Through Baptism, every Christian has been consecrated, ordained, and installed into the ministry. . . Every Christian is a teacher of the Gospel.**"

But the question of the ministry remained. Walther attempted to describe the office of the public ministry as set-apart, a preaching office that God had instituted for the sake of order. Walther tried to avoid confusing this pastoral office with the priesthood of all believers, but he emphasized that God calls the pastor to his office through a congregation. Many of his colleagues then went on to claim that the pastoral call was indeed based on the priesthood of the believers in the parish. Conceptions of the universal priesthood were competing with those of the set-apart office of the ministry. The result was the schism that developed later between the Missouri Synod and the followers of Loehe.

Loehe was opposed to giving the laity a prominent role in church affairs. He feared that in such a case pastors would be subordinated to the will of their congregations. He wrote: "One thing is regrettable. When our good people arrive over there and breathe the American air they become imbued with democracy and one hears with amazement how independent and congregational they think about church organization. They are in danger of forgetting the high, divine honor of their office and becoming slaves to their congregations." [13]

After the Missouri Synod was organized in 1847, Loehe expressed this fear directly in a letter to Walther:

"With heartfelt sorrow we have noted that your synodical constitution, as it now stands, could not completely meet the model of the first congregations, and we fear, certainly with complete justification, that the fundamental mixing of democratic, independent, congregational principles in your constitution will cause greater damage than the mixing of the princes and secular authorities have brought to the church in our homeland. Careful attention to the many teachings of the holy apostle about the organization of the church and Seelsorge in general would have taught the dear lay brethren something different. A constitution is a dogmatic adiaphoran [Ed: a matter not essential to the faith], but not a practical one." [14]

Professor John H. C. Fritz of Concordia Seminary, Saint Louis, writes, "[Loehe] did not believe that every Christian has all the rights and privileges of the Office of the Keys, nor that the Christians, as spiritual priests, transfer their rights, when calling a pastor, to such pastor for public administration, and that in this wise the office of the ministry is established in a congregation, and that, therefore, the office of the ministry is derived from the spiritual priesthood of all believers. Not through the local congregation, said Loehe, but through the Church, that is through the congregation and the clergy, the Lord calls and ordains men for the ministry. Loehe believed that, according to Scripture, the clergy *(das Ministerium)* is entitled to a voice in the calling of a pastor, and he was not satisfied to admit that ordination was simply a church ceremony, which publicly attested the validity of the call....Loehe, however, was not of the opinion that the existing differences were a departure from the Lutheran doctrine and constituted a cause for rupture," as many of the Missouri Synod pastors insisted. [15]

Arland Hultgren of Luther Seminary, Saint Paul, Minnesota: "It is fair to say that most Lutheran pastors regard their own ordination as a trust committed to them in an ordered way that continues a succession - an apostolic succession, in fact—that is not purely a matter of theological correctness, but symbolized by ordination from a minister of the Word and Sacraments who has gone before." [16]

On September 7, 1844, Walther published the first issue of *Der Lutheraner* (The Lutheran). Its circulation was helpful in making connections among the various companies of Lutherans in the General, Michigan, and Ohio synods and other places such as Frankenmuth where Loehe missioners had gone. Its stated purpose was "to prove that the Lutheran Church is the true Church of Christ, not a sect. It is to unite the divided members of the Lutheran Church, to recall those that are fallen away....Consequently, every article must stand the test of the Holy Scriptures and the Symbols of the Evangelical Lutheran Church."

This paper served as an instrument to bring together Lutherans committed to the Lutheran Confessions and the writings of the Lutheran Church fathers. When F. C. D. Wyneken read it, he said, "Thank God there are still real Lutherans in America!" *Der Lutheraner* became a thorn in the flesh of any who were Lutherans in name only. Many ridiculed Walther and charged him with rehashing antiquated opinions of men long dead and gone. (By his many writings Walther might have amassed a fortune. He never accepted payment for his books, pamphlets, and editorial work. All such income went to the synod treasury. Walther died a poor man.)

The Ohio Synod had become a disappointment to Loehe and his *Nothelfers*. It was torn by discord, partly over the use of English and partly over theology. The confessional Lutherans along with Loehe opposed seminary classes in English, believing that their theology would be weakened in translation. These conservatives also opposed

using the words *Jesus spricht* (Jesus says) with the words of institution of the Lord's Supper. They believed that this weakened faith that
Jesus was present in the bread and wine. Unable to win their arguments, the Loehe men and other confessional pastors withdrew from
the Ohio Synod in 1845.

On September 13-18, 1845, F. C. D. Wyneken, Friedrich Winkler
(who had left the Ohio seminary), Wilhelm Sihler, and twenty other
pastors, eleven of them Loehe men, met at Cleveland to separate from
the Ohio Synod and to plan a synod that would be genuinely Lutheran.
Walther was invited but could not attend. So he had written to Ernst
supporting the plan for a new synod and expressing the wish of the
Missouri men for an organic union of truly Lutheran pastors and congregations. F.A. Craemer and the other Loehe pastors had been disappointed with Friedrich Schmid's lack of Lutheran convictions. They
left the Michigan Synod to take part in the new synod plans. The group
at Cleveland drafted a constitution. They authorized Ernst, Sihler, and
Friedrich Lochner to explore the possibility of including the Saxon
Lutherans of Missouri. When Ernst informed Loehe of these plans, he
replied that he was in favor of association with the Missouri group.

The three men went to Saint Louis in May 1846, where the Loehe
men first met Walther face to face. When Walther heard them preach in
Saint Louis, he shed tears of joy over their sound Lutheranism. The Ohio-
ans and the Loehe men were just as impressed with the Missouri Saxons.

The joint planning group was made up of Loehe men Sihler, Ernst,
and Lochner; and for the Saxons Carl Ferdinand Wilhelm Walther, G.
Loeber, E. Keyl, O. Feurbringer, C. Gruber and G. Schieferdecker. They
spent a week redrafting the constitution written in Cleveland. It was
discussed in the Saint Louis congregation. On May 20 it was signed by
the Saxons and the Loehe men.

In July 1846, another preliminary meeting was held at Fort Wayne
in Sihler's residence. The constitution draft was reconsidered and
signed by sixteen pastors. Fourteen were Loehe men: W. Sihler of Fort
Wayne, A. Craemer, Johann Nichael Gottlieb Schaller, Georg Ferdinand
Sievers, Friedrich B. Lochner, Edward Baierlein, Moltke, E. A. Brauer,
Hoyer, C. J. H. Fick, Adolph F.T. Biewend, Karl J.A. Strassen, Heinrich B.
Wunder, and C. H. R. Lange. There were four Saxon pastors: G. H. Loeber
of Altenburg, Missouri, C. F. W. Walther of Saint Louis, Ernst G. Keyl of
Milwaukee, and Theodore J. Brohm of New York; and a Saxon lay del-
egate, Fr. W. Barthel from Saint Louis.

In 1848 the Ohio Synod surrendered to conservative influences and declared its total adherence to the Lutheran Confessions. But it was too late to bring back the Loehe men who had by then joined the Missouri Synod. [17]

The German Evangelical Lutheran Synod of Missouri, Ohio and Other States was founded April 26, 1847, in what today is St. Paul's United Church of Christ, Chicago.

An amendment to the constitution draft was proposed by Trinity Church, Saint Louis (C. F. W. Walther, pastor), and adopted. This amendment declared that the relationship of the synod to the individual congregation would be that of an advisory body and that the synod's resolutions would have no binding effect until adopted by the congregation as not contrary to the Word of God and suitable.

This amendment flowed out of the concept that the authority of ordained pastors and of the synod is only that which has been delegated to them by congregations from the priesthood of all believers, who along with the apostles received from Jesus the Office of the Keys (Matthew 18:19).

Seven of the eleven voting pastors were Loehe men and three of the four lay delegates were from congregations founded by Loehe men. Of the forty-one pastors and ministerial students on the charter roster of the Missouri Synod, twenty-one were Loehe men, all the men sent by Loehe to America up to that time but one. By the time a break developed between Loehe and the Missouri Synod in 1853, Loehe had sent eighty-four men into that church body.

That year at Missouri's request, Loehe deeded the Fort Wayne Concordia Seminary to the new synod. In 1861 the seminary was moved to St. Louis. In 1875 it relocated to Springfield, Illinois, where today it trains a large enrollment. [18]

The first officers of the new synod were C. F. W. Walther, president; Wilhelm Sihler, Ph.D., vice president; F. W. Husmann, secretary; and Mr. F. W. Barthel, treasurer. Walther offered *Der Lutheraner* as the official organ of the synod. It was accepted. Walther was retained as editor, and a committee on publications was appointed.

The synod took control of the log-cabin classical college and theological seminary near Altenburg, Missouri, which the Saxons had established in 1839. It was moved to Saint Louis in 1849. Out of its humble beginnings grew today's great Concordia Seminary.

In 1850 F. C. D. Winkler, then pastor of the original Old Trinity Congregation in Saint Louis, was elected the second president of the Missouri Synod and served in that office until 1864. Professor J.T. Mueller wrote, "Twenty-five years after its organization, in 1872, the Missouri Synod numbered 428 pastors and 251 parochial school teachers." [19] Mueller does not mention the number of congregations.

Missouri's Constitution

Missouri's constitution set an organizational pattern different from that of the older synods in America. The Missouri Synod was a union of both pastors and congregations, not merely an organization of clergymen. Everything possible was done to safeguard the independence of the congregation, and yet the synodical president was vested with a great deal of authority. The president controlled the theological examination of all candidates for the ministry. He was overseer of the doctrinal soundness of all pastors in service. He was mandated to visit every congregation and check on the doctrine and life of pastors and teachers and to examine the congregation's spiritual condition. In theory the congregations had final authority, but in actuality the synod officers had more power over the congregations and pastors than those in the older synods. A strong person such as C. F. W. Walther could easily shape the synod according to his beliefs.

As stated, Loehe was uncomfortable with Missouri's constitution. He wanted magisterial oversight (teaching authority) to ensure that his pastors would preach and teach the truth in accord with the Lutheran Confessions. He quoted, "If ordination is interpreted this way, we shall not object either to calling the laying on of hands a sacrament. The church has the command to appoint ministers; to this we must subscribe wholeheartedly, for we know that God approves this ministry and is present in it. It is good to extol the ministry of the Word with every possible kind of praise in opposition to the fanatics who dream that the Holy Spirit does not come through the Word but because of their own preparations." [20]

So Loehe did not fear Walther's control over the synod. What Loehe feared was that Missouri's constitution placed the pastors under the will of their congregations. However, his wish to work with this Lutheran group that was so committed to Scripture and to the Lutheran Confessions prevented him from protesting strongly against the synodical organization.

Loehe's fears of lay dominance should have been allayed by the clerical control that developed at synod meetings. The organizational meeting in Chicago April 26, 1847, consisted of eleven voting pastors and four lay delegates. Five years later the synod, meeting at Fort Wayne, had 41 voting pastors and nine lay representatives.

The Argument Spreads to the Buffalo Synod.

A dispute then arose elsewhere with Missouri concerning the nature of the church and the ministry. This argument, from which Loehe could not stand aside, had been going on for some years between Walther's group and Johannes Andreas August Grabau, senior minister and head of the Buffalo Synod. In 1839 Grabau had led a thousand Prussians to America after King Friederich Wilhelm forced a Lutheran and Reformed church union in Prussia similar to that in Saxony and Bavaria. This made Grabau a natural ally of the Saxon Missourians. Loehe felt kinship with both groups.

The problem was that the Buffalo and Missouri groups developed opposite ideas of the nature of the church and the ministry. Missouri had to overcome the authoritarian ways of Stephan. Grabau had trouble when some people in the congregation he pastored at Buffalo, New York, rebelled against his authority. Walther's solution was to give more power to the congregation; Grabau's answer was to stress the authority of the pastoral office. A flood of writings from both sides changed the argument into literary warfare that continued for twenty years. The argument was full of excessive statements on doctrine by both sides. This was part of the setting in which Missouri's doctrine of the ministry was forged.

Loehe tried to mediate in the struggle. He sympathized with Grabau's emphasis on the importance of the pastoral office more than with Walther's view that the pastor has no authority other than that given him by the congregation based on the priesthood of believers. But he urged that each group should tolerate the other's viewpoint in order to work in concord for the gospel.

The thanks Loehe received for his efforts was to be attacked by both sides. The Missouri Synod convention of 1850 asked Walther to draw up an official doctrine on the church and the ministry. The relationship between Loehe and the synod cooled. But Loehe kept some pressure on the synod to end the conflict when he stopped sending students to the Fort Wayne seminary.

The synod invited Loehe to come to America to review the Lutheran scene and consult them in person concerning the nature of the church and the ministry and the minimum doctrinal agreement required for church fellowship. When Loehe declined, the synod, determined to make any effort to maintain unity with its founder, sent Walther and its new president, F. C. D. Wyneken, to meet with him in Germany. In October and November 1851, the two men were guests in Loehe's home. They felt such unity with him that the Missourians consented to continue to study the question of the church and the ministry and Loehe agreed to continue to supply them with pastors. Perhaps influenced by Loehe, Walther and the Missouri Synod founders refused to license candidates for ministry or permit the hiring of ministers without a giving them a call.

Who Can Call the Missionaries?

Missouri's position that calls could be issued only by a congregation made it difficult to send pastors out as missionaries into completely unchurched areas where no congregation existed to call them to minister. In order to provide for evangelistic ministries, the first constitution of 1846 called for the office of an Explorer (*Besucher*). The first explorer was Carl Fricke, a layman and candidate for ordination, sent to gather information that might lead to the organization of congregations among German Lutherans. The Besucher could distribute literature; when invited to do so, he could preach and teach and consult about organizing reading services (*Lesegottesdienste*) and family devotions. The dilemma was that the Besucher's work was to be exploratory, preliminary, and necessarily superficial. But German Lutherans could not be satisfied with superficiality. Fricke toured southeastern Wisconsin with few results. He soon accepted a call in Indiana.

At the 1848 Missouri convention it was proposed that the synod should extend a call to a man qualified "to serve the scattered Lutherans with Word and Sacrament." But this ran into the insistence that a call could be extended only by the unknown people who would be served. A compromise was accepted that "a Besucher might consider himself called to work among the scattered and forsaken Lutherans only to the extent that the law of brotherly or neighborly love and the authorization of Synod gave him call to help them fulfill in their stead the duty incumbent upon them."[21]

Thus tentatively authorized, Explorers were sent into virgin territory. An Explorer looked first for Germans, then asked if they were

Lutheran. If the Germans were pagan or Methodist, the Explorer was to try to persuade them to set about becoming pure, confessional Lutherans."Aside from purely physical hazards and distresses the greatest obstacles he encountered were sectarian denominations, spiritual quackery, religious syncretism, frontier materialism, and just plain indifference." [22]

It was intended that a pastor under call to an established congregation might take time off and make exploratory trips. In November 1848 Pastor Friedrich Lochner searched southeastern Iowa from his base near Collinsville, Illinois, and demonstrated that some benefits might be possible from such an effort. But no other pastors proved able to spare such time away. After 1850 the office of Explorer fell into disuse for a number of years.

In 1856 the president of Missouri's Northern District sent Pastor Georg Ferdinand Sievers of Frankenlust, Michigan, to explore the Territory of Minnesota. He studied possible work among the Chippewa Indians who had been moved from Michigan to a reservation near Brainerd, then the area around Fort Snelling and southeast in Carver County. He celebrated the sacrament where he found communicants sufficently orthodox without worrying about the technicalities of ministerial call.

That same year the Western District heard Pastor C. August Selle urge the revival of home mission work. He asked for the office of itinerant minister, which he called *Reiseprediger* (traveling preacher) rather than *Besucher* (Explorer). The Explorer was sent to locate the needs for ministry. The new office might be permitted partially to meet those needs. Under this plan Selle and others directed work in southeastern Iowa, California, and Kansas. The 1863 convention agreed that the itinerant might preach, but he could administer the sacraments only in genuine emergency.

The *Reiseprediger* was the ancestor of today's mission developer. In 1865 the Missouri Synod authorized this person to conduct ministries as exceptions to the rule for the sake of love. This was considered a temporary and emergency solution to the doctrinal dilemma, but the position became permanent. After 1865 the synod more and more accepted the theory that congregations through the synod may extend a valid call to service in noncongregational forms of ministry.

Like the Lutheran Church—Missouri Synod, the Evangelical Lutheran Church in America and its predecessors also have usually not been willing to ordain candidates to minister in noncongregational work. Such candidates must normally be ordained through acceptance first of a call to parish ministry. After three years of parish work, the candidate is eligible for call by the ELCA to noncongregational work. But the ELCA and its predecessors, as sending churches, have always extended calls to their missionaries.

The Saginaw Colonies Multiply.

As the Missouri Synod was being organized the migrating fever in Bavaria continued. The revolution of 1848 was near. Loehe had been thinking of a broader approach to colonization. The German immigrants in America were so widely scattered, the church could not hope to follow them wherever they went. So, why not concentrate German Lutheran immigrants in selected regions? In the spring of 1847, Loehe sent Johann Heinrich Philipp Graebner, one of his students, with twenty-two Franconian families to settle a second colony eight miles east of Saginaw, seven miles northwest of Frankenmuth. These settlers had an easier time getting started because of the help and experience of the Frankenmuthers. They named the settlement Frankentrost (Franconian consolation). Today that congregation is Immanuel Lutheran Church on Highway 46, a congregation of the Missouri Synod.

With Frankentrost and the two colonies that followed, Loehe did not try to select the persons who would emigrate. His plan, however, was to persuade Lutherans who planned to settle in America to choose the Saginaw area. He established revolving funds from which to purchase land, sell the land to settlers, and reinvest the returning proceeds in more land.

In 1848, Pastor Georg Ferdinand Sievers (See chapter 1, "Indian Missions—Loehe's Dream") led the settlement of a third colony named Frankenlust (Franconian desire) near the Saginaw River about six miles northwest of Frankentrost and five miles southwest of Saginaw Bay. Here they did not have the virgin forest to deal with, but a small prairie along the riverbank with grass as high as a man. The first worship services were held in the homes they built. Then they built their church between the two arms of the Squ-qua-ning River. After German custom, ninety-three acres of parish land (*Pfarrgut*) was set aside for the church's use and income.

Pastor Sievers wrote: "We had the pleasure of dedicating our newly-built Frankenlust chapel on Nov. 21st [1849]. It is built of convenient logs, 28 ft long, 24 ft wide, dressed inside with raw clay. My few school children and the ladies of the vicinity made wreaths and garlands as well as they could from pine and autumn greenery. On the wall, over the altar was written in evergreen: St. Pauls [sic] Church." This congregation became Saint Paul Lutheran Church of Saginaw, today a congregation of the Missouri Synod.

From Frankenlust Pastor Sievers established many congregations in the surrounding area that joined the Missouri Synod. In 1849 he took over from Craemer the Saginaw services he had been conducting. The first services there were held in private homes. Later the smithy of a man named Adam Gauder served as a church center. On November 30, Pastor Ottomar E. Cloeter, one of Loehe's missioners, arrived from Germany to become pastor of that congregation. It was named Holy Cross Lutheran Church, today a congregation of the Missouri Synod in downtown Saginaw.

Part of the congregation soon felt uncomfortable with Cloeter's Lutheran confessional preaching. A more liberal group of twenty-two separated from Holy Cross. Learning that Pastor Friedrich Schmid at Ann Arbor had kindred leanings, they called him to be their pastor in Saginaw.

CHAPTER 3

FRANKENHILF

L oehe decided to organize a colony of poverty-stricken Bavarians to send to Michigan both as a mission group and as a "settlement for the poor." At that time many people in Bavaria lived in poverty. Some were unable to marry for lack of the three hundred guilder required to receive a marriage license. As a result, many young people lived in common-law marriage without commitments made under law. Loehe had in mind a settlement that would become an industrial center with a match factory, mills, and so forth, where poverty-stricken colonists could find employment when they arrived. He would name the colony *Frankenhilf* (Franconian help).

Loehe wanted to buy all the tillable land east of the Saginaw River between the Saginaw Bay and Frankenmuth. But he lacked money. So he interested affluent friends in Nuremberg, who loaned him money on which he would not be required to pay interest as long as the money was used for developing his mission colonies.

In the spring of 1849 Loehe instructed Pastor G. F. Sievers of Frankenlust to buy land for this colony. At a very low price, Sievers bought 1,592 acres on the Cheboyganing River eight miles northeast of Frankenmuth and six miles east of Frankentrost. The land would be sold to indigent people who would in time pay off their debt. Carl Gottlob Amman, a Swabian from Memmingen, represented the lenders who had furnished the capital for the land. He was placed in charge of the Frankenhilf colony.

Amman was not a pauper like those in his care. He was able to buy and pay for his own land. He would deal out the rest of the land that had been purchased by the colony fund, stand by the new arrivals with advice and assistance, and help the new settlers find work such as building roads at colony expense. A man of many skills, he was able to teach a variety of trades.

Loehe reported to his Neuendettelsau mission society:

"So, then, there is land available for a fourth colony. In the hearts of such as are interested in the cause, a thought comes to the surface again, namely, of a colony of poor people who in the fatherland have no prospects to marry. True, those who have undertaken our plan cannot open an asylum to such as are without any means whatever. Our poor would have to possess so much at least as is needed to pay their fare to America. But it is possible to let them have a piece of land and a cabin, and on days on which their own land would not need their work, these people could be given employment and wages, so that they could gradually pay off their land and their cabin. Over there on the Cheboyganing River there soon may blossom a flower of heavenly mercy." (George Fritschel, *Quellen and Documente*.)

In the spring of 1850, Amman led a number of families out of Germany on this mission. The families had obtained the means for their journey from friends and relatives. There were several students in Amman's group, bound for the preaching seminary at Fort Wayne. The company left Bremen on a sailing ship on April 18, 1850. For thirty-two days, Amman comforted those suffering from *Mal de Mer* (sea sickness). He served as chaplain, leading devotions and Sunday worship, as he put it, "despite the ridicule of the evil-minded."

A comparatively swift passage brought them near New York on May 10, when they were becalmed for ten days. On May 20, Tuesday after Pentecost, a tug boat towed them into New York harbor. A medical staff came on board, and the medical examinations of 280 immigrants were completed in half an hour.

In New York the colonists were met by Pastor Hermann Kuehn, one of Loehe's students who had arrived earlier. Kuehn had heard of Loehe's plans for the Frankenhilf colony. He informed Amman that he was ready to serve as colony pastor and would like to join the company.

They took a steamer up the Hudson River to Albany, where, Amman charged, they were cheated by the inn-keeper. This was followed by an uncomfortable thirty-six-hour train ride to Buffalo. There they boarded a steamer bound over Lake Erie for Detroit. Some of the colonists decided to stay in Detroit. They found acquaintances who offered to find work for them. This seemed preferable to a life in the wilds without money.

Because steamer service on Lake Huron was irregular, the rest of the company decided to finish their journey by sail boat. But contrary winds extended a two- or three-day journey to eleven days. Near Saginaw Bay the ship was becalmed for four-and-one-half days.

When the company debarked at Saginaw Bay, it was met by Pastor G. F. Sievers, who invited them to an overnight stay at his Frankenlust colony near the Saginaw River five miles across the plain. The next morning they boarded a boat that took them to Saginaw.

There the remainder of the colony broke up. Some learned that German laborers could find work in the saw mills of Saginaw or Saginaw Bay. Others were invited to hire out in the colony at Frankenmuth. Only two families remained to begin the Frankenhilf colony, those of Carl Gottlob Amman and his cousin Michael Schwarz.

Life would have been easier for Amman had he purchased a farm for himself in either the Frankenmuth or the Frankentrost colony. Had he looked only to his own interests, he would have done so. But when he took leave of Wilhelm Loehe at Neuendettelsau, he committed himself and his family to a mission that he would not abandon.

The Amman and Schwarz families with Pastor Hermann Kuehn arrived at Frankenmuth on June 6, 1850, where they stayed in the Missions House. (This house had been built for Ojibway children, and was now used to house immigrants.) The Frankenmuth people brought their belongings from Saginaw out to Frankenmuth by oxcart without accepting the twenty dollars Amman offered.

As soon as he arrived, Amman visited the 1,592 acres Pastor Sievers had set aside for the new colony and selected 160 acres to purchase for his own family's farm. He started building his cabin on land that is now part of the cemetery of St. Michael's Lutheran Church at Richville.

On June 16, writing from the Frankenmuth Missions House, Amman sent the following to his parents, brothers, and sister in Memmingen, Germany (parenthetical material supplied by the writer):

> "No doubt you have been curious for some time to know how large this (new) colony is. Do not be disturbed if I tell you, as of now, my family [which included the Schwarzs] is the only one that will go there [to the

Frankenhilf land]. Already on the boat two single men decided to defect. Most of the others, persuaded by friends, left us in Saginaw Bay. Two families came as far as Saginaw City. They had to remain there, however, to take work as laborers, so they could earn enough to pay the debts they had accumulated en route.

"Herr Pfarrer [Mr. Pastor] Kuehn was advised not to undertake a farm operation, for it could be a hindrance to his pastoral work. So he dismissed his two hired men and his maid.

"Cousin Michael Schwarz and my hired man are with me. On Monday, June 10, we looked up the land.... It was traversed by a clear creek of drinkable water, covered by beeches, sugar maples and oaks—not too heavily, so easily cleared.

"There I had them begin the building of a cabin for us. I bought 160 acres and am hopeful to have 20 acres cleared by next summer.... The Frankenmuthers have assured me I can depend on them for help. The most difficult task will be to build the road....

"Here [at Frankenmuth] the [log] houses are still as the settlers built them originally, a disheartening sight for the newcomer. But one becomes accustomed to it and before long feels at home. When our home is completed, I will send you a drawing of it. Everyone has his home in the center of his property. Consequently Frankenmuth is quite extensive. It covers an area five English miles long and two miles wide. In the entire area no one locks his door. Here in the midst of the woods we live as safely as in a large city....

"Prices here are not low except for maple sugar, salt and venison. I have eaten more venison since I am here than in my entire life before. An Indian will sell you a heavy quarter of venison for 24-30 cents.

"The woods are beautiful and pleasing. Among the flowers which grace our garden (at the Missions-house), we find wild cherry trees, gooseberries and currants, the last not very productive.

"A multitude of song birds and others with more beautiful feathers nest here. But unfortunately [there are] also guests which are a nuisance to man and beast, mosquitoes.

Their sting causes considerable pain. But one gradually becomes accustomed to them and after a time notices them no more. Where much clearing has been done, they retreat. Compared with the woods, we have none here.

"How long we will remain here [at Frankenmuth] I cannot determine. If others who have purchased land already should not arrive, it is possible that we shall remain here until spring, for I have planted a small plot to beans and potatoes. In the meantime work [at our log cabin] would continue. Still, if the work there develops rapidly, I plan to move there [to the new colony site] possibly this fall." [23]

On August 17, Amman's log cabin was completed, and at its dedication Pastor Hermann Kuehn preached in the Michigan wilderness for the first time. But soon, his ship congregation having melted away, Pastor Kuehn accepted a call to a congregation in Illinois (see Amman's letter excerpts in chapter 5).

Loehe expected that the first settlers in his colonies would attract others and spread German Lutheranism in all directions. One congregation would lift and carry another. Other Americans might avoid the Germans and so permit a solidly German region to be established. His expectations were fulfilled. In 1847 Frankenmuth had 153 people, forty-eight of them voting members. A year later there were 203 people, sixty of them voting. In 1852 there were 345 people, ninety-three voting. The second church built in 1852 measured 40 x 74, 24 feet high at the walls. The church Frankenmuth built in 1863 measured 63 x 126 with a steeple 168 feet high.

George Fritschel reported that in 1922 Saginaw County had twenty-one Lutheran congregations. St. Lorenz at Frankenmuth was the largest with 2,215 souls. Saint Paul Church in Saginaw was next with 1,500, Saint John in Saginaw had 1,300, and fourth in size was Saint Michael of Frankenhilf (Richville) with 1,124. The rich fruit of what was sown in the first colonies included a concern for parish schools, "the like of which is seldom encountered, and a churchly atmosphere flourished in beautiful bloom...If one could have established the colony idea in other states, what a blessing would have resulted!... Fourteen pastors and teachers have come from Frankenmuth and three are presently students at the seminaries. The congregation has four schools, five teachers, 174 school children and only three children of the congregation do not attend parochial school."

CHAPTER 4

THE BEGINNINGS OF WARTBURG SEMINARY AND WARTBURG COLLEGE

More German Lutherans kept migrating to all four colonies. To keep them together and with their church, Wilhelm Loehe decided in 1850 to build a *Pilgerhaus* (pilgrim house) or hospice at Saginaw as a temporary home for immigrants on their way to one of the colonies. There they could rest and learn English while they looked for land to build on.

During Walther's and Wyneken's visit with Loehe in 1851, they had reminded him that the Missouri Synod badly needed a teacher-training school. There was no such Lutheran institution anywhere in America. Many congregations in the Midwest were looking for Lutheran teachers for their parish schools. But because the Missouri Synod was already appealing to Germany for funds to expand Concordia Seminary in Saint Louis, they could not think of attempting to establish a normal training school. They hoped that Loehe would come to their aid.

Loehe agreed to help. For some time Loehe, too, had felt that the American church needed teachers as well as pastors to care for youth. He also believed that teachers could break the path for missions by establishing Christian schools in unchurched communities. The idea of a pilgrim house was expanded to plan for this even more serious need and Loehe raised money to build both.

Loehe considered placing the teacher seminary in Detroit where one of Loehe's young pastors, Johann Michael Gottlieb Schaller, was working. Loehe had sent Schaller so that the Americans might profit by the splendid gifts of this young "Timothy." Schaller first pastored a congregation in Philadelphia and joined the Missouri Synod. In 1850 he served in Baltimore. At the 1850 convention of the Missouri Synod, Schaller was convinced by Walther's arguments that Loehe had fallen into error. His concern for truth was greater than his respect and love for his spiritual father. That year he became pastor of a church in Detroit and later vice president of Missouri's Northern District.

When Loehe attempted to place the seminary under Schaller's direction, he may not have been aware that Schaller had begun to differ with some of Loehe's opinions. The word Loehe received was that Schaller had his hands full with his blooming congregation and could not undertake leadership of the institution. Loehe also found that with the modest means he had at hand it would be difficult to buy a site in expensive Detroit and that the maintenance of the institution would be costly.

So in 1852 Loehe turned to the Saginaw colonies where the outlook was more favorable. Land and living costs were cheap. A ring of congregations was blooming. The support of the proposed seminary seemed assured.

Since the institution was to serve both as a hospice and a seminary, it would need space for the family of the director and about twelve students, as well as for a number of immigrant families. A rather large building was planned.

A Bavarian candidate named Hacker presented himself for work in America, and Loehe had him in mind to serve as director of the seminary. But Hacker's wife was unwilling to undertake life in the Michigan wilderness. At the same time that Hacker was in Loehe's study declining Loehe's call to the seminary, thirty-one-year-old Georg M. Grossmann appeared for final instructions to teach in America. Born in Gross-Bieberau, Hessen-Darmstadt, Grossmann had served as a teacher in Land Hessen since graduating at age nineteen from the Teachers Seminary at Friedberg, north of Frankfort am Main. On June 19, 1846, he had married Nanny Steppes, daughter of Captain Steppes of Friedberg, and he had already fathered some of his children who eventually numbered twelve.

Grossmann had been converted during his late twenties under the influence of Pastor Christian Dieffenbach of Schlitz in Land Hessen. At about the same time Grossmann met Loehe at a church dedication in Hessen-Nassau. Loehe asked him to consider work as a missionary in America. Grossmann consulted his wife. She was entirely in accord. Convinced of Grossmann's gifts and faith, Loehe decided to send him to the University of Erlangen to deepen his theological education. When Grossmann was finished with his preparation, Loehe gave him the title "Inspector."

George Fritschel, son of Wartburg's pioneer professor Gottfried Fritschel, wrote this narrative for the seventy-fifth anniversary of the Iowa Synod:

> Because the time of his departure for America was near, Grossmann had come to Neuendettelsau to receive his last instructions from Loehe. It was then that he learned that five students were about to leave for America and that Hacker, their called teacher and leader, had just decided to decline the call.
>
> After Hacker left his study, Loehe said to Grossmann, "Now tell me, Inspector, if *you* were director of this seminary, could you expect your Nanny to go into such primitive circumstances as we have in Saginaw?" Grossmann answered, "There is no question that my wife will go wherever God places me." Loehe said, "Thus is the Word fulfilled 'Before they call, I will answer.' At the instant when an unreliable man leaves me with a problem, the best solution is already at hand. Consider the matter thoroughly, consult your wife, and let me have your definite answer tomorrow."

The next morning Grossmann came to Loehe's study to accept the position of leader of the seminary and to discuss the details of the undertaking. Since the school was to be built in Saginaw, it could not be part of any of the four colonies. The seminary would serve Saginaw's Holy Cross Congregation by operating an elementary school on its behalf, and Holy Cross's pastor Ottomar E. Cloeter would be asked to assist at the seminary.

Johannes Weege Sr. and Johannes Weege Jr., master carpenters and cabinetmakers, were sent to Saginaw to direct the building of the hospice-seminary. They arrived with their families as part of a group of Hessian settlers in August 1851. (The two Weege men were identified as "senior" and "junior," but were not father and son. They may have been uncle and nephew.) "Senior" Weege was soon known also as "Der Kantor" when he agreed to lead the unaccompanied singing at the worship services conducted in Amman's home.

Several lots were acquired in Saginaw so that the seminary students might raise vegetables. Those students who were able to pay for their support were expected to do so. Others would receive aid from Germany.

The following year, on April 15, 1852, Grossmann sailed from Hamburg, Germany, leading five students and a company of Bavarian farmers who wanted to settle in the Franken colonies around Saginaw. Under the influence of Loehe, the emigrants entered on the journey with the understanding that, if possible, they must stay together to preserve their healthy German culture. In Hamburg the group had formed a ship congregation and called Grossmann as their pastor. He was ordained on the Sunday before they sailed. They arrived in June at the mouth of the Saginaw River on Lake Huron, five miles northeast of the Frankenlust colony.

From there they sailed sixteen miles upstream to the town of Saginaw. On the way they passed the tributary Cheboyganing River on whose bank upstream and southeast lay Frankentrost, and farther east Frankenhilf. At last they saw the smoking chimney stacks of Saginaw's saw mills from which they could hear the daylong screech of saws and smell the pleasant odor of fresh-sawn wood. There they were welcomed by Pastor Cloeter.

Relatives and friends of the new arrivals came twelve miles from Frankenmuth on oxcarts to take many of the pilgrims to their mission hospitality house or to their homes. Immigrants who had no friends or relatives in the new home also found shelter with little or no effort. Fritschel wrote, "Hospitality then was so great and the joy of being able to harbour someone from the Fatherland so genuine, that they almost quarreled over those without attachment."

Frankenmuth now had a saw mill, a grain mill, a physician (Dr. Koch), and three stores. Pastor Craemer had gone to teach at the Fort Wayne seminary in November 1850. Pastor Karl Roebbelein had come from Hanover, Germany, on May 2, 1851, to succeed Craemer.

Grossmann, his family, and his five seminary students were taken to Cloeter's parsonage in Saginaw. Holy Cross Church in this saw-mill town was a 42 x 24 foot house built of lumber by members of the congregation. All the other Lutheran churches far and wide were log structures. The Grossmanns and his students found temporary shelter in the homes of the Holy Cross congregants.

The Weeges had assembled building materials for the hospice-seminary, but construction of the *Pilgerhaus* had not yet begun. So Grossmann rented a vacant store. The shelves and counters in the store served as bookcases and study tables. A dining table was made from a large block of wood and a door. For lack of beds, the students slept on the floor.

Grossmann and his students helped the Weeges build the *Pilgerhaus*. However, newly arrived pilgrims never needed it. By the time it was completed, the first three colonies had been established. Pilgrims headed for these colonies or Frankenhilf found hospitality with relatives and friends while they were getting settled. Also, the location of the *Pilgerhaus* in Saginaw was an inconvenient place for settlers to live while they cleared land and built homes in the colonies.

So the new building served only the teachers seminary. A large school was not intended—the original plan was for six students and one instructor. When Grossmann arrived with his first five students, all of them were so advanced that they expected to graduate within a year. The sixth student did not arrive until a year later.

On July 1, 1852, with his five students, Grossmann opened in that Saginaw store the first Lutheran teachers seminary in America. Intended to serve the Missouri Synod, it was the seed of what later became the Iowa Synod's Wartburg College and Wartburg Seminary. The building was finished and the seminary occupied it that fall of 1852. The seminary received a glad welcome from the colonists and their pastors. There is no record of the exact date it came into use or when it was dedicated. At the dedication, Pastor Cloeter delivered the address. The students sang in the choir. Classes probably continued until July 1853, with brief vacations around holidays.

CHAPTER 5

THE FRANKENHILF COLONY
TAKES ROOT

On March 31, 1851, Karl Gottlob Amman wrote to his parents,

"Reliable reports from Pfarrer [Pastor] Loehe inform us that we may expect a large contingent [of Frankenhilf colonists] in the spring. This is very gratifying news. It will expedite the formation of a congregation.

"The situation here is still very bad. Toward the end of last August, our Pastor Kuehn...received an order to assist an ailing pastor in Illinois, for the shortage of pastors is so great. Now a congregation there has called him to be their pastor. It is a group of twenty families without any spiritual attention, and he feels conscience-bound to accept.

"Naturally I did not consent to this at first and have written many letters. In Frankenmuth also at a pastoral conference, I pleaded the cause of our future congregation. However, I did not want to compel him (Kuehn) to return. I did not want it on my conscience if that congregation would be neglected. So I have given my consent, cherishing the hope that the Lord of the Church will send us a shepherd of souls again. The enclosed letter to Pfarrer Loehe was written for that purpose.

"Since the church at Frankentrost is six miles away, and the church at Frankenmuth is eight miles from us, we conduct our own worship services here in our house. Occasionally Pastor J. H. P. Graebner from Frankentrost pays us a visit. The education of the children falls on me, of course. It is very time consuming. In other respects we are quite content in our solitariness, wishing only that our loved ones were here with us."

With only Amman's family on the scene, the Frankenhilf beginnings were discouraging. Amman had to sit alone in the wilderness through the winter of 1850-1851 with his family, his hired man and his cousin Michael Schwarz. He wrote in the letter quoted above, "Now I have additional worries because I am now alone. And if I could not begin it trusting in God, I would rather forsake it."

Loehe decided to send more colonists. In June of 1851, a year after Amman's arrival, Michael Gruber arrived at Frankenhilf with his wife. Late that fall Pastor Johannes Deindoerfer (unmarried) led the families of Carl Glave, Heinrich Dahl and Paulus Popp to Frankenhilf. Deindoerfer made his home with the Ammans. On the third Sunday of Advent, Deindoerfer conducted his first worship in a room that Amman had included for this purpose when he built his own log cabin.

Shortly after Pastor Deindoerfer arrived, he met Elizabetha Katherina Weege, daughter of Johannes Weege Sr., now the colony's chief carpenter and cabinetmaker, and sister of Heinrich Weege who later came from Germany to complete his theological studies in the seminary at Dubuque. The Weeges were members of Cloeter's church in Saginaw. The Deindoerfers were married the week after Easter 1852. Amman shared his home with the newlyweds.

On December 12, 1852, Amman again addressed his parents:

"Through the kindly provision of Pfarrer Loehe, we now have a faithful shepherd of souls, Pastor Johannes Deindoerfer. He was married about six weeks ago. He married Katharina Elisabetha Weege in Frankenhilf with Pastor Graebner [Frankentrost] officiating on Oct. 18, 1852, and they presently live in our house. Here we also conduct our divine services. Conditions are quite crowded and as a church not very impressive. Nevertheless, our services are solemn and blessed.

"Our congregation consists of thirteen families and two unmarried men, and we have decided to build a church. Last week we began construction. Most likely it will not be completed this winter because among this small membership we have several indolent Christians who do not display great enthusiasm and thus handicap the better ones. Still, here it is better than in the congregations of Germany.

No one is compelled to join. Each one desiring membership must face a test concerning his faith and life. Manifest sinners and those openly professing unbelief are excluded. Naturally it is difficult to protect oneself against hypocrites, for no one can see into the heart.

"Since Herr Pfarrer is here, our children receive the best of instruction and I am relieved.

"For the construction of the church, parsonage and school house, I have donated ten acres. I will have only 200 paces to church. Once the school is built, it will be no farther than at home.

"500 more acres have been bought east of us [by the colony], and it is expected more will be purchased to the south. This will be a great help in developing our congregation....

"Our little Christina is a dear child, born September 14, 1851, now age 15 months. She has never been sick and already for some time she has been able to walk alone. Kaethe, though she appears sickly, is rugged and tough. Gottlob and Anna (daughter by Amman's first marriage, who later gave birth to the first generation of Schuchmann children at Saint Sebald) are developing nicely, and in several years, we hope, will be a real help for us."

Listed in the church records with the Amman family is Christoph Ludwig Buder, who was probably a relative. (Saint Sebald records show that he left Frankenhilf with the Ammans in 1853. He was age thirty at that time.) Included in the above letter, Amman wrote, "Buder arrived here safely. On advice of Riethmaier in Frankenmuth he remained there for a time to familiarize himself with the work. I deemed it wiser for him to undertake at once to work his own land. He was with me for fourteen days and has received 40 acres on time-payments. It would be better for him if his bride were with him now. His near-sightedness makes it difficult for him to do everything alone. He is well taken care of, has very fine neighbors with whom he finds lodging and board." Buder attended the Eucharist for the first time on the Second Sunday in Advent, 1852.

Fort two years, Pastor Deindoerfer conducted worship in the Amman home. The colony added a number of families.

In June 1851, after a long and lonely winter all alone in the wilderness, the Frankenhilfers joyfully greeted Mr. and Mrs. Michael

Gruber. It is interesting that this thrid founding father of the congregation and his wife were still alive and they helped celebrate the 50th anniversary of the congregation in 1901.They were the only founders still alive and early church history records that they were the first in tehe congregfation to mark a golden wedding anniversary on April 27, 1901 of the congregation's anniversary year.

Then in the autumn of 1851, three more families arrived and were joyously received by the three already living at the primitive settlement. These included the families of Messers P. Popp, Glave and H. Dahl. The following year, in 1852, came the families of J. Schwab, M. Schwab, A. Heinlein, P. Gress, G. Bauer, M. Huber, G. Kamm and L. Sippel.

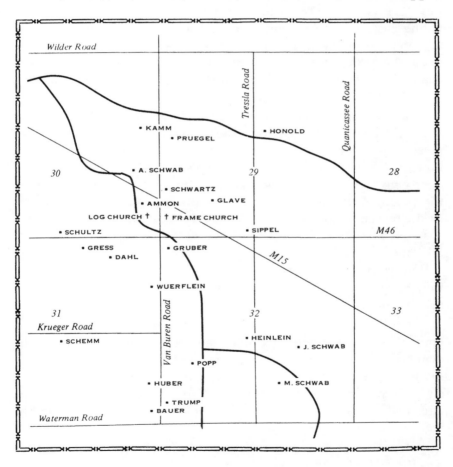

Map courtesy of Saint Michael Lutheran Church, Richville, Michigan

And helping to complete the founding period with their arrival in 1853, were the families of L. Trump, J. Honold, J. Schemm, A Schwab, M. Pruegel, K. Wuerflein and F. Schultz.

With these added families, the committed Christians among them decided in the spring of 1853 to organize a congregation (see the account of the organizational meeting in chapter 8).

Missouri's 1852 Synod at Fort Wayne

Established as a confessional body faithful to the Lutheran Book of Concord, the Missouri Synod spread rapidly in both organization and influence. By 1852 when the synod met at Fort Wayne (June 21 to July 3), it claimed 114 pastors. Present at the synod were forty-one voting pastors (whose congregations had joined the synod), twenty advisory pastors (who had joined the synod but could not vote because their congregations remained independent), and nine lay delegates. Twenty voting and thirty-three advisory pastors were absent.

Since Loehe had advised him to join the Missouri Synod, Deindoerfer also attended. With Pastors Graebner and Roebelein of Saginaw, he traveled to Detroit, where they joined other pastors in a pleasant journey to Fort Wayne. There Deindoerfer met for the first time the leaders of the young synod. Presiding was Wyneken, the pioneer who eleven years earlier had first brought to Loehe's attention the plight of pastorless Lutherans in America. Adam Ernst, the first Nothelfer sent by Loehe, was also there. Ernst, wrote George Fritschel, "had not become a learned man. However he had what balances much education, a true heart, a burning love for his Savior, and a will to endure sacrifices that few equalled." Loehe's second Nothelfer, George Burger, had died. Wilhelm Sihler, one of the first university scholars sent by Loehe, also attended.

C. F. W. Walther dominated the assembly with his talent and influence. Also present were Friedrich August Craemer, pioneer of the Indian mission and then professor at the Fort Wayne seminary; Theodore Julius Brohm, cofounder of Concordia College at Altenburg, Missouri, and then pastor of Trinity in New York City, where he faithfully looked after Lutheran immigrants; Friedrich Lochner, pastor of Trinity in Milwaukee; and J. M. G. Schaller from Detroit.

The Concordia Seminary founded by Loehe and Sihler in 1846 was the central institution of the synod at Fort Wayne. Over the years Loehe had time and again filled its classes with scholars and practically maintained it. What Concordia had done over the years to alleviate the synod's shortage of pastors and to promote the synod's sensational growth could hardly be exaggerated.

The spirit of the synod assembly was brotherly, although it seemed to Deindoerfer that President Wyneken spoke too sharply of the Buffalo Synod and Grabau's doctrine of the ministry. Although Deindoerfer did indeed agree with Wyneken that the ministry was not a "privileged state" that God set over the church as a ruling hierarchy, he was glad when the synod decided to do everything in its power to end the quarrel. The synod offered to negotiate quietly with the Buffalo Synod in order to keep the argument out of the news. What more could the synod do? This spirit of peace, evidenced also in other cases, caused Deindoerfer to decide to join the Missouri Synod. Since his Frankenhilf congregation had not organized as yet, he became an advisory member.

Because the Synod now extended geographically from New York to New Orleans and it was impossible for many pastors to attend synodical meetings, the synod assembly divided the Synod into four districts.

The Deindoerfer Road

Women colonists had to carry their flour through forests and swamps from Frankenmuth to Frankenhilf. There was no road between the two settlements. Finally, under the direction of Pastor Deindoerfer, the people of both colonies joined hands for the building of a road. The trail was long known as the Deindoerfer road.

Amman wrote (in the above letter):

"Most inconvenient was the fact that we had no road to drive on for 9-10 weeks. We had to carry all provisions and tools to the site. Worthy of thanks is the fact that the Frankenmuthers helped us work on the road. Nevertheless it was our [Amman's, his hired man's and Michael Schwarz's] lot to do the greater part, and since it was at a most inconvenient time for us to do the work, it was difficult for me to keep my people in a good mood.

"After the road was finished, I at once bought a pair of strong oxen for $55 and a wagon for $40 which proved a great help. After a portion of the woods had been cleared, I selected the most suitable site for the house, on a slight incline near a creek. During the hot season [of 1850], the work was very tiring. So the building of the house did not progress as rapidly as I had wished. But on September 11, we were able to move in, heartily thanking God that our carrying back and forth [from Frankenmuth] had come to an end.

"After we were settled here, my plans were directed mostly toward winter-seeding as much land as possible. Since one can sow rye here until Saint Martin's Day [November 11], I was able to prepare a nice piece—but not as much as I had planned earlier.

"According to the books, clearing the land is much easier and less expensive than it is in reality. When one considers the multitude of trees, many of them of immense size; when one observes not only the cutting but that it is necessary to burn all the foliage, great masses of it plus the rotted wood, then one is in danger of losing courage before a portion is finished.

"But then one realizes what can be accomplished with the help of God. It was indeed a real pleasure when I saw the greening wheat I had sown, where only four months ago there was nothing but dense forest.

"[Because of the stumps] such a field is not as nice to behold as the fields in Germany. To remove the stumps would take too much effort, so they remain in the fields until they rot away, a matter of 6-10 years.

"When [rye] seeding was finished, we still had time before winter set in, which was very early this year, to build a barn. I had also begun the [summer] kitchen and cellar [a building separate from the house for canning, washing, and ironing in summer without heating the living quarters]. But I could complete neither because of the arrival of snow.

"I have no reason to complain, but rather to sing praises, for the Lord has helped me faithfully. Of all the Germans in the surrounding area, I was able to accomplish the most in our first year. All of it called for great effort and considerable money, but it was well invested....

"It is possible that we may soon have a road to Saginaw City. That would make this shopping center nearer for us than for the Frankenmuthers.

"There is no one living within five miles to the east of us. Reliable reports from Pfarrer Loehe inform us that we may expect a large contingent in the spring. This is very gratifying news. It will expedite the formation of a congregation.

"By this time, no doubt, you are anxious to know how our house looks....Up to the roof it is built of logs, laid one upon another, faced for the interior and with the bark removed on the exterior. It is about 13 feet to the roof. In the center there is a plain door, leading into a vestibule. To the right is our living-room with a bedroom adjoining, to the left a room with a private entrance [designed to serve also as a worship center for the congregation]. Upstairs there are three small rooms and a loft. That is the full height. It measures 30 feet in length and 20 feet in depth. Compared to other local construction, it is a large house. Since it is built for living purposes only, it is sufficiently large.

"For the time being our baggage will serve as closets. The bedsteads are homemade.

"The [summer] kitchen will be added on to the house, the cellar next to the kitchen. On the side of the kitchen is the bake-oven and the well. A small projecting roof [porch] will be added to the house. The yard surrounding the house is planned for an orchard. Eighteen fruit trees are already planted. To the west of the house is the barn and barnyard."

In spite of poverty, the colonists were a contented group, ready to share with their neighbor even at great sacrifice. When a colonist had no flour, his neighbor loaned him his last money to purchase flour in Flint.

Loehe was not responsible for all the plans for the Saginaw colonies, which often were but partially fulfilled. He received ideas from his friends in the colonies as well as from consultants at Neuendettelsau. The idea of a *Pilgerhaus* was proposed by Mr. Wilhelm Sommer. The idea of a colony for the poor came from Pastor Cloeter at Saginaw. In fact, Pastors Cloeter and Sievers (at Frankenlust) had purchased land near Frankenhilf before their proposal for the colony reached Loehe. Loehe concurred with the idea and made funds available to purchase more.

Soon Cloeter realized that while his colony for the poor looked fine on paper, it would not be easy to establish. He wrote to Loehe:

"This is what it will take to establish a colony in the midst of the wilderness, five to seven miles from every inhabited place (that is a day's journey into the bush): much courage and also money, much money. The necessary courage will be hard to find among people in Germany who have been unable to escape from poverty and who have resigned themselves to this fate. The only person who can have such courage is the man who does not keep looking to his own interests and his own welfare in this world, but has an eternal perspective and so serves the church. I would like to call this 'religious courage.'"

Then Cloeter suggested that because such poverty-stricken people could find good work in Saginaw, Loehe should consider building a pilgrim house there as their shelter until they could afford land and make a start for themselves. The pilgrim house-seminary was built, but, as explained in chapter 4, was never used to shelter penniless colonists.

Deindoerfer did not drop the idea of a colony for the poor entirely. When well-to-do families purchased land at Frankenhilf, they provided jobs for the poor. The self-sufficient colonists included Amman, Schwarz, Bauer, Buder, Dahn, Glave, Gruber, Kamm, Popp, Pruegel, Schultz, Schwab, Sippel, and Trump.

Loehe wrote to Deindoerfer: "You, my dear brother, are so brave to aspire to founding a colony of the poor in Frankenhilf, I find it good and fine. I go along with it. However, we leave it to you to decide how to carry this out. It seems to me that the colony treasury has fulfilled its purpose. Without it there would have been no Frankenmuth, Frankentrost, Frankenlust or Frankenhilf. There would be no neighborly, homelike colonies that, in contrast to cosmopolitan places, are predominantly German."

Life and Progress at the Seminary

In the summer of 1853 in Germany, Loehe was making arrangements for another class to replace the first five graduates at the Saginaw seminary. An additional student, Christian Kraenzlein, who was apparently very young, arrived in July 1853.

From the agreement that Grossmann had signed, life at the teachers seminary followed a strict regimen. There were instruction and study periods with chapel times morning and evening. There was some free time after meals. The courses of instruction included religion and teaching methods for elementary schools, where pupils would learn arithmetic, history, geography, and German. English was not yet offered. Since Grossmann was a skilled musician, he probably taught choral and instrumental music.

After that year of study, the first class of five students had passed their examinations and was ready to graduate. There is no record of the date of the first commencement. Gerhard Ottersberg in his history speculated that since the next class was to sail from Germany in August, "it seems likely that (the commencement) took place in September." [24]

The original plan was probably to register one class at a time at the Saginaw seminary and to graduate it before the next class arrived. But because immigrants were not using the space saved for them in the Pilgerhaus, it was possible to house two classes together.

CHAPTER 6

THE DOCTRINE
OF THE MINISTRY

By 1852, ninety-three missionaries had been trained and sent to America by Loehe. The four Saginaw colonies, their seminary, and the Fort Wayne seminary were in business and prospering. But for Loehe all this was to lead to heartbreak.

The tension between the Missouri Synod and Loehe over the doctrine of the ministry had abated following the conference Loehe had with Walther and Wyneken in the fall of 1851. Following the Fort Wayne Synod in 1852, the conflict erupted again. Loehe's respect for the episcopal traditions of the church, both east and west, made it difficult for him to accept the Missouri Synod emphasis on congregational rights and the inclusion of "democratic, independent, congregational principles" in its constitution. Loehe firmly believed that the democratic model is at odds with the authority of the Word of God, the Lutheran Confessions, and the great tradition of the church—especially the creeds, the teachings of the first Councils, the Liturgy, and the Office of the Ministry. Loehe maintained that these constitute a treasure entrusted by the Holy Spirit not to be put at risk through popular vote. Loehe was sensitive to Article 14 of the Augsburg Confession in which the Lutheran reformers had expressed their "deep desire to maintain the church polity and various ranks of the ecclesiastical hierarchy."

Ironically, in spite of Walther's verbal dedication to the flexibility required by congregationalism, when confessional difficulties arose between him and Loehe, Walther proved the one unable to bend. So much so that ex-Missourian Father Richard John Neuhaus has stated,

> "Always for Lutherans who would be evangelical catholics the question is the church.... Lutheranism, we can perhaps agree, has had much to say about the gospel, but

little about the embodiment, the bearing and the being of the gospel that is the church—one, holy, catholic and apostolic. I have often reflected that Lutheranism's most coherent doctrine of the church was that advanced by C. F. W. Walther in his claim that the Missouri Synod and those in complete doctrinal agreement with it constitute 'the true visible church on earth.' Coherent and irredeemably sectarian. For some it made sense, however. In the fall of 1990 I was explaining once again to my mother, then 87 years old and the widow of a Missouri Synod pastor, why I became a Catholic. 'Yes, yes,' she said, 'you've told me all that before, but there's one thing I don't understand.' 'What's that?' I asked. 'I don't understand why you had to leave the *Church*.'" [25]

In the words of John Hannah, "Walther and the whole of the [Lutheran Church—Missouri Synod] for many years practiced ministry much from the catholic tradition while spouting congregational rhetoric" [26]

So, in their efforts to protect the doctrinal purity of the pastors affiliated with Missouri Synod, Walther and Wyneken have been described as having exercised more teaching authority than that which they verbally opposed and charged Loehe with advocating for the church. If this was the case, it may have been this authority used by teachers who followed Walther and Wyneken that provided the church so many scholarly leaders who were catholic in the faith and dedicated to Scripture and the Lutheran Confessions (Paul R. Hinlicky, Christa Ruth Klein, Leonard R. Klein, Martin E. Marty, Jaroslav Pelikan, O. P. Kretzmann, and Arthur Carl Piepkorn, to name a few). Richard John Neuhaus, trained by the Missouri Synod, is considered by some to be not only one of the most influential persons in the Lutheran and Roman Catholic communities but among all American intellectuals. Their stories may illustrate the value that a strong magisterium can have for any church body. [27]

The irenic resolutions of the Fort Wayne assembly resulted in no reduction of stress between Missouri and Buffalo. And from his distance Loehe was unable to moderate the conflict. Loehe seems to have been more adjustable than Walther and Wyneken. He held a position between those in the Bavarian state church to whom the Lutheran Confessions meant little and Walther who believed that Luther and his colleagues had spoken the final word in the development of

Lutheran teachings. The result was that many Missouri leaders decided that Loehe had taken the side of Buffalo against them.

Unable to settle their differences with Missouri, in 1853 the Buffalo men Grabau and Heinrich von Rohr visited Loehe in 1853. After Grabau met with Loehe and a conference of pastors associated with him, they agreed that on some things neither the Word of God nor the Confessions spoke clearly; there are "open questions." But when they returned to America, the Buffalo leaders found that neither their own synod nor the Missourians were satisfied to leave disputed matters unresolved by calling them "open questions." Loehe had failed as a mediator and his friendship with Grabau cost him the good will of the Missouri Synod.

Bitter conflict developed between the Buffalo Synod leaders who sided with Grabau and those who agreed with the Missouri Synod. The Saxons welcomed into their midst disaffected pastors and congregations from Grabau's group. Many Buffalo clergy resented Grabau's strict control. The climax came in 1866 when the Buffalo Synod ministerium considered a charge of false doctrine on the Church and the ministry against Grabau himself. The ministerium found Grabau guilty of error and urged him to correct his position. He refused. A minority remained loyal to him, but in 1866 following a colloquium between the two synods, the majority negotiated with the Missouri Synod and were accepted there. This reduced the Buffalo Synod from twenty-seven pastors to four. [28, 29]

After Grabau's death in 1879, the Buffalo Synod gradually modified the views that had caused the conflict. Influenced by the democratic mood in American churches, it gave up practices of banning, excommunication, and dictatorial authority over congregations. At the time of its merger with the Ohio and Iowa Synods in 1930, Buffalo had forty-four pastors, fifty-one congregations, and 10,341 members.

The Conflict Reaches Michigan

At the conference in Frankenmuth following the amiable Fort Wayne synod assembly, the synod's work was reported and discussed. To their surprise, Deindoerfer and Grossmann heard spoken a false report that Wyneken's Fort Wayne speeches criticizing Grabau and the Buffalo Synod had also been directed against Loehe. It was said that Wyneken suspected Loehe of wanting to erect a priestly dominion; that this was why Loehe emphasized the divine institution of the pastoral office and ordination.

Walther was present and he also spoke critically of Loehe. This evoked a response in support of Loehe from Frankenhilf's Deindoerfer and the Saginaw seminary's Inspector Georg M. Grossmann. Hoping to bring about peace, Grossmann defended Loehe's principle of "open questions."

Deindoerfer pointed to the negotiated settlement between Wyneken, Walther, and Loehe in 1851 on the differences on the doctrine of the ministry. After that meeting, both Wyneken and Walther had said of Loehe, "Here is no priestly pride to be seen. Here Christ's spirit rules. Here beats a faithful Lutheran heart." Deindoerfer wondered, How could Loehe have changed so mightily in two years?

George Fritschel reconstructed some of the lively discussion in his *Aus den Tagen der Vaeter,* translated by Herbert M. Prottengeier, condensed and edited here (see Foreword). In presenting the Frankenmuth discussion, Fritschel marked the speakers only by the first two letters of their names. The writer was able to identify all but "Pl." and "Br."

Pl.: "Our teachings are the Word of God. Therefore, all who refuse to accept them are false teachers and lying prophets."

Georg Grossmann: "May I ask that you explain these teachings to me more clearly. I must say that I have not seen a statement that this position on the doctrine of the ministry is the Word of God?"

Pl.: "What can be clearer than this teaching: The holy ministry is the authority to carry out the rights of the spiritual priesthood in open office by reason of joint interest (*Gemeinschaftswegen*)?"

Grossmann: "I have read this sentence repeatedly. But I must emphasize that it is certainly not clear to me. What is to be understood by the 'spiritual priesthood.'?"

Pl.: "Under 'spiritual priesthood' I understand exactly what Scripture understands in 1 Peter 2:9, 'But you are a chosen race, a royal priesthood, a holy nation, God's own people, that you may declare the wonderful deeds of him who called you out of darkness into his marvelous light.' I would like to know how you understand this verse."

Grossmann: "I understand this verse as in similar places, such as Revelation 6:1, '(He has) made us a kingdom, priests to his God and Father'; 2 Moses 19:6, 'You shall be to me a kingdom of priests and a holy nation'; and Isaiah 61:6, 'You shall be called the priests of the Lord, men shall speak of you as the ministers of our God; you shall eat the wealth of the nations, and in their riches you shall glory.' In all these places the children of God are shown God's purpose for them. God had accepted them in mercy though at times they were not his people and had fallen from grace and had made them his people. As Israel in the Old Testament was the nation that God had selected among all the nations to be his people, so also we Christians are God's people of the New Testament."

Karl Roebbelen: "Then you find that in this place reference is made only to the fact that Christians are God's own?"

Grossmann: "Let us start with 2 Moses 19:5: 'Now therefore, if you will obey my voice and keep my covenant, you shall be my own possession among all peoples, for all the earth is mine.' Those were the words which Moses in the name of God was to convey to the people as God wanted to make a covenant with them at Mt. Sinai. Observe the parallelism of the thoughts where the same substance is brought twice in different words. And now Peter applies this to the Christians to whom he is writing. In the entire first chapter, he holds before their eyes all that God has done for them. This is the foundation for his warnings in the second chapter. First he speaks in general, then he speaks of individual Christian virtues."

Br.: "But it reads clearly and distinctly that we are priests, and you do not want to say that this applies to pastors only, but that it applies to all Christians. Isn't that so?"

Grossmann: "Most certainly the entire first and second chapter of Peter applies to all Christians without exception. Let us, however, read the Word in context. It is not proper to tear one part out of context. 1 Peter 2:12-5: 'So put away all malice and all guile and insincerity and envy and all slander. Like newborn babes long for the pure spiritual milk, that by it you may grow up to salvation; for you have tasted the kindness of the Lord. Come to him, to that living stone, rejected by men but in God's sight chosen and precious; and like living stones be yourselves built into a spiritual house, to be a holy priesthood, to offer spiritual sacrifices acceptable to God through Jesus Christ.' Here it states specifically that the Christians are to act as a holy priesthood, to offer spiritual offerings, acceptable to God through Jesus Christ."

Pl.: "And as each Christian is a priest, he has thus the rights of priesthood, that means he has the right to preach, baptize, pray, admonish, etc."

Grossmann: "Does that stand here?" As far as I see, it means only that the Christians, as spiritual priests, have the responsibility to offer spiritual offerings, acceptable to God. If I am to believe you that the work of preaching, baptizing, etc., is meant, then you must first point that out to me. I don't find it here."

Roebbelen: "Well, what do you find here? Of what do the spiritual offerings mentioned here consist?"

Grossmann: "Hand me a concordance, then I will cite the places in which the offerings of Christians are mentioned. I will not name the many places in the Psalms other than: Psalm 50:23, 'He who brings thanksgiving as his sacrifice honors me'; or Psalm 119:108, 'Accept my offerings of praise, O Lord, and teach me thy ordinances.'

"I will only cite Hebrews 13:15-16, 'Through him then let us continually offer up a sacrifice of praise to God, that is, the fruit of lips that acknowledge his name. Do not neglect to do good and to share what you have, for such sacrifices are pleasing to God.'

"And then I think of St. Paul admonishing the Romans in 12:1, 'I appeal to you therefore, brethren, by the mercies of God, to present your bodies as a living sacrifice, holy and acceptable to God, which is your spiritual worship.' The following chapters then show how we Christians in all the situations of life should do God's will and live holy lives as children of God. That is the worship service, that is the sacrifice that God expects from every Christian and to which Peter points us."

Graebner: "It seems to me that you overlook what plainly stands here, that we should proclaim the wonderful deeds of him who has called us 'out of darkness into his marvelous light.' Don't you agree that this refers to sermons such as the one you delivered last Sunday?"

Grossmann: "I have never viewed these words in this way. I do not believe that is the sense of the Apostle's words."

Br.: "Of what then does the apostle speak?"

Grossmann: "Simply of the pious living of the Christians. Whenever Scripture speaks of the duties of the Christian, Scripture counts it the duty of the Christian to let his light shine before the people, 'that they may see your good works and give glory to your Father who is in heaven.' It seems to me that Christ and Peter said exactly the same things in different words. Both speak of duties, not rights."

Pl.: "Why will you not admit that it says here that every Christian in his own being owns the preaching office, that he then transfers it on the command of Christ to the one who through this transfer becomes a called servant of the church?"

Grossmann: "Why? Simply because it is not so stated. Nothing is said that a transfer occurs, nor can anything that is spoken of be transferred to another person. In the Old Testament one had to allow another to bring the blood and the offerings demanded by God. But the offerings of the New Testament must be brought individually by each spiritual priest. Can I let anyone else bring my body as an offering to God? If God demands anything of me, I must do it. I cannot do it through another. He wills that I proclaim his virtues."

Roebbelen: "But it says plainly that we are priests. Didn't priests have the duty to preach the Word of God? Weren't the priests the teachers of Scripture?"

Deindoerfer: "I would not say so without additional comment. It wasn't the priests who taught the Word of God in the Old Testament. It was the prophets. Priests had to instruct the people about offerings (Malachi 2:7). But we do not hear that Samuel or Elijah or Elisha organized priest schools. They organized prophet schools. 'Prophet' is the Greek idea of the German 'preacher,' with the distinction that the prophets God sent were inspired by God, while we preachers take our knowledge from the inspired Word of God."

Grossmann: "I would add that 'declare' (1 Peter 2:9) and 'preach' in our mode of speech are two different things. When one wishes to inform me of anything, whether he is a servant of God or not, he declares it to me. However, 'preaching,' according to our form of speech, is speaking in the name of and at the behest of God. I think that the real meaning of the word 'declare' is never used as a synonym for 'preach.' The word that Luther translates into `preacher' often means `servant.'"

Deindoerfer: "I am astonished that so much is read into the quotation (1 Peter 2:9). Out of the passage we are discussing we can and will only take this for ourselves and our congregation members, that we are God's chosen people. We want to preach into their hearts the splendor of their position as Christians. And then not to forget the end, that God demands of them that in all and every way, by word, by their daily life, their doings, their omissions, they must show their faith and thus declare the wonderful deeds of him who called them to his light. The result will be that the honor of God will be more widely known. Then they will let their light shine. Then their entire life is an offering acceptable to God."

Pl.: "Brother Deindoerfer, can I tell you openly what I do not like about you? Yes? It is that you believe that you understand God's Word better and that you can interpret Scripture better than our fathers, even Dr. Martin Luther. You must understand Scripture in the light of the fathers. If you would first of all set yourself at the feet of this God-sent prophet of our times [Ed.: Walther?] and learn from him how you should understand this, then you would not have such foolish ideas. You must first analyze the places. One must admit that Luther and the fathers had a better understanding of Scripture than oneself. Then you would very soon see that this point is the foundation point from which we can see that it treats of the public (*oeffentliche*) priesthood and how it is no other than this common (*allgemeine*) priesthood that is transferred to the pastor. That is your mistake. One can only be sure of the agreement with Scripture (*Schrift maeszigkeit*) of any doctrine (*Lehre*) when it can be pointed out that it agrees with Luther and the fathers."

Deindoerfer: "I also feel that I know Luther somewhat. And if I know Luther, then it is good that he doesn't hear you. Don't think ill of me, but I believe if he were here he would box both of your ears and say, 'What are you making of me? What I say I always want to have approved by Scripture.' I do not find what you find in the 1 Peter 2:9 reference. One must also read Luther's words on any subject in the context of which he speaks."

Roebbelen: "Well, dear brethren, time has run out. We still have time for further discussion in the morning. I think we can do no better than to recommend to both Brothers Grossmann and Deindoerfer that they examine the subject once more and not only read but also to study the fine citations from the fathers which are composed so masterfully. Then it can be no other than that they will be entirely united with us. *For it is so clear that our teaching is Luther's teaching* [emphasis added], and Luther's teaching is God's Word. You don't want to teach anything that is not God's Word, do you?"

Br.: "I would then suggest that we talk over tomorrow what seems to me to be hierarchy. I mean the difference found between our synod and Pastor Loehe over church regulations (*Kirchen Ordnungen*). There is no reason for us to dispute further over the question of the pastoral office as we have no prepared data (*vorlage*). We can discuss it again at the next conference."

All agreed and adjourned. That evening Grossmann preached at the worship service.

The Conference Confronts Its Differences with Loehe.

Roebbelen: "This morning we want to discuss the differences between us and Pastor Loehe on the church office. How do we want to go about this?"

Pl.: "I see a highly dangerous departure from Lutheran teaching in Pastor Loehe's position. He would take her God-given Christian freedom from the congregation."

Deindoerfer: "That would certainly be a most dangerous and Godless undertaking. But it almost seems to me that we understand something else in the words `Christian freedom' than you do. I understand under the 'Christian freedom' that Christ has earned for every single Christian and therefore for each congregation of Christians that which Luther says so gloriously in his writing 'The Freedom of the Christian Man': 'A Christian through faith is a free lord and subject to no one; a Christian is the most dutiful servant of all and subject to everyone....No one on earth has power to command him in spiritual matters; there God and God alone is his Lord.'"

Pl.: "But Loehe will not recognize the God-given rights of the congregation."

Grossmann: "You can't mean, can you, that Loehe would shove the occupant of the office (*Amtstraeger*) in between God and the individual Christians!"

Pl.: "As you who have spoken in opposition to me agree entirely with Loehe, tell us what your position is concerning the sentence: A congregation owes obedience to the pastor in all things not contrary to the Word of God."

Grossmann: "The answer is very easy. The sentence is entirely false. I would not say 'in all things contrary' but 'in all things demanded (gefordert)' in God's Word. Exactly because a Christian is under God's commandments, one can only demand of him what God's Word says."

Roebbelen: "But Pastor Loehe has criticized our church regulations. He blames any poor conditions in our congregations on our regulations."

Deindoerfer: "But he has emphatically declared that thereby no doctrines, no teachings of Scripture are involved. The question is only what regulations are most beneficial for the church. That certainly is an entirely different question. It becomes a matter of human choice, a consideration of worth and value....God has actually appointed no regulations for the church. He has left this to man entirely, and the church is free to make workable church regulations according to the need of the times."

Roebbelen: "Do *you* mean, I will not ask does Loehe mean, that the preaching office, the pastor, has the right to institute good church regulations?"

Deindoerfer: "Do you mean as an authority? No. The entire duty of the pastor for which he has his right from God is to feed the congregation with the Word and Sacrament. All other things belong in the sphere of the worldly and there the pastoral office has no right to prescribe anything. But truthfully I believe that a pastor understands more about good church regulations than any layman and that his advice should be good...."

Roebbelen: "Why do you see danger in our church regulations that leave everything in the hands of the congregations?"

Grossmann: "I can probably answer this as follows: If all congregations were as mature spiritually as Frankenmuth, Frankentrost and Frankenlust, there would be little danger. But let us look at the history of the church in Saginaw. As Pastor Cloeter here in Saginaw insisted on carrying out church discipline, as he undertook to exhort sinning members to repentance, what happened? A large part of the congregation met and formed another congregation.

Or let us take Frankenhilf. All who know Frankenhilf know that side by side with mature and experienced (*erfahrenen*) Christians whom one can trust in anything, there are such who in Germany kept the church at a distance, and who here had to be won again through faithful pastoral care (*Seelsorge*). This poses the question: How should one compose external regulations (*Ordnungen*) for the work of the visible church? This is the place where our thinking parts."....

Deindoerfer: "I was at a synodical meeting recently. I noted that the pastors were the principal speakers and that the lay members only voted or did not even vote. That looks very good on paper. With that one can flatter many lay members. The synodical organization can still become a modified monarchy or aristocracy in spite of it.

Whether one cites the regulations or not, it is and will be the case that the pastors already because of their education and experience will wield decisive influence. If this were agreed to as a proper procedure, it would hardly be a hierarchy because it would be established and recognized as a human regulation."

Roebellen:"It is true that our pastors take the lead at our synodical meetings. But I do not place all pastors on one level. Those with insight and experience will always have a greater influence than those who have less. I would not place Professor Walther on the same level with a young pastor who has just entered the office—despite the fact that some young pastors feel that they understand everything better than all the others together. Professor Walther, to me, stands higher than a dozen others."

Grossmann: "It is particularly in the matter of calling pastors that Loehe fears that impure elements in the congregations or uninformed people may do damage. He wishes by means of good church regulations to prevent bad regulations which simple people might propose without harmful intentions."

Pl.: "Then Pastor Loehe wants to dictate to the congregations who their pastor should be, like a little pope."

Grossmann:"You must not always point to the ridiculous or to the worst. What Loehe would like to see is this, that the synodical president or the most responsible pastors be consulted. He fears that failing a good church regulation, congregations will simply take no advice. He fears further that eventually disorders will occur to the detriment of the congregations."...

Talk continued along these lines. It was concluded that the two brethren should reflect more on the matter. They were certain that these two would then agree with the others. The meeting adjourned.

Grossmann combined his visit to this conference with a short visit to the Deindoerfers. Karl Gottlob Amman with his team took them home from Frankenmuth to his house where the Deindoerfers lived. As they parted, Roebbelen gave Grossmann a very friendly invitation to visit him soon so they could discuss the matter further.

After Grossmann and Deindoerfer left, Roebbelen said to the others, "One thing is clear to me, these two are not dangerous enemies. They honestly mean well. We do not want to allow the differences that have arisen here between us to cause us to view them with squint eyes. We should rather hope that they are soon taught better."

CHAPTER 7

WHAT IS THE PREACHING OFFICE?

G rossmann took advantage of Roebbelen's invitation and visited him at Frankenmuth. He came to discuss the differences because their significance had become clear to him and it concerned him greatly.

Roebbelen: "You do not want to accept the description of the preaching office which was given at our conference. What do you have to criticize?"

Grossmann: "The description reads, 'The holy ministry is the authority or power to carry out the rights of the spiritual priesthood in open office by reason of joint interest.' I can accept that. But there are a number of points that do not seem clear and tend to lead to error."

Roebbelen: "Will you name them to me?"

Grossmann: "In the first place it says here that the holy ministry is a power or authority; secondly that this power consists of carrying out the rights of the spiritual priesthood; thirdly in open exercise of office; and fourthly from joint interest. One can say that, but it seems to me that here is something more easily thought than one can prove."

Roebbelen: "Let us take last, 'joint interest.' What is dark there?"

Grossmann: "I think of two meanings there. First, it can mean that a number of Christians join together and every single member turns his share over like an artisan partnership. Or, because one really cannot think of the office as split into shares, every Christian has the pastoral office in his spiritual priesthood. Every Christian is in his own being a pastor. Then each relinquishes what he should do and appoints a qualified man to act as his substitute. Thus a member of the congregation could come to the pastor and say, 'Pastor, I wasn't present at your election and call. Naturally I want you to substitute for me and I hereby turn my office over to you.'"

Roebbelen: "Why shouldn't one be able to visualize such a substitution?"

Grossmann: "Because as far as I know Scripture nowhere speaks thus, that one can turn over his spiritual priesthood like that. You must admit that this is not in the Scripture passage we discussed in our recent conversations. There it was only said what Christians are and what they as Christians must do. But there was no discussion that they should or could turn their Christian priesthood over to another. If I should believe that or teach that, one must cite me clear quotations for it. There simply are no such citations or you would have quoted them. Then the matter would have been settled. You only quote Luther, and what he wants is entirely different....

"Walther wrote in *Der Lutheraner*, 'We must confess that one is occasionally startled with certain of Pastor Loehe's explanations in his publications, where he speaks of the church and how she should be formed. One may arrive at the idea that questionable (*bedenkliche*) principles are at the base. Then hear the excellent man himself, not only when with glowing eloquence, on holy places, he sweeps all before him, but also when he opens his heart in private conversation, in simple speech. One learns to know the man more closely, full of the most precious simplicity, honesty, mildness and humility, with his high regard of every child of God and of every good thing, which and where he finds it. Then all doubts vanish and one must say, 'Here is no trace of priestly pride to find; here is humility that forgets self and only thinks of the church, the worthy maid and her bridegroom. Here reigns Christ's spirit; here beats a faithful human heart.

"'As we did not agree on every expression regarding the disputed teachings during our recent stay in the home of Pastor Loehe, we can assure the dear readers with happy confidence that an agreement was reached in truth and love, through God's grace and kindness which is of higher value than an agreement which has its authority vouched for by forcing one another's signatures to narrow formulae.'

"And that quotation from Walther is the way I also understand Loehe. When you always hold the congregations in the foreground, it seems as though Christ is at the same time forgotten."

Roebbelen: "That certainly is not our intention, and one dare not understand us that way."

Grossmann: "Let me just refer you to two quotations from Loehe. First, 'When we ask the question, Who gives the office to the pastor?, the simple answer is that God gives the office through the service of the whole congregation. He is and remains author and founder of the office in general and giver of the office to individual pastors. He does not first make the congregation holder and possessor of the office so that she passes it on further and the pastor receives it from the congregation second-handed.' Secondly, 'the Lord himself gives the office using the entire congregation as his organ. The congregation does not give away her rights or privileges. She does not waive for some few the rights of the many, who then do not have them. But she gives the Lord's office as a servant of the church in that she has the Lord's command for the disposition of the office and the Lord thus works his wishes through her directly.'...

"When one describes the pastoral office, why does one not speak of Jesus and his service instead of authority and rights and joint interests? I fear, and my experience confirms, that superficial and frivolous (*leicht-fertig*) congregational members get the idea that `We are the ones who make the pastor. We give him our rights and we can always take them back.' People could be led falsely by this kind of thinking to forget entirely Christ in whose Name and by whose command they had called this hired man and servant of Christ. I know you don't want that but you give opportunity for the people to arrive at such false conclusions. If you speak as Scripture speaks, this cannot happen. That is why I do not use the words `authority' and `rights'."

Roebbelen: "You don't deny that Christ has given his congregation certain rights?"

Grossmann: "No. I would not deny what you are trying to say. But your way of speaking easily leads to error. Right here I would ask you, Where does Scripture speak of the rights of Christians in this sense? At least to my recollection there is no place where rights are spoken of in this way. On the contrary, I find that often the duties, tasks, service, and work of the servants of God are discussed."

Roebbelen: "But the Christians also have certain tasks. To carry out these tasks, they do have a right?"

Grossmann: "I would say they have a duty. And when one speaks of the spiritual priesthood, the Christians here have a big duty, namely, to proclaim, to make known the great virtues of him who has called them. I say a big duty because it contains use of every means by which the eternal salvation (*Heil*) in Christ can be made known and spread." ...

Roebbelen: "What form would you then propose in order to express what you want to say?"

Grossmann: "The holy preaching office, instituted by Christ himself, is the service in which a qualified and properly called servant of Christ edifies a congregation by preaching the gospel and administering the Sacraments. Wherever a congregation calls a pastor for this service, it deals as a part of the chosen people and kingly priesthood in that it thereby proclaims the virtues of God. I believe that would contain everything in the other definition in the sense in which I recognize it as a teacher of holy Scripture."

Roebbelen: "And what is your attitude toward me, if I am of the opinion that the common priesthood and the open preaching office are only different things in form and not two different things standing side by side? And when I am even of the opinion that the individual Christian, to carry out in good order the task given to all, relinquishes his share in favor of the pastor who then does what otherwise all should do?"

Grossmann: "Then my position is that I leave you the right to prove this to me out of God's Word. And as long as you until now, I would say, in erroneous manner maintain that this is the teaching of God's Word, I am prepared to deal with you as my brother. I consider your opinion (*Meinung*), as long as you have not proven it to me out of Scripture, to be a human opinion. I view it (do not take offense at my reference) as wood, straw, stubble, which you have built on the foundation laid from God's Word. The foundation is the teaching of the office as the service ordained by God. The small difference that arises as you disagree with me on one point cannot part our unity in the faith. And I am certain that when we view the subject according to the Word of God and lay everything else aside, the Holy Spirit will also lead us to unity in this. How do you see the matter?"

Roebbelen: "I also do not consider the matter to be divisive. It seems to me that the main thing between us is the question of church regulations. And when you say it is not a matter of doctrine (*Lehre*), but a matter of church life (*Leben der Kirche*), I cannot deny you fellowship of faith (*Glaubensgemeinschaft*) because we do not think alike here. I also hope that more exact reflection will still lead us together. I would like it if we could also discuss the question of what our Confessions teach on the subject. But we can do that another time." (Excursi 1, 2, and 3)

Excursus 1. Mary Todd, assistant professor of history at Concordia University, River Forest, Illinois, writes in an article titled, "Thinking about History: The Missouri Compromise": "Lutheran understanding of the ministry depends on the tension between the two principles of a priesthood of all believers and a set-apart office of ordained ministry of Word and Sacrament. But the [Lutheran] Confessions do not address these two principles in juxtaposition. Rather, it is the office of the ministry that is so carefully explicated. There is in fact only one reference to the priesthood of all believers in the symbolical books, and even that is in the context of the right of the Church to choose and ordain ministers. Luther's focus on the universal priesthood had been an element of his early career as a reformer, but as the reformation progressed, his stress of that aspect of ministry dimmed. Instead, the overarching emphasis of both the later Luther and the Church over time has been on the office of public ministry.

"Lutherans find this paradox of ministry difficult to translate into everyday understanding.. Because it's not easy being people of paradox, while we subscribe in principle to both aspects of ministry, we find it hard to reconcile them in the life of the Church. And so they tend to exist in a not-so-creative tension. Misunderstanding of each has at times led to conflict between clergy and laity; misunderstanding of both over time has been a perpetual feature of congregational life. Misconception of the universal priesthood can find it in competition with the set-apart office, leading to power struggles, elevation of the ordained ministry and devaluation of the ministry of the laity, and vice versa. Difficulty in retaining right relationship or balance between these two complementary but different aspects of the ministry of the Church has left Lutherans open to persistent charges of an inadequate theology of the ministry and of the Church." *Lutheran Forum* 31, no. 4 (Winter 1997): 46.

Excursus 2. John A. Stoudt, pastor of Emmaus Evangelical Lutheran Church in Ridgewood (Queens), New York, writes in an article titled, "The Office of the Holy Ministry as Dispensator Sacramentorum": [John Gerhard 1582-1637] "makes it very plain that the act of presiding at the Holy Communion is not committed to all the baptized people of God, but rather to the properly called and ordained ministers of the Church. Luther never said that all Christians are allowed to preside at celebrations of the Mass; he did assert that Christians (as opposed to pagans) are the only ones who possess a faith that makes them `worthy' or `fit' to make use of the Eucharist by receiving the the Lord's Body and Blood. The royal priesthood created through Baptism, is consequently, not the same thing as the office of the public ministry....

"The priesthood of all believers and the office of the public ministry are not identical or interchangeable. Each has its own proper Christological dimensions, and we Lutherans should know better than to mix them up. Such confusion would reduce the office of the holy ministry to a mere function within the Church." *Lutheran Forum* 31, no. 4, (Winter 1997): 53.

Excursus 3. Frank C. Senn, pastor of Immanuel Lutheran Church in Evanston, Illinois, writes in an article titled, "The Use of the Means of Grace: An Exercise in the Critique of Church Statements": "In the ELCA [Evangelical Lutheran Church in America] lay members of synods and churchwide assemblies as well as clergy vote on church statements. This represents a development within American Lutheranism that reflects the democratic spirit of the American nation. The earliest meetings of the Ministerium of Pennsylvania from 1748 on gave voice but not vote to lay delegates. By a century later lay delegates were regularly voting at synod conventions. Some Lutheran church bodies achieved virtually an equality between clergy and laity in synod assemblies because each congregation was represented by its pastor and a lay delegate. The ELCA has constitutionally mandated that the clergy should never outvote the laity by specifying that the ratio in assemblies of this Church shall be 60 percent lay/40 percent clergy. So the highest teaching authority in this Church is given to persons who do not have 'a regular call' (*ritus vocatio*), as Article XIV of the Augsburg Confession puts it, to exercise the public teaching ministry in the Church. The ELCA Constitution defines the Churchwide Assembly as the highest authority in the Church, and pastors and congregations can be disciplined for disregarding the ELCA Constitution. But this arrangement seems to be in conflict with the Lutheran Confessions, to which pastors subscribe at their ordinations and which are also enshrined within the constitutions of congregations as the norm for faith and practice. Thus, you see that we have a conflicted situation built right into the structure of the ELCA which raises the question of what kind of authority lies behind any statement of this Church." *Lutheran Forum* 31, no. 2, (Summer 1997).

CHAPTER 8

FRANKENHILF'S FUTURE— WITH LOEHE OR SYNOD?

T he doctrine of the ministry question arose at Frankenhilf the following spring of 1853. A meeting was being conducted in Amman's home to organize the congregation. The latest group of immigrants had established themselves in the colony as well as possible with the help of the early settlers. Pastor Deindoerfer asked everyone to attend the meeting, which replaced the customary Sunday afternoon worship. (George J. Fritschel's narrative [30] based on minutes of the meeting, gives an account from which the following is drawn.)

A number of the members had been content to attend only the Sunday morning worship. Even that was a gain for some, because in Germany they seldom attended public worship at all. But at Frankenhilf, living among faithful church-goers, they felt constrained to follow the colony pattern. Besides, there was no inn where one might spend time on Sunday. Also, if they tried to avoid attending church, Amman or L. Sippel admonished them in a kindly manner and a visit could also be expected from the pastor.

So, on this Sunday, when the congregation met to organize, all members of the colony showed up.

The meeting opened with a hymn. Deindoerfer prayed for the aid of the Holy Spirit. He then stated that the time had come to organize a congregation that would take responsibilty for its own affairs. Since here in America the government does not concern itself with the Church as was true in Germany, the Church must govern its own affairs.

Deindoerfer had distributed copies of a constitution (*Gemeinde Ordnung*) which Loehe had written for the colony. The members had read it, and Deindoerfer had reviewed it with most of them on his visits. He said that establishing a congregation is an important matter and therefore a secretary should first be chosen to record accurately what was decided so that one could at any time refer to what had happened. On nomination of Sippel, Amman was chosen as secretary.

Amendments to the constitution were suggested. Paragraph 24 had read: "We lay the confessional money (*Beichtgeld*) on the altar as thankoffering, not as pay for absolution, but as an act of love. The gift is for the pastor who pronounces absolution." Amman proposed to drop the whole paragraph. First, confessional gifts were customary only in certain parts of Germany. Secondly, instead of making confessional gifts, people should increase the pastor's salary. Third, confessional gifts were not being made at Frankenmuth. The proposal to drop the paragraph had unanimous approval.

At Amman's suggestion, the last paragraph was also deleted: "Falling away from the Confessions automatically results in separation from our colony. Our colony consists of Lutherans only." Amman felt that anyone who left the Lutheran faith also left the congregation or was excommunicated. That was self-evident. Because colony land was sold only to Lutherans, the Frankenhilf congregation could consist only of Lutherans. Pastor Loehe insisted that land adjoining the colony should be purchased now at the current low price, as far as their means would reach, and sold only to Lutherans. But how could one force anyone to move away from the colony if he afterward should leave the Lutheran church? Having purchased his land, he could not be forced to sell it. The congregation agreed with Amman.

Next came the question of support of the pastor. The constitution read: "The yield of the parish land as well as all pastoral honoraria and perquisites belong to the pastor from the day of his installation."

Loehe had established forty acres of parish land to be used for pastoral support (*Pfarrgut*). Amman paid twelve dollars to begin a Funding Treasury (*Fundierungskasse*). As soon as they were able, each colonist was to pay 13 cents for each acre they owned into this treasury. The pastor's salary would be paid from this treasury once Loehe's support of Deindoerfer came to an end. Up to that point, Loehe had paid Deindoerfer's salary from the Poor Colony Fund. Otherwise Amman would have had to provide the pastor's entire support, since no one else had any money.

L. Sippel said that this looked fine on paper, but to date the forty acres of parish land had not produced one dollar. So far the pastor had not received any honoraria, and there would be few for a long time to come. One could not expect Mr. Amman to keep the pastor in his home and feed him indefinitely. That must be the duty of the congregation. If the pastor was expected to accept what he could get from the congregation, it was a little bit too much to die on and very much too little to live on. It had become a bad situation, especially when one considered that most members had come with practically no means. Sippel knew however that Pastor Loehe intended to provide the pastor's salary for some time in the future.

Pastor Deindoerfer then explained that Pastor Loehe had sent him over in response to the plea of this congregation which had accepted this constitution previously (before they left Germany). When Loehe founded this colony as a colony for the poor, he provided for it. The forty-acre parish tract was intended for later times when it would probably bring in enough for a pastor to live from its proceeds. Pastor Loehe had given Deindoerfer enough money to arrive at Frankenhilf, had since sent him more, and wanted Deindoerfer to tell him how much he needed. The mission fund entrusted to Loehe would take care of it. Of course, Pastor Loehe asked that he be assured that the congregation wanted his help and support and would be worthy of it.

Thereupon, Mr. Sippel wanted to know what Pastor Loehe's priorities were concerning the Frankenhilf congregation. Deindoerfer replied that it concerned Loehe that the Frankenhilf congregation actually be and remain a completely Lutheran congregation in teaching and practice. In America it would be easy for another spirit to enter a congregation—for example, when another pastor would be called to head the parish.

Mathias Schwab: "Pastor, what then is your position to Pastor Loehe?"

Deindoerfer: "Pastor Loehe directed me to this congregation when he sent me over. The congregation, then only the families of Amman and Schwarz, had turned to Loehe asking that he might furnish them with a pastor. As Pastor Loehe intends to sustain this congregation and pay my salary until the parish land, or the congregation along with the proceeds from the parish land, raises the necessary maintenance, I have pledged to Pastor Loehe that if I receive a call from another congregation, or if I decide to resign for other reasons, I will inform him of the reasons why I wish to accept another call etc. I thus do not give up the work of this congregation unless he knows about it."

Michael Schwarz: "Then we would have nothing to say about it?"

Deindoerfer: "In case this should happen, the congregation probably would know nothing of it until I have Loehe's answer. Then I naturally could not accept another call until this congregation agreed. I am bound to this congregation until you agree to my stepping out of my work here."

J. G. Kamm: "Could we obtain another pastor when you leave? Would Pastor Loehe help furnish us another pastor? Would he then pledge himself for the support money for this other pastor?"

Johannes Trump: "When and as long as as Pastor Loehe protects and looks after this congregation, it seems to me, it must follow that he must be satisfied with the pastor. If we expect him to furnish all the pastor's salary or at least the greater share, then I feel he has a right to have something to say about it when we call a pastor."

Amman: "It seems the same to me as to Trump. If I had to pay all or at least most of an undertaking, I personally would not demand to have everything to say about it, though it would not be entirely unjust for me to do so. But I would at least insist that that I have a voice in the matter and that I had a right to enter the discussions."

Michael Huber: "Would Pastor Loehe agree? Should it happen that Pastor Deindoerfer should leave us, which I hope will never come about, would he furnish us a new pastor? Would he furnish the necessary money?"

Deindoerfer: "Certainly he would. He is vitally interested that this congregation bloom and develop. Think what he did for Frankenmuth, Frankentrost and Frankenlust. These no longer require his care. And so Frankenhilf will be able to eventually stand self supporting."

Sippel: "That will take years. Thus it appears to me that we as a congregation should decide to place ourselves under the advice and guidance of Pastor Loehe as long as we require his help. We would thus oblige ourselves, because he supports or at least helps support our pastor, to deal with him as they deal with a patron in Germany— the patron in Neuendettelsau, for instance, in the event of a vacancy would propose a pastor."

Paulus Popp: "That's exactly as it was with us at home. There the consistory elected one of the three he presented. Who are the consistory here?"

Deindoerfer: "There are no consistories here. Here the congregations have united into a large body. It is called a synod. Our synod is the Synod of Missouri, Ohio and other States. The synod elects officers, and President Wyneken is obliged, when a congregation wishes, to name and propose pastors whom he trusts would serve the congregation correctly."

Sippel: "Pastor, how would it be if we confer the right and duty on Pastor Loehe for as long as he is in some respects our patron, or I would rather say our fatherly friend, helper and advisor, to advise us in such matters as are usually dealt with by the synod?"

Popp: "I am for that fully."

Amman: "As I know that Pastor Loehe wishes us only well, I believe that such faith in him would bring him much joy."

Others expressed themselves in similar terms. There was full unanimity.

Deindoerfer: "It seems to me that this is the unanimous opinion of all members. It pleases me that the congregation itself wishes to establish the matter in this way. I am convinced that Pastor Loehe will be entirely satisfied. Should I now put it to a vote that it may become a recorded decision of the congregation?"

Sippel: "Yes, put it to a vote. But ask each one individually so we may know who is for it and who is against it."

Deindoerfer: "Well, I believe no one has anything against the proposal that if Pastor Loehe pays the pastor's salary and helps us build the church, the congregation promises to seek his advice when calling a pastor. I ask for a vote. Each say free and openly what he feels about it."

Some simply said "yes." Others declared that they considered the proposal to be correct and inexpensive. So full unanimity was shown in support of the proposal. Secretary Amman recorded it in the minutes, which he then read. Then all signed the constitution, the *Kirchenordnung der evangel. lutherisch. Gemeinde Frankenhilf* (Constitution of the Evangelical Lutheran Congregation of Frankenhilf). It was signed by the first founders from the families of Amman and Schwarz who came in 1850 to those who had arrived by the twenty-third Sunday after Trinity 1852: J. Deindoerfer, pastor; Carl Gottlob Amman; Michael Schwarz; Heinrich Dahl; Paulus Popp; C. Glave; J. G. Kam; L. Sippel; J. Schwab; and Georg Bauer. (Note: See Appendix V Constitution, etc.)

Pastor Deindoerfer said that he would send a copy of the minutes with his next letter to Loehe.

This was the founding of what became both Saint Michael's Lutheran Church of Richville, Michigan, a congregation of the Missouri Synod, and Saint Sebald Lutheran Congregation of rural Strawberry Point, Iowa. The Saint Sebald group broke away from Saint Michael's and moved to Iowa that same fall. The warm and unanimous vote of confidence in Wilhelm Loehe expressed at this first meeting of the Frankenhilf congregation in the spring of 1853 was to change in less than three months. By July, in response to rumors fomented in the other colonies, the sentiment would turn from unanimous support to majority suspicion and then to outright rejection of Loehe's sponsorship.

The meeting next discussed how to complete their church building. This log church was 25 feet wide and 36 feet long. Some were pessimistic. The church had been erected in the fall as far as the roof. Trees had been felled. Timbers had been sawed into correct lengths, trimmed with broad axes and fitted to each other. Now boards and shingles were required for the roof. Planed boards, sills, windows, doors, and floor boards needed to be purchased at great cost. Where would they get the money?

Pastor Deindoerfer announced that Johannes Weege, Loehe's superintendent (*Verwalter*), had been instructed by Loehe to lay aside from the moneys repaid by earlier colonists at Frankenmuth enough for the church building at Frankenhilf. So the necessary money would be on hand. This brought a joyful response. They decided that as soon as time could be spared from farm work, they should go at finishing the church and start building a parsonage.

If all had had the enthusiasm that Amman and one or two others showed, the church would soon have been completed. But there were a number who time and again had excuses. The few zealous ones could not handle the heavy work alone.

Deindoerfer had written to his father and relatives asking for gifts for a small bell. Amman had news from his relatives that in Memmingen a considerable number of guilders had been contributed for another bell. It seemed that the little chapel (*Kirchlein*) was about to receive these gifts.

After the chapel, the parsonage was to head the list, for it was almost too much to expect Amman to share his house with the pastor's family much longer. No one dreamed that he would continue to do so the following winter in Iowa. And the pastor did not foresee that the bells would never reach the chapel. He, too, had no notion of the heavy days that soon lay ahead for him.

Scripture and Creed

Like Grossmann, Deindoerfer, too, visited Pastor Roebbelen at Frankenmuth. Roebbelen had urged him soon to bring his young wife Katharina Elisabetha for a visit. [31] The young pastor from Frankenhilf did so at the next opportunity. It was a nice day, so they were on the way early and wandered through the gloomy forest. The road ran between the rows of trees like a deep ravine. They could easily understand how Karl Amman and his companions had become lost in the forest three years ago and had to spend the night in the pouring rain.

Walking with laughter was almost as fast as riding with leisurely oxen over stumps. Here and there they passed a clearing with a log dwelling. They heard the bells of Frankenmuth sounding through the woods as they drew near. Friends of missions had sent these bells to the first settlers. On one was the figure of Saint Lorenz after whom the Frankenmuth Church was named. Under it was the inscription "Concordia 1580, *res parvae crescunt*" (small things grow through unity). The bells hung from a scaffold beside the steeple-free log church. The congregation was talking of building a frame church, now that the log church could no longer hold all the people.

As they walked, the young pastor viewed the future hopefully. His Frankenhilf also had good prospects for growth, though the original plan to make it entirely a welfare colony would only be partially fulfilled.

They arrived at Frankenmuth and the two pastors were soon engaged in earnest conversation. The arguments turned on the use of Scripture and the Lutheran Confessions. Deindoerfer said that his approach to Scripture teaching on a question was to study Scripture in context, study the Confessional document in the context in which it was written, and then compare the two for accuracy in his understanding. Roebbelen called the Confessions the voice of the church telling us how to interpret Scripture. "Why would we have the Confessions if they did not, as the voice of our church tell us how we should interpret Scripture? And particularly when we consider who has given us these glorious explanations of the Word of God. These men whom God has allowed to stand up as prophets and witnesses of recent times against the papacy have really had a greater measure of enlightenment from the Holy Spirit than we have. The best and most God-acceptable way and means of penetrating the Scripture is certainly that we set ourselves at the feet of these men and let them teach us."

In the afternoon the two men argued from Scripture and the Confessions whether the pastoral office is transferred to the pastor from the priesthood of individual Christians or from the congregation as a community.

Roebbelen: (after much discussion) "It seems that we are not far apart on the subject. You attack the subject from a different side than we do. You do not ask first what Luther says about it and thus do not understand the Confessions according to Luther's way. You do not recognize in the Confessions the correct decision given by the church itself about what Scripture says. You go directly into Scripture....I am afraid that is a method that may easily lead one astray. For what are we compared to the great theologians that God has given our church? One should not hold such gifts of God cheaply."

Deindoerer: "I don't intend to do that. I do believe it is correct to go directly to Scripture. Should I thereby possibly arrive at an erroneous opinion and should I understand Scripture wrongly, I will certainly seek information and instruction from the great teachers, so that I may check (*nachpreufe*) my work and find my error. On the other hand it will not confuse me if, among the great theologians I find differing opinions as is the case in the matter before us. That will drive me next to check the viewpoint in which I differ from others. And if I see that they are mistaken and that no mistake lies before me, what brings me to this certainty must be that it is based on Scripture."

Roebbelen: "Where do you find my error in that I have arrived at a conviction other than yours?"

Deindoerfer: "Number one, that you first want to go to the great teachers, although that need not lead to error directly. You only decide to prefer one to another when they are not unanimous. Number two, in your Scripture choices, after the pattern of your teaching fathers

[Wyneken and Walther], you select passages which do not apply at all to the establishing of the pastoral office. Thirdly, in your method, as you make these Scripture passages the beginning of your thinking and then, in some manner (*gewissermassen*), you spin your thoughts and probably without realizing it, through your final conclusions you go beyond Scripture and arrive at something certainly is not found in Scripture."

CHAPTER 9

THE TENSION GROWS

The question of the pastoral office and its transfer soon stirred all the people in the Saginaw valley. At first only the pastors debated it. But then they discussed it with the more mature lay persons, of whom there were many among the Franconian immigrants. Because Luther was quoted so often in *Der Lutheraner* and in sermons, some lay people had *Luther's Works* sent to them from Germany. These works were read diligently also when neighbors met. The pastoral call became part of daily conversation, for the pastors preached about it when the Sunday lessons gave opportunity and even when they did not.[32]

Deindoerfer and Grossmann remained entirely on the defensive. They did not say, "Your viewpoint is a human theory which does not agree with what Luther wrote in the Smalcald Articles." They did bring up the question, "If God has given the preaching office to every Christian, that is to every man, woman, and child, and the pastor obtains it from them, does every member give a quit claim deed, so to speak, when they call the pastor? How does that agree with the fact that the office is given directly to the entire church? Does the church have the office indirectly...through the possession of the single members?"

But Grossmann and Deindoerfer avoided speaking to the question more than was absolutely necessary because the other pastors were not agreed on the subject themselves.

Finding Walther and his colleagues unwilling to yield to his wish for a strong teaching office in America and especially in his Michigan colonies, Loehe tried to withdraw his missioners from the newly-organized Missouri Synod. But the great majority of the ninety-three men he had sent to America forsook Loehe and followed Walther and Wyneken. The only contact Loehe had left with the Missouri Synod had been through his relationship with the colonies he had begun in

90 • The Pilgrim Colony

Michigan. But the first three were now affiliated with the synod. Only the Frankenhilf colony stood with him. In the months that followed, the Franconian lay colonists picked up distorted news of their pastors' debates. Fears spread that Loehe was too authoritarian and wanted to take away their God-given freedom.

Except for Deindoerfer, the colonial clergy, supported by Wyneken, Walther, and other Missouri Synod leaders, thought it intolerable that the head of the seminary in their midst [Grossmann] should hold to Loehe's beliefs, which they charged were not only undemocratic but unLutheran. From his Holy Cross Church pulpit in Saginaw, Pastor Ottomar E. Cloeter criticized Grossmann as he sat in the congregation. Cloeter suggested that Grossmann, Amman and Deindoerfer leave Michigan and work in some state where there were no congregations of the Missouri Synod. [33]

The other colonial clergy joined Cloeter in focusing pressure on Grossmann. He had earlier been invited and even pressed by Pastor Cloeter to join the Missouri Synod. Grossmann refused because he, like Loehe, disagreed with Missouri's congregational emphases. His position caused so much conflict that Grossmann was for some time placed under discipline at Holy Cross. [34]

Cloeter became increasing vocal in expressing bitter feelings toward Grossmann and Deindoerfer. He spoke in such a manner from the pulpit that people kept glancing to where the Inspector of the seminary sat, turning to see what impression it made on him, because it was clear that Cloeter's words were directed at him. It no longer helped to point out that except on one or two points, they were entirely united in doctrine.

Because popular slurs hit home, some spoke of Loehe's "'Romanizing' teachings on the pastoral office." From this the less informed went on to say, "Loehe has fallen from the faith and has become a teacher of error." Not all people were against Loehe. Numerous lay persons raised questions that the pastors were hard put to answer. Johannes Weege Sr. reported that a number had become so disgusted with the controversy that they wanted to leave the colonies if only they could sell their land.

The Spring Conference

The time for the colony pastors' 1853 spring conference drew near. After what had been said at the fall conference of 1852, Loehe's teachings would be further debated. The more the neighboring pastors observed that their arguments and references caused no change in Deindoerfer's and Grossmann's positions on the doctrine of the church and ministry, the less likely it appeared that the two would ever yield. The mood became bitter. The former hearty greetings were gone. The other pastors no longer visited the two. Cloeter in Saginaw withdrew from teaching at the seminary.

The conference consisted chiefly of arguments repeating Scripture references used at the previous conference and in private conversations. Roebbelen tried unsuccessfully to mediate and to lead the meeting to the point where both sides could set forth exactly where the deviation from each other occurred. The Franken pastors maintained that Loehe did not listen to the "voice of the church," that he held himself wiser than "the ancient teachers" who they claimed taught that in the call the pastoral office was transferred from the laity to the pastor. They insisted that this was the teaching of the Confessions. Whoever understood the quoted passages in a different way had departed from the "pure teaching of God's Word." and could probably be carried in the synod as an erring brother, but only for a time.

George Fritschel reconstructed from his sources the following dialogue [35]:

Pastor P.: "Because Grossmann and Deindoerfer here deviate from the clear teaching of the Lutheran church and thus have a false and unLutheran teaching, can I still in spite of this recognize them as brothers in the faith?"

Pastor H.: "For true unity in the faith an absolute unanimity must occur. Didn't Pastor Walther say in regard to Loehe, 'The more important true unity is that which penetrates the last threads in unraveling a teaching.' That is the true unity we demand....Certainly we must be first united in principle, then the unity must also extend to the finger tips."

P.: "The question arises for me if we shouldn't now demand that Grossmann turn the seminary over to us. If he doesn't do so, it seems to me that we are dealing with a schismatic school that will tear the unity in our midst apart."

Grossmann: "I cannot give away what does not belong to me. I could not resign if you demanded it of me. The institution does not belong to me. It belongs to the Society for Inner Missions [in Germany]. I am under call by that same society. I can only hand my resignation to them. And as the institution does not wish to establish dissension but to serve the synod, that is my call and I have pledged myself to it."

H.: "Then I propose that we state that we are of the opinion that we have an institution at which a teacher stands who does not agree with us but agrees with Pastor Loehe and that we can no longer tolerate him in our midst. We must demand that the institution is either turned over to synod or locked shut."

Grossmann: "What would synod do with the institution if Loehe surrenders it? Synod still solicits gifts from Germany for the seminaries at St. Louis and Fort Wayne. Can she maintain a third institution?"

Roebbelen: "Brothers, don't overdo the matter. Grossmann has spoken correctly. There is no quarrel between us in connection with the teaching of the holy preaching office. Thank God, we are united in that. We should tell of that and not of our difference; otherwise we will never come together."

Cloeter: "We will never come together."

Grossmann: "Brethren, think what you do. The teacher seminary should and wants to serve no one but the synod. In a few months the first five students will have finished the prescribed plan of instruction. You visited the seminary repeatedly. You were present at the examination. You testified that what was taught was right. Don't you want these parish school teachers? Do you want them to go elsewhere?"

Roebbelen: "Under no circumstances. We must have them."

H.: "Will you, Grossmann, refer them to synod?"

Grossmann: "What else? Loehe has founded this institution for the synod. My instructions and call are for the purpose of preparing them for the synod. If I did otherwise, I would be wrong. Naturally, as long as Loehe must sustain the institution, its teachers and seminarians, I am responsible to him, not to you. I wish nothing more than to live with you in peace and to work for you. And in that the difference that lies between us is of no hindrance. It has little to do with the teaching about the pastoral office. And in practice, it certainly means nothing."

Deindoerfer: "I must express myself on one thing. If you exaggerate the disunity as has happened today, then you simply make it impossible for us to live in peace with you. You drive it to the breaking point."

S.: "Here it is either/or. Since our teaching is the right one, your teaching is false. And we cannot endure false teaching."

Grossmann: "Consider what you are doing. We are fully united with you in what a pastor should teach. We teach what the Confessions teach. We differ on one point that never came up before and was therefore never treated as part of Christian doctrine. You have set up a theory that we cannot accept because God's Word says nothing about it."

Deindoerfer: "Do you want to throw us out because of this difference? Do you therefore wish to withdraw the hand of a brother from us. Do you want to ban us for that reason? How can you justify that before God?"

Wyneken's Visit

Pastor Cloeter at Saginaw became increasingly hostile. [36] Once he had to be away from his pulpit so he suggested to his congregation that the services be dropped. One man asked if Inspector Grossmann would also be absent and why he could not preach. Cloeter answered, "He cannot preach because he is a false teacher." A storm arose. When the men came home from the meeting and told their wives about it, the women protested vehemently because there would be no services for two weeks and that Grossmann was called a false teacher. They had to call another congregational meeting at which it was decided that Grossmann should preach and that he was not a false teacher.

Fritschel copied the following from the report Grossmann sent to Loehe at Neuendettelsau [37]:

One day there was a knock at the door of my study. Pastor Cloeter entered. Greetings had hardly been exchanged when the following conversation took place.

"Brother Grossmann, I have come to inform you that you stand under church discipline because of your false teaching."

"After this first grade of admonishment, then the second, and after unfruitful warnings the third, will banishment from the congregation follow?"

"No."

"So I am thus sentenced to remain in church discipline all my days and to stay away from the Sacrament of my Savior if I don't become a Missourian? Under such circumstances nothing else remains for me, except to part myself from a congregation whose pastor misuses his holy office in such a manner. I therefore herewith declare my resignation from your congregation."

"I shall report this resignation to President Wyneken."

Grossmann's report to Loehe continued:

"Horror (*Grauen*) and shock still grip me every time I think of this offcial outrage by a Lutheran pastor. But this outrage served in the hands of the Lord to show us Loeheans the path we should follow. Wyneken did not keep us waiting long."

Wyneken allowed Grossmann to come to Cloeter's parsonage to tell him his story. Cloeter could not deny that these had been the proceedings. Wyneken showed himself a man who did not handle people with kid gloves (*Glacehandschuhen*). Wyneken demanded immediate revocation (*Widerruf*), and he was not satisfied with that. He demanded that Cloeter admit his injustice (*Unrecht*) and ask Grossmann for forgiveness. Thereupon Grossmann declared that, in that case, his resignation from Holy Cross Congregation was voided.

What more Wyneken said to the pastor was never revealed. After that Cloeter acted somewhat friendlier, but in his sermons he warned about the danger of the "hierarchy" in the Lutheran church. The most dense hearer knew who was meant.

Wyneken also visited Grossmann personally to speak with him as his president. He listened to the instruction in the seminary classes. Grossmann had informed Wyneken that the seminarians he had brought with him from Neuendettelsau were ready to serve as parish teachers. He asked Wyneken either to attend to the examinations personally or to appoint examiners. Wyneken did the latter. He expressed regret over the situation in Saginaw County and blamed Loehe for it.

It was clear to Wyneken that neither Deindoerfer nor Grossmann would be convinced to change their opinions on the doctrine of the church and ministry, and he had no other Scripture proofs to offer. So he shrank from complaining about the situation. "Should you have gone to Iowa or California where we have no congregations, then we could continue next to each other in peace," he said. "Then we would not have to testify against you."

"Mr. President," said Grossmann, "do you view these differences of opinion (for they can be nothing more than that because the Word of God says nothing about it) actually to be so large and significant? Must our unity of belief be broken over the question if Christ transfers this office through the congregation in the call or whether the individual Christian in a way gives a quit claim deed?"

"In our teaching, dear Grossmann, there can be no differences. The matter may be big, it may be small. There we demand unity into the last threads of carrying out the teachings. In teachings there are no opinions." [38]

Addressing the struggle on the doctrine of the Church and the Ministry, J. L. Neve summarized the positions of Loehe and the Missouri Synod leaders:

"While Walther emphasized the invisibility of the true Church, Loehe maintained that, according to the Augsburg Confession, the Church is the visible assembly of those who have the pure Word and Sacraments, *no distinction being made between the visible and invisible Church* (emphasis added). Loehe was unable to approve the 'doctrine of transference,' according to which the ministry was merely the exercise of the spiritual priesthood of all believers.

"He sided with Walther against Grabau in declaring that the office of the ministry was only to feed and lead with the Word and Sacraments and had no right to set up as ordinances things not expressly commanded in the Word of God. But according to his views, the ministerial office had not been committed to the spiritual priesthood of individual Christians, but to the Church as a whole. Not every individual Christian can therefore transmit his personal share, but the Church as an entity, must transfer the office instituted by Christ." [41]

After seventy-eight years of debate Missouri's position was set forth again in 1931 in its *Brief Statement of the Doctrinal Position of the Missouri Synod* prepared by a synodical committee headed by Dr. Franz August Otto Pieper and adopted in 1932 by the synod:

"Since it is by faith in the Gospel alone that men become members of the Christian Church, and since this faith cannot be seen by men, but is known to God alone, I Kings 8:39; Acts 1:24; II Tim. 2:19, therefore the Christian Church on earth is invisible, Luke 17:20, and will remain invisible till Judgment Day, Col. 3:3, 4.

"In our day some Lutherans speak of two sides of the Church, taking the means of grace to be its 'visible side.' It is true the means of grace are necessarily related to the Church, seeing that the Church is created and preserved through them. But the means of grace are not for that reason part of the Church; for the Church in the proper sense of the word consists only of *believers,* Eph. 2:19, 20;Acts 5:14. Lest we abet the notion that the Christian Church in the proper sense of the term is an external institution, we shall continue to call the means of grace the 'marks' of the Church. Just as wheat is to be found only where it is sown, so the Church can be found only where the Word of God is in use...." [42]

"But why, when no Word of God is at hand for it, but only a theory that one sets up by making the spiritual priesthood the starting point? Then through a sort of deductive thinking (*Consequenten*), one comes to a conclusion. I then see this conclusion as a correct or false human conclusion. Should that part us?"

"We cannot at all endure that you represent Loehe in the midst of our congregations. If Loehe insists on continuing his work in America, why doesn't he go where we do not have the duty to oppose him? It would be best if he actually discontinued his work here. He has started so much in Germany and has enough work there. *We no longer need him!*" (Emphasis added.)

"Then it happens to Loehe as it sometimes goes with parents who have given their possessions over to the children. After the children no longer need the parents, they turn from the parents and eventually the parents wander into the poorhouse."

"No. Loehe has done infinitely (*unendlich*) much good for the Lutheran church in America. In times to come one will probably first really appreciate it when the harvest has been gathered. I personally thank Loehe infinitely much. As I went to Germany to seek healing for my ailing throat, Loehe led me to clarity on Lutheran teaching. Up to that time I was fundamentally a unionist (willing to share worship with non-Lutherans). Loehe taught me to recognize the glory (*Herrlichkeit*) of the Lutheran church. He influenced me very much. Then he encouraged me to write the *Notruf* letters about the distress of the Lutherans in America and to have them printed. He helped me write them and saw to it that they were printed."

"I never heard that from Loehe."

"And when one thinks of how he prepared his *Nothelfers* [helpers in need—see chapter one]. Without Loehe, the Saxons in Missouri and the *Nothelfers* would never have met. The founding of the Missouri Synod was mostly his doing."

"Why then can he not work with you any more. You know he is prepared to do so."

"No. That is past. We can only work together with him when we can hope that he will leave his opinion and step over to us. And when we cannot do this ourselves, how much less can we expect this from him."

"Do bring other proofs, proofs from God's Word instead of the Fathers, and we will be the first to let our opinions go."

"We have no other proofs. And if these proofs do not satisfy, then we simply cannot convince. They should be entirely sufficient."

"Would you take over the Teacher Seminary and develop it if I resign my position and Loehe conveys the property to you as he did the Indian mission and the Fort Wayne Seminary?"

"No. In the first place, we cannot accept any more from Loehe now that it has been determined that he will not go along with us. Secondly, we are in no position to maintain the Teacher Seminary. I endure many a weary hour because the funds we raise for our institutions do not reach what is needed."

"What should we do then?"

"I can give you no advice. It would seem best if you two [Grossmann and Deindoerfer] would return to Germany and Loehe would confine himself to training deaconesses and his other Romanizing things (*Dinge*)."

"Well, Mr. President, you know that neither of us can act independently by ourselves. We are both called for our work by the Society for Inner Missions affiliated with the Lutheran Church of Bavaria. We have promised that as long as we are wholly supported by them, we will seek instructions from them."

"That is perhaps a sort of popery such as Loehe wishes to establish."

"No more so than when you as president expect to be informed when a pastor obtains a call from another congregation so that you can help in the call of his successor. In doing this, you are not a pope in any way."

"Very good. Soon after my return home, I shall write to Pastor Loehe. I hope he will not allow it to come to a rupture in these blooming congregations. I can forsee that if it continues as at present, it will come to that. Cloeter's stumble shows that conclusively. If that happens, the growth of the church would be forever damaged."

This was Wyneken's last visit with Grossmann. He had to break it off to go to Frankenmuth and Frankentrost, carrying out his duty as president to visit the congregations whenever possible. He did not go home by way of Saginaw, where Grossmann lived, but through Flint. From Pontiac he could ride the railroad train.

Grossmann remembered Wyneken's remark: "Should you have gone to California or Iowa, we would not have the duty to oppose you." Grossmann said, "This sentence caught fire with me. I thought of the words of Abraham, 'Let there be no strife between you and me... for we are kinsmen.... If you take the left hand, then I will go to the right...etc.'" Wyneken had hardly left when Grossmann laid out the map of America. "I had to find out where 'Ei-oh-way' lay. As a green German, I had only *heard* of a state named Iowa."

On the map Grossmann saw that Iowa lay west of Lake Michigan and Wisconsin. Grossmann hurriedly borrowed a riding horse and rode to Frankenhilf to confer with his friends Deindoerfer and Amman.

George Fritschel wrote of Amman, "This layman, intelligent and highly interested in the church, was well able to understand the theological quarrel, and he concurred entirely with his pastor."

It was the spring of 1853. Grossmann wrote to Loehe that in view of the fact that the Missouri spirit could not endure a deviation from the Missouri conception of any teaching point, only fighting and mischief could grow out of their continuing in Saginaw City. They advised Loehe to remove the seminary and his entire missionary work to Iowa. But since foresight is better than going ahead without investigation, they had decided to send two scouts out to view the land and people of Iowa personally. If everything was found to be satisfactory, they could settle in Iowa the following spring of 1854.

Before the scouts left, Deindoerfer went to Saginaw City to serve as sponsor for one of Grossmann's children who was to be baptized. He also came to further discuss the "blow" (*Schlage*) of Missouri's hostility. The walking caused Deindoerfer to develop a sore foot. Because the doctor feared blood poisoning, he stayed at Saginaw two weeks. When Amman came with his team of oxen to take Deindoerfer home, Amman brought further disturbing news. The quarrel was now burning in the small congregation at Frankenhilf. The storm would soon break. [39]

That summer of 1853, each Frankenhilf member was expected to contribute seventeen days of labor each on the construction of their church. For his additional labor, the foreman J. G. Kamm was repaid by others through work on his farm. Their goal was to celebrate the church's dedication in September. Some were so eager that they left their own work undone and were ready to help at all times. Others let their fellow members work on the church, while they did their own farm work. Because these "had no time," it was necessary to postpone work on the church building. Summer came before the church was at last under roof.

Worship services were now transferred from Amman's house not many steps away to the uncompleted church. But as construction went on, the congregation was stirred by false rumors that Loehe was making a grab for power. Heated meetings were held. Some members threatened to leave unless Loehe would surrender title of the church property to the congregation so that it might, as the other three colonies had done, join the Missouri Synod.

CHAPTER 10

THE FRANKENHILF SCHISM

T he storm broke the first Sunday after Deindoerfer's return from Saginaw: July 24, 1853. The Frankenhilf congregation was assembled in Amman's house church. Deindoerfer and Grossmann were both present. Excitement filled the congregation. Expecting the worst, Amman had asked Grossmann to write minutes of this important meeting. [40]

The Frankenhilf people had learned through relatives and friends who lived in both places that the Frankenmuth and Frankentrost congregations had broken off fellowship with Loehe. The Frankenhilfers repeatedly heard: "What have *you* done? You have sold your Christian freedom to Pastor Loehe. He can do whatever he wants with you. He can take your pastor away and give you another whom you do not want." The labels placed on Loehe's practices gave them goose flesh: "It's Romanism, hierarchism, as when a Roman Catholic bishop supplies the people with any pastor he wishes." Loehe's "tyranny" against the Frankenhilf congregation was only the beginning of his plans to enslave the congregations. Several said that there should be a statement in the constitution that the congregation belonged to the synod.

One charged that Loehe had published a book, the second edition of Loehe's *Agenda*, in which the liturgy was very "Catholic." The people of the four colonies were unaware that all their pastors had for years conducted their worship from Loehe's *Agenda*.

Those who knew of his deaconess motherhouse in Neuendettelsau also charged that Loehe had established an order of nuns. Loehe had embarked on an evil path. He was on his way to Rome. The Frankenhilfers heard this from the other colony pastors or from members of their congregations.

The question had arisen, "To whom does the parish land belong?" Some went to the courthouse and found the land recorded in Loehe's name. Then Trustee Amman had to hear bitter complaints from some who absented themselves from heavy work on the new church: "We don't want to work just so that Pastor Loehe can obtain a church from which he may later exclude us. We want the land and the church in our own name or we will not work on it." Those who had never contributed much labor were more agitated than those who had done most of the work.

Deindoerfer wrote Loehe:

"However, there were only a few who muttered and just those who had never been been heartily enthusiastic about the church. The muttering reached its high point when the president [Wyneken] came to Saginaw about the seminary matter and there, as in Frankenmuth, praised the freedom of the congregation and dared to say that through our teaching [Deindoerfer's and Grossmann's] the congregations were robbed of their glorious freedoms and rights. Our people [at Frankenhilf] soon heard this from Frankenmuth zealots. They blew into their ears about 'priest rule' that could come if it were not already present....They should glad to be free from the German bondage which they would not submit to in the new country. Now our congregation's resolution leaving title to the church and parish land to the Society for Inner Missions was attacked, and also the fact that the Frankenhilf congregation stands under the leadership of the German friends.

"Through smart advisors from Frankenmuth, the distressed farmers suddenly discovered that they had never really understood our congregation's resolution. Now they saw the light. The uproar became open..."

President Wyneken had declared on his arrival that he would never submit to such slavery. Because of this and all the charges against Loehe that had come to their ears, many Frankenhilfers came to the congregational meeting with their minds set to rescind the resolutions of their spring organizational meeting. For that reason Deindoerfer had asked Grossmann to come and write the minutes. Present for the meeting were: Amman, Bauer, Gruber, Huber, Kamm, Popp, Schwab, Schwarz, Sippel, and Trump—the entire congregation. A number of new settlers had not yet joined.

After the opening devotions, Deindoerfer stated that he had a number of questions to lay before the congregation. The first question: "Did anyone have anything to criticize as to the Scriptural correctness of the pastor's teaching and preaching? Had he ever preached anything that did not agree with God's Word?" All answered with a decisive "No."

The second question: "Was there anything objectionable about the pastoral care he had given, the application of God's Word in his practice?" Several spoke up and declared that in sickness and in need the pastor had stood by them faithfully. One said that the pastor at first earnestly admonished him because he seldom showed up at services. For this he was grateful, since this had awakened him from his spiritual indifference. Another wanted to know the reason why the pastor was asking such questions.

Deindoerfer answered that during the two weeks he had been confined at Saginaw with a foot infection, there had been much talk about "priest domination." He wished the congregation to express itself if he had in any way taken for himself any of their rights or in any way made demands that one could call "priest domination." How had anyone arrived at this expression?

The phrase *priest domination* bit like lightning. Schwarz spoke first. He had spoken about "priest domination," but not in reference to Deindoerfer. It looked like priest domination to him when the congregation could not elect a pastor and Loehe would appoint one even if they didn't want that particular one.

Deindoerfer: "Who has said that Pastor Loehe wanted to force a pastor on the congregation or that the congregation was not allowed to elect its pastor?"

Schwarz: "Wasn't that Loehe's intention? Isn't it priest domination when Pastor Loehe expects the congregation to ask his advice?"

Deindoerfer: "If this congregation became vacant and President Wyneken proposed suitable pastors, would that also be 'priest domination'? There has never been any suggestion that the congregation could not choose its own pastor."

Amman: "No. No one has said that. We all know it. And outside of that, Loehe has demanded nothing. Last spring Pastor Deindoerfer suggested that Pastor Loehe wished that the congregation express itself so that he may know if he can henceforth happily protect and benefit the congregation. Then we agreed that we would not act without his advice as long as he carries the burdens of the congregation. That is as far from priest domination as when a son asks his father for advice in important matters and the father expects to be asked as long as he supports him with money."

Sippel: "Look at our church constitution which Pastor Loehe wrote. There it is expressly stated that the congregation must elect their pastor and exactly how that is to be done."

Amman read the minutes to the meeting, and Schwarz had to concur. So Grossmann wrote, "The congregation answers with a unanimous 'No'. The fear of 'priest domination' has not arisen from the official acts of the pastor." He read the last sentence to the congregation and everyone agreed, "That is correct."

Deindoerfer: "The third question: Is there anything to criticize about the pastor's behavior?" Minutes: "The congregation answers with a unanimous 'No' and declares that the accusation of being unconciliatory or disobedient to authority is false."

The fourth question: "At the spring congregational meeting called principally in connection with the establishment of a charitable foundation in Frankenhilf, did the pastor try to persuade anyone to remain with the German Society for Inner Missions instead of joining the Missouri Synod?" The congregation answered "No." Only Popp found a persuasive message in the casual remarks Pastor Deindoerfer made at the close of the meeting: "No one will oppose it and no one could oppose it." Besides Popp himself had voted to remain with the Society.

The fifth question: Had Pastor Deindoerfer tried to persuade the congregation not to join the Missouri Synod? The congregation gave a unanimous "No."

The sixth question: Why is there now a demand to break the word given to the German friends? What are the points that the congregation feels in conscience bound to demand?" The discussion included talk both for and against remaining with the Inner Mission Society.

Amman: "After all that Pastor Loehe has done for Frankenhilf and its congregation, wouldn't it seem thankless and faithless if we did not wish to consider him a fatherly friend and listen to his advice in all important matters? It is not a demand that Loehe sets up, but it is a condition that every decent human and Christian must view entirely self explanatory. Just consider. He sent Pastor Deindoerfer over and has supported him so far. He has promised to continue this support which might well extend into years."

(For the following Fritschel used fictional names, for which the writer uses numbers):

1: "That is all true. But the danger is always present that if Pastor Loehe wishes he can lock the doors of this church because the deed is not in the name of the congregation but in the name of Pastor Loehe as trustee of the Society for Inner Missions. That does look like priestly rule. And then there is grave danger that Pastor Loehe could prevent the congregation from exercising its holy right to elect a pastor. Although until now he has shown so signs of such ideas, who can prevent them?"

2: "Please tell me who except Amman, Schwarz and I have given money to the church. I don't deny that others have given work. But the few dollars that the three of us gave just about paid for the nails. But there were also boards, windows, doors etc. Who paid for that? The Society for Inner Missions paid for that. I mean that one must be a jackass [Esel] to say the Society did that for itself. It did it for us. And when the deed stands in its name, that is very proper. I am entirely in favor of the resolution adopted at the spring meeting."

3: "For my part I don't want anything to do with priest domination. We had to endure it in Germany and should thank God that we are free from that yoke."

4: "Well, well, (No. 3)! That sounds real nice to hear about Christian freedom, especially from you. That doesn't come from you originally. You heard it in Frankenmuth. Let someone else believe that you suffered under priest domination in Germany. I know how eagerly you attended church. And now you want to talk big."

1: "We demand that the congregation join the synod and that our resolution of last spring be rescinded."

5: "Yes. I demand it, and if the congregation doesn't do so, we will leave the congregation."

6 and 1: "Yes, we will do that."

2: "When did you reach that decision?"

3: "Last night."

1: "You dumb fool. You shouldn't have said that."

The dissidents held to their opinions. Some who worked particularly hard at the church demanded that it become the property of the congregation or they would resign. They refused to sign the minutes showing that when each question had been asked of them there had been no criticism they could make of Deindoerfer or Loehe.

7: "Pastor, let the four go their way. We others remain with the previous resolution. One could not fatten the smallest pig on the moneys which the four might contribute in the next five years. The rest of us naturally cannot do much, but we are not thrown entirely on our own resources because the friends in Germany have promised to help. Others will come, too; so the congregation will grow. If the four want to leave a Christian congregation because priest domination might occur some time, they show of what spirit they are children. It sounds grand to speak of Christian freedom that Christ has won for us, as though this freedom consists of a congregation conducting its business without any fatherly counsel. Such speaking is most blasphemous. The Christian freedom won for us by Christ is that we are free from sin, death and the power of the devil."

Deindoerfer: "There is no object for me to set forth any more questions. I recommend that everyone think the matter over carefully again and next time present in writing what the final decision of each actually is...

"I wish to inform the congregation of one other thing. I must make an emergency journey. I would not do so except that it is absolutely necessary."

2: "Then Brother Amman will have to read the sermons."

Amman: "No. I will be absent, too."

Deindoerfer: "I have asked Pastor Graebner of Frankentrost to hold afternoon worship services and to conduct any other pastoral services." So the meeting closed.

Grossmann wrote to inform Loehe of the unhappy turn of events. Deindoerfer and Amman would soon begin the trip to Iowa. They did not know that the reports of the temper in the Franken colonies had already caused Loehe to decide to move his stakes further west. Letters were enroute to America in which Loehe directed that Grossmann or Deindoerfer should explore Minnesota or Iowa for good land to recommend for settlement. In the letters Loehe released both men of their calls to serve the colony and the seminary and freed them to do what they deemed best. He would support them to his best in further work at other places that they might select.

The Scouts

On July 25, 1853, the morning after Frankenhilf's congregational meeting, young Pastor Johannes Deindoerfer and Karl Gottlob Amman, the upright Swabe and founder of the Frankenhilf colony for the poor, set out for Iowa. Amman's son Johannes had just been born on June 12, but because their hearts were heavy from yesterday's disappointments, he resolutely joined his pastor in an assignment they both felt to be God's will.

In spite of Deindoerfer's recent sore foot, their first day's journey went thirty miles past neighboring Tuscola, the county seat, on a plank road over swampy land to Pine Run and Flint. The next day, July 26, they rode nine hours by stage to Pontiac in time to board the train for Detroit, where they arrived two hours later.

They avoided visiting friends in Detroit so that no one else would learn of their intentions. On July 28 they took a morning train for Chicago. Later Amman reported, "Chicago itself is significantly larger, has in part beautifully built brick houses, and a rapidly increasing sea port. As near as I can recall, nine new railroads go in various directions from there, and more are planned. Numerous large and beautiful churches are ornaments of the city. But the city lies low and it would be unhealthy there if Lake Michigan did not spread out next to it. We saw masses of German workmen go to the railroad buildings in the morning."

The most direct route to Iowa was by rail to Davenport and from there to Iowa City where they knew of a land office. But they took a steamer up the coast of Lake Michigan to Milwaukee, where Amman had a cousin whom he wished to contact for information and advice. Deindoerfer wrote: "The inhabitants of Milwaukee are divided into three groups of about equal size, Yankees, Germans, and Irish. Norwegians are also in the vicinity." A mighty dome symbolized Rome's witness—twelve bishops had come there to help dedicate the cathedral.

Amman's friend lived eight miles out of town on a plank road. After they had obtained much useful information, a slow freight train took them seventy-one miles in ten hours to Janesville, Wisconsin. Here the land was even better than in Michigan. They moved on to Galena, Illinois, in a small "snail" stage coach. It was Sunday, July 31. The coach would not continue until the next day. That evening the travelers visited a Methodist church.

On August 1, Amman and Deindoerfer arrived at Dubuque. They were impressed with the city's position. The Mississippi connected the city with Saint Paul and New Orleans, and by way of the Ohio River with the eastern states. Railroads would soon be built to this place and across Iowa. The city was about as large as Milwaukee and contained two thousand Germans. Hearing that Dubuque had a land office, and that the government still had much land for sale northwest of there, their plans to go to Iowa City faded.

Germans in Dubuque seemed to be Roman Catholic or practically unchurched. But the scouts were told of German Lutherans concentrated at Guttenberg, Garnavillo, and Davenport.

The official at the land office was helpful when he learned that they wished to establish a colony of German Lutherans. German settlers were most welcome. He showed them that there were only small frangmentary plots left along the river. It would be necessary to go inland. He suggested Clayton County about sixty miles northwest of Dubuque. It lay along the edge of the prairie with much woodland and many springs of water. He recommended sections 2, 3, and 4 in Township 92 (now Cass Township) and sections 26, 27, 28, 33, 34, and 35 in Township 91 (now Sperry Township). This land lay northwest of Strawberry Point with its single log store, six miles southeast of Volga and twelve miles south of Elkader.

The land agent referred them to Captain James Morley, a U.S. Army veteran and a former surveyor who lived in that area, who had purchased much of the recommended land from the government and was holding it for resale.

The trip went slowly because Deindoerfer became ill on the way. When they arrived, they were disappointed by the sandy prairie west of Strawberry Point. Then Amman and Deindoerfer found James Morley. He gave them a ride on a stoneboat pulled by oxen. They moved north and east through slopes and valleys into his claim. Here was good land with woods and meadows, springs and brooks, equal to anything in Michigan. This land was said to yield fifty to sixty bushels of corn to the acre. They inquired about grist mills, saw mills, the price of lumber.

Instead of returning to Saginaw the way they had come, they went to Garnavillo where they had heard there were many Germans. They found an almost completed church to which a Reformed pastor had been called by a German flock.

On August 9, at the river town of Clayton six miles east of Garnavillo, they waited for a steamboat to continue their trip home. Deindoerfer sent a letter to Frankenhilf:

"Our mission we have fulfilled. After a difficult tour on foot, including going astray many miles, we have found a suitable place. It lies about 60 miles northwest of Dubuque, about 25 miles west of the Mississippi. It has all the resources we need: prairie and timber, springs and brooks, good land, high location, mills and stores nearby (no large stores), and many Germans in the near towns and surroundings. But no city is near. Dubuque is far off and the other towns are so small you can hardly see them....

"The land near the cities is all bought up. Iowa City is too far from the Mississippi, and it would cost too much to get there."

About August 15 Deindoerfer and Amman arrived back at Frankenhilf and found that Loehe had sent a letter advising that they should indeed move the colony to Iowa or Minnesota, since his support for the ministry in Michigan was no longer desired.

Loehe had intentionally refrained from turning over to the Missouri Synod title to the teachers' seminary and the 1,592 acres on which the Frankenhilf colony was located. His experience with the other three Saginaw colonies and the Fort Wayne seminary had taught him that once he gave up control, he also lost his influence over them. So, with sadness he agreed to their leaving Michigan. He wrote:

"We are a society for inner mission. Mission is never at home; it is a pilgrim. When it has wrought its blessing in one spot it moves on and carries its blessing to other places. When we were done in Fort Wayne, we went on farther to Saginaw County. Now we are through in Saginaw County, so we are going farther." [43]

Loehe felt no ill will toward the Missouri Synod. He wrote, "I do not feel myself separated from them, and I am happy that through this synod so many thousands of people have received and still receive God's Word and all that is in it." [44]

This good will was reciprocated by Missouri's leaders. C. F. W. Walther wrote in *Der Lutheraner* "Our synod, the German Evangelical Lutheran Synod of Missouri, Ohio, and Other States, which at the close of its last convention (1851) already had ninety-two members, was originally composed of two elements. The one is the Saxon Lutherans who in 1839 emigrated to Missouri; the other is a host of Lutheran pastors who since 1843 have been sent over almost solely through the efforts of Pastor Loehe in Bavaria, and the congregations which at least partially have been organized by their efforts. It has been precisely the latter group whose entrance into our synod year by year has brought it so rapidly to its significant membership figures....

"Next to God it is Pastor Loehe whom our synod must almost solely thank for the happy increase and rapid strengthening in which it rejoices; it must rightly honor him as its real spiritual father. It would fill the pages of an entire book if anyone would try even in short summary to relate what that dear man has with tireless zeal and in the most self-denying manner done for our Lutheran Church and particularly for our synod during a good many years." [45]

James L. Schaff, of today's Trinity seminary, Columbus, Ohio, described additional benefits from Loehe, "It was a negative contribution that Loehe's work gave the Missouri Synod some serious antagonists....The ongoing controversy with the Loehe men in the Iowa Synod sharpened the acumen of the Missouri theologians. Even if this can be termed only vaguely one of Loehe's contributions, it nevertheless was a development for which he was the catalyst." [46]

The decision to move both the seminary and the colony surprised the local clergy, who now invited them to stay. But Grossmann and Deindoerfer believed that no reconciliation would be possible without abandoning Loehe and his principles. They could not in good conscience agree to this.

It would be painful to leave because the new Saint Michael congregation at Frankenhilf was busy erecting its first building on four acres of Amman's donated land. Built of hewn logs, 25 x 36 feet, the church interior was finished with planed, knot-free boards. J. G. Kamm directed the construction. He built the pulpit and baptismal font from plans drawn by Pastor Deindoerfer. Purchased material had been paid for by Superintendent Johannes Weege Sr. from the colonization fund as promised.

But preparations for moving nevertheless began immediately. At the seminary, final examinations were conducted. Georg Grossmann advised the five graduating teachers to accept calls to teaching positions in congregations of the Missouri Synod. Three seminarians followed the Inspector's advice. They were Simon, who later became a professor at the Springfield Seminary; Riedel, who served as a teacher at Frankenmuth for many years; and Jacob Brater, who became the parish teacher at Frankenlust.

The youngest student, Christian Kraenzlein, had recently arrived at Saginaw. He and Karl Beckel, accompanied the pilgrims to Dubuque where they became the seminary's first theological students; Beckel became its first graduating candidate for ordination to the ministry.

Inspector Grossmann made it known that the seminary was for sale, and he soon had a buyer. He also attempted to collect from people in Frankenmuth the money Loehe had advanced them from his Frankenhilf fund. He sent instructions to New York that the new seminary students who were already enroute should not go to Saginaw but should follow the seminary directly to Dubuque.

Amman found a buyer for his farm. Johannes Weege Jr. would have to remain in Saginaw temporarily until he could sell his farm in Hesselust and because he had numerous transactions to close out for Loehe's four colonies.

Freight goods from Germany arrived in Saginaw for Amman: the two small bells that personal friends and relatives of Amman and Deindoerfer had sent. They took the bells along to Iowa.

At the parting, Grossmann, Deindoerfer, and Amman found that they still had many friends in the colonies, many of whom did not agree with the verdict of condemnation against Loehe and his followers. They considered it a wrong (*Unrecht*). But what could they do? They could not come with the pilgrims because all that they owned was invested in their farms. The land held them fast.

The parting from the pastors varied. Roebbelen was the most friendly. He deplored the fact that Grossmann and Deindoerfer could not accept Missouri Synod's teaching on the pastoral call. He called their departure a sin: "God cannot go before you, so he will follow you with his chastizing switch!" He thought his zeal a service to God.

The other pastors in the colonies were surprised that the Loehe people would leave so soon. They had hoped that by their united firmness they could cause Grossmann and Deindoerfer to change to Missouri's position. Now they were bitterly angry that the two were going away. But the two preferred the physical hardships of the Iowa frontier to another winter of continuing charges of heresy by their brothers in the faith.

In Missouri circles, Grossmann and Deindoerfer were later described as breakers of the church community. All church fellowship with Missouri was revoked for them. By stepping out of the synod they had put themselves and their followers under the ban of excommunication.

Roebbelen at Saginaw still acknowledged them as brothers in the faith. He referred in *Der Lutheraner* to a sermon in which he had asked his Frankenmuth congregation for funds to send to Grossmann in support of the seminary in Dubuque:

> "I therefore declare that recently released explanations by Pastor Loehe's emissaries in Iowa, who recently reopened their teacher's seminary (which is no longer simply a teacher's seminary) have moved me to feel that their continued contrary stand is only in the realm of church organization. I have asked for a contribution for the seminary in Iowa as a gift of love presented to those who stood grounded in one faith with us but cannot convince themselves that their expression of one, lone, subordinate article in the unity of the Lutheran teaching structure (because of a lack of insight into the inner cohesiveness of all teachings) is either a concession to error or results in error. I have as little ground to withdraw this plea, because the need of our brethren in Iowa is great" (Dated at Frankenmuth, October 13, 1854).

This was the last friendly word in *Der Lutheraner* about the Iowa pilgrims in the next fifty years.

The Pilgrims Take Their Leave

On September 4, 1953, in its still unfinished building, Saint Michael church conducted a meeting at which the church property was formally transfered to those members of the congregation who had turned against Loehe. Amman asked that the congregation elect someone to succeed him as secretary and benefactor (colony leader), since he would probably leave the colony before the end of the month. Michael Schwarz was elected secretary.

Pastor Deindoerfer presented a letter from Pastor Loehe in which Loehe declared that he had noted with grief that anyone in Frankenhilf as well as in the other colonies had discovered hierarchial desires behind his actions and had repaid with ingratitude what he had done with the best of intentions. True, he had a right to dispose of the congregation's possessions and to sell them for other purposes; his friends in Germany who had given the money to buy these possessions had now given him permission to sell them. But Loehe did not wish to do this. He instead gave full ownership of these possessions to the Saint Michael congregation.They should join the Missouri Synod, and they should do what they pleased with the parochial lands purchased from his colony funds.

Deindoerfer said,"As Loehe for the sake of peace has now closed his work in Michigan, let it not be said that he in any way accepts the sinful doubting of your benefactors in Germany.The behavior of some in the congregation has been ugly and unholy. The pretense that a priestly rule could grow out of Loehe's sponsorship was pitiful. It showed an immature and unchristian mind when some members said they would resign if the congregation did not join the synod. Pastor Loehe will now continue his mission work for neglected Lutherans in the state of Iowa."

Deindoerfer announced that everything the congregation had at hand from Loehe was to be a gift to the congregation. The materials turned over to Saint Michael Church were listed in the minutes: the church building with all the lumber lying about it (provided that the lumber be used only for the church building), the pulpit, the altar and altar paraments, benches, baptismal dish, two white covers, a black drape, a crucifix, two tin candlesticks, an altar Bible, a hand written liturgy, a tin chalice, a tin paten, a host box with its leather case, a tin baptismal dish, a baptismal ewer, a bier, an offering bag with a handle (*Klingelbeutel*), a homeopathic apotheke with instructions, a bed stead, and a table.The colonial fund had paid for the window frames, several hundred feet of floor boards, glass, putty, screws, nails, and carpenter work. Any outstanding bills would be paid by the congregation.

Deindoerfer then stated that Loehe's German benefactors had invited him to join in their new work in Iowa. He gave the reasons why he considered this call a godly one that he would accept. Continued work by him at Frankenhilf would be hindered by the unfounded and sinful mistrust that existed there. He now asked for the concurrence of the congregation in this decision. Several, particularly Kamm, objected, but could not deny the mistrust Deindoerfer had observed and given as the reason for his decision to leave.

Wilhelm Sihler, first vice president of the Missouri Synod, who lived hundreds of miles from the scene and could only go by hearsay, wrote in *Der Lutheraner.*"What did Pastor Deindoerfer, this more mature brother, do next? He tried to influence his congregation in

Frankenhilf to settle in Iowa. While he succeeded with one member, he left the whole congregation in the lurch and made off to Iowa with the one [Amman], taking along the bells, altar decking, etc., that belonged to the congregation in Frankenhilf, and all this with the encouragement and understanding of Pastor Loehe, who would have found it difficult to approve of his joining our synod.... [S]neaking silently out of Synod and later giving no conscience-bound reasons cited from God's Word for his leaving." [47]

The next meeting was conducted on Tuesday, September 6, at 12:30 P.M. At this meeting a benefactor (colony leader) and two trustees were to be elected by ballot. L. Sippel was elected benefactor, Michael Gruber and Matthew Schwab as trustees. Resigning benefactor Amman reported on the debts of the congregation.

Amman was asked if he wanted to give land from his adjoining farm to the church. He offered to give two acres if the congregation would buy four more acres. The congregation bought four acres from Amman for four dollars. He also asked that twelve dollars be returned to him that he had paid into the treasury because of paragraph 25 of the constitution, even though no one else had contributed. The congregation voted to pay him back.

Deindoerfer said that he would probably leave during the next week. But he could not leave without assurance that the congregation would still be led by and provided with God's Word and the Sacraments. He recalled that this was his duty. He proposed that the congregation without delay turn to the Missouri Synod to ask for supply of its spiritual needs. The synod could either provide another pastor or see to it that a neighboring pastor serve them. Since the congregation could hardly expect a pastor of their own at once, it would probably be best to seek help from a neighboring pastor.

Schwarz moved that the congregation itself compose a letter to President Wyneken. Deindoerfer said they could have one of the neighboring pastors write the letter. Then Deindoerfer was asked to write it in the name of the congregation. On the next Sunday at the early service, the letter should be read to all and signed.

Several members of the congregation still refused to agree that Deindoerfer should give up his office: "Why not let the four [dissidents], who certainly have no valid grounds for their complaints, simply go their way?" The congregation could do all right with the help of Loehe's German friends. If Deindoerfer left and Loehe withdrew his hands, the congregation could not expect a pastor of its own for decades.

Deindoerfer explained that this positively could not be. To keep peace, Loehe wanted to search out an entirely new field for his activity. And Deindoerfer himself could find no pleasure working in a region where his brethren looked upon him as an apostate (*abgefallen*) and treated him as such. "I don't care to let my life and work be soured and stunted by constant strife—all the less because the doctrinal disagreement is not a fight between me and the Missouri Synod, but a disagreement that concerns the entire Lutheran church."

It was not easy for Deindoerfer to part with some of the members. The innocent had to suffer with the guilty. He pointed out that there could be no talk of blessed labor for a pastor when part of the congregation accepts the position taken by his opponents. Where that is the case, the pastor must resign. He was sure that the congregation could not obtain another pastor in the near future, as no pastor could live more than a month on the funds that the congregation would be able to raise.

When the Frankenhilfers got home and told their wives of the meeting, they became even more aware of the situation they had created for themselves. "Where will we go to church? Should we send our children to school through the forest to Frankentrost or Frankenmuth?" Several went to Amman and Sippel (their resigned and newly elected leaders) and wanted to take it all back. But they were told, "The separation has taken place. Now you would like to have it otherwise, but only for your own sake. That would last only a short time. It is too late."

As Deindoerfer had predicted, after he left, the congregation had to get along for nine years with afternoon or mid-week worship services conducted by Pastor John Henry Philip Graebner, who in 1847 helped establish the congregation at Frankentrost. Saint Michael Church did not secure its own pastor until January 4, 1862. Then Pastor G. Bernthal was installed and served there his entire career of fifty years (1862-1912).

CHAPTER 11

THE PILGRIMAGE TO IOWA

Summer was over. On Sunday morning, the Feast of St. Michael and All Angels, September 25, 1853, the twenty-five adult colonists who stayed at Frankenhilf dedicated their new Saint Michael Church with Pastor Sievers of Frankenlust conducting the service that Deindoerfer had expected to lead.

The previous week, the other Frankenhilfers had made their farewells and left for Iowa, except for Johannes Weege Jr. and his wife, Anna. Weege's duties kept him in Saginaw until the following spring.

There is no recorded list of names of the pilgrims who left Michigan. But eighteen people whom we know from the story were the four Ammans, two Deindoerfers, at least four Grossmanns, four Weege Srs., two Weege Jrs., (temporarily left at Frankenhilf), and students Beckel and Kraenzlein. Deindoerfer's church communion records also show a man named L. Buder who faithfully communed from Deindoerfer's arrival in Michigan through 1862 at Saint Sebald. Emilie and Elizabeth Grossmann were married within twelve years after they arrived in Iowa. Of the twelve children born to the Grossmanns, probably more than these two were born before the migration to Iowa.

Led by Amman, one group of twenty-two men, women, and children went by boat to Detroit. From Detroit some pilgrims took a ten-hour train ride to Chicago. Others took a lake steamer.

Grossmann and Deindoerfer with their small families drove all the way from Frankenhilf in an open wagon drawn by two horses. This saved train fare and they needed the team in Iowa where horses were more expensive than in Michigan.

The railroad travelers debarked from the train at Chicago and stayed together. Soon a German errand boy discovered them. "Hey, fellow countrymen, where do you want to go? Can I help you? Do you want a good German guest house?" At this Guest House of Berlin, they met those who had come by steamer. The Grossmann and Deindoerfer families arrived with their team and wagon. It was September 30. All were together again.

Grossmann and Amman consulted together. Both were nearly out of cash. Grossmann said, "But you sold your farm. You must have some spare money and could lend me some?" "I sold my farm alright, but I don't get the money until spring. You sold the seminary building and collected debts owed in Frankenmuth. I thought you could lend me some money." "The buyer is not sure he can raise the cash. And on most debts in Frankenmuth, I received good words as well as bad ones but very little money."

The money supply was near the end. How would they get to Dubuque? They held a council of war. About two-thirds of them with Deindoerfer and Amman would take the train to Freeport, Illinois, with trunks and cases. The trunks would be left at Freeport until money could be obtained. Grossmann and the others would come along with the wagon on which everything possible was heaped.

On October 1 at midmorning, the larger group left on the train, while Grossmann and the smaller group started out with the wagon. The train arrived at Freeport after 1:00 A.M. At 11:00 A.M. they drove on in stage coaches. About noon on Monday, October 3, they ferried across the Mississippi. Deindoerfer and Amman sought out the same Dubuque hotel where they had stayed on their scouting trip. The innkeeper was glad to see them again. They arranged for quarters for the entire group, and no one asked about their money. They had paid out their last cent on the journey.

Grossmann and his group followed over the prairies of northern Illinois. They sought night refuge from farmers between the towns. It was an unwritten law never to refuse hospitality, and farmers did not ask as much pay as would be required in the towns. They passed through Freeport and arrived at Galena. The day before they had eaten only bread and milk and sausage, purchased from the farmers. Grossmann spent his last cent buying food for all at the local inn.

They reached the river at the village of Dunleith (now East Dubuque). They saw scattered houses on the Dubuque side of the river, behind which were the forested hills. Grossmann said, "How do we get over the river? Our money is gone." A girl on the wagon said, "Mr. Inspector, I remembered that I had a gold piece in a dress, and I have found it." She handed him a half dollar.

Soon a ferry boat touched shore to unload its wagons and passengers. Then the call, "All aboard." Their wagon and passengers went on the ferry. The bell rang, the horses that powered the ferry went on their treadmills, and the boat left the bank. Grossmann kept his group together, his watch in one hand and the half dollar in the other, as the ferry captain collected his fares. "How much?" The captain looked the group over and said, "Fifty cents." The watch went back into its pocket.

When they neared the opposite shore, there stood Amman and Deindoerfer, who greeted the group with open arms. Soon they sat together peacefully in the German inn. Since the inn could not accommodate them all, some were moved to another hostel The fact that they now had a valuable team encouraged the two lodging houses to open their doors to the pioneers.

Since inns collected their bills when the guests left, the leaders counted on having a number of days to raise the money they needed. Grossmann remembered that Loehe had promised to arrange with a New York bank to honor drafts made by Grossmann and Deindoerfer. They hoped that one of the three banks in Dubuque would accept such a draft. Finley, Burton and Company and the Langworthy Brothers both refused.

At the newest and smallest bank, Jesup and Company, the clerk brought them to Mr. Jesup. He looked at their paper and asked their names. "You two came from Michigan as missionaries among the Germans?" Jesup then explained how he knew all their plans. A stranger had come to him twice, asking if they had drawn money here. The stranger had detailed the work Deindoerfer and Grossmann had done in Michigan. He asked Jesup to watch for them so that if possible the stranger might be of help to them.

Neither Grossmann nor Deindoerfer recognized the name of their benefactor. But Jesup said, "Gentlemen, what can I do for you?" They explained their needs and that their belongings were still in Freeport. They described Loehe's promised arrangement with the New York bank, but admitted they did not know if the agreement had been worked out.

"How much do you need?" "Fifty dollars." Without a word, Jesup left and brought them fifty dollars. "Is this really enough?" He would send their draft to New York. They should return in about ten days for the answer. He dismissed them, suggesting that they should feel free to seek his advice on any need that troubled them.

CHAPTER 12

THE PLANTING OF SAINT SEBALD

Winter would come soon. The plan was that most of the colony would stay in Dubuque while Deindoerfer and Amman went on with their families to Clayton County. There they would build a parsonage-church and a cabin. The rest of the colony would follow in the spring.

It was about October 18 when Grossmann and Amman reappeared at Jesup's bank. Jesup received them into his office with great friendliness. He said he had not yet received a reply. "Do you need money?"

"We can certainly use it. We have had the trunks and cases shipped from Freeport. We have made some purchases and paid some of the hotel bills."

"When would you travel to Strawberry Point?"

Grossmann said, "We have decided that under the circumstances part of the group and I will stay here. Deindoerfer and Amman will go on and make a beginning for our colony."

"Then you will need money for the two families to travel on?"

"That is what we are waiting for."

"How much money do you need?"

"We have to pay the rest of the hotel bill and make purchases for the immediate future of the colony. It will take one hundred dollars."

Without a word Jesup produced the money. "Here is one hundred dollars so that you need not be held up here. I am pleased that you, Pastor Grossmann, will remain here. I hope you will decide always to remain in Dubuque. We need many citizens like you. I am sure you will like it here."

"But you have had no answer from New York. You don't know if our draft will be accepted. We cannot accept your money until you do."

"I have no doubt that all is in order. You must make haste. The winter will come soon. You dare not lose time. Just go. The rest will turn out all right. Come back in two days. Better yet, I will inform you as soon as the rest of the money is available."

Deindoerfer and Amman bought their supplies. Two days later a message came from Jesup, "Come and get the rest of the money." The bank had accepted the draft.

Deindoerfer and Amman took the trail to Clayton County and sheltered their families at Elkader. There at the county offices they selected an 80-acre tract of forest for their church and 120 acres for Amman's farm adjoining the church land on the west. By December Amman had built a log cabin and his family moved into the first house of the new settlement. They named the budding colony "Saint Sebaldus" in memory of the first missionary who had brought the gospel to their ancestors in Bavaria. It was a name already carried by a famous cathedral in Nuremberg.

The new colony later became popularly known as "Sanct Sebaldus am Quelle," meaning "Saint Sebald by the Spring." This spring was the first source of water for the Deindoerfers. Today, diminished to a small trickle, it still flows in the valley below the parsonage and may be reached by a short path from the northeast corner of the cemetery.

> "Stout, sturdy oak trees are still lifting their gnarled limbs toward the sun, `giants in the earth' powerful sentinels guarding hallowed ground, where saints did pray and labor, and did 'keep the faith.' And he that seeketh may still find the place where at the feet of the most beautiful of forest trees there sprang forth the cool, clear water of the well-known 'Spring of Saint Sebaldus,' and he may still follow the tiny rill where its rippling waters meandered down the slope until the thread of silvery sheen was lost in the mossy undergrowth of white oak, and red oak, and maple, and elm, and butternut, and walnut, and hickory, and many, many another tree that God had made.
>
> "A little way up the hill was the parsonage that served as a church and parsonage in one. Almost at the top of the hill there was and still is the little cemetery, and just beyond its enclosure you see the old, white, frame church that was erected after the old parsonage could not accommodate those that came to worship on the Lord's Day." [48]

It was November when Amman and Deindoerfer first arrived at Saint Sebaldus. Deindoerfer found a small deserted log cabin nearby, where he and his family stayed until they almost perished of cold. Amman then built a board partition through his one-room cabin and invited his pastor's family once more to share his roof as they had done at Frankenhilf.

During the long winter they began to build the parsonage-church, the second house of the settlement. Amman (see chapter 4) had happily written to his parents concerning the church under construction at his Frankenhilf location, "I will have only two hundred paces to church." Now this hope was to be fulfilled in Iowa. His Saint Sebald home adjoining the church property would be about two hundred paces from the new church.

The 45 x 32 foot parsonage-church was built of sawed lumber instead of logs. The building material was hauled from Volga, where White & Son operated a saw mill. Many times Amman and Deindoerfer drove up and down the hills without getting any material or only half a load. Shingles were made by Deindoerfer, split from blocks of oak. He was aided by two young colonists that Grossmann sent from Dubuque. Floorings had to be hauled twenty-five miles from Clayton and were laid months after the Deindoerfers moved into the house. For lack of funds, the walls were not plastered, but the laths were covered with wallpaper.

CHAPTER 13

THE SEMINARY BEGINS AGAIN

G rossmann had planned to locate the seminary at the Saint Sebald colony. But with neither seminary building nor colony to go to as yet, he and students Beckel and Kraenzlein stayed in Dubuque. On November 3, 1853, the five students promised by Loehe arrived from Neuendettelsau via New York: Christian Bauer, Paul Beck, Conrad Duerschner, Wilhelm Krauss, and Heinrich (Henry) Weege. They brought with them Loehe's consent for the teachers seminary to remain in Dubuque.

Grossmann rented a vacant house for the seminary at 511-513 Garfield Avenue near Eagle Point Park. A stable built of stone stood in the back yard. The rent was twelve dollars per month, later raised to fourteen dollars. Grossmann bought lumber from which he and the students made tables and benches, bedsteads, an altar, and a pulpit. To save trucking, all supplies and furnishings (including a stove) were brought home by the students in a wheelbarrow.

The Seminary's New Home

The teachers seminary reopened in Dubuque on November 10, 1853. Thus began the second year of the normal school that eventually developed into Wartburg College and Wartburg Theological Seminary. The house also provided the Grossmann family's home. The inspector's study served as a classroom and on Sunday as a church.

Soon other Lutherans found their way there for worship. When the room became crowded, they learned that the courthouse could be used for Sunday services. That Advent the first worship services were held in a hall at the courthouse.

Grossmann and his students immediately found opportunities for mission work among Dubuque's German citizens. By the Christmas season, German Lutherans who had been attending other denominations came to Grossmann's services in spite of being labeled "bigots." This group founded Saint John, the mother Lutheran church of Dubuque, with Grossmann as their pastor.

Grossmann and his students soon located other German Lutherans nearby to whom they ministered at Sherrill's Mount, Tete des Mortes, and French Settlement.

Student Karl Beckel opened a parish school for children. He began with Grossmann's oldest daughter Emilie as his only pupil and soon had ten enrolled. The parish school gave the six seminary students practice in teaching methods. Though Grossmann was already thinking of converting the normal school into a theological seminary, this change did not take place until a year later. Early in 1854, Grossmann wrote Loehe that all his students were preparing to become teachers. The curriculum included Bible history and the catechism, English, grammar, geography, church history, ancient history, and music—including piano and violin lessons. Grossmann sent Loehe a list of texts and supplies that future students would need to have with them when they arrived, along with clothes and bedding.

Grossmann and his colleagues now communicated to Loehe the need to train preachers for prospective congregations in the Midwest. In response, Loehe commissioned Pastor Konrad Sigmund Fritschel to serve with Grossmann on the theological faculty. Fritschel had just completed his studies at the Neuendettelsau seminary with a public testimonial that rated him as superior in classical languages and equal to university graduates in theology. Loehe intended Fritschel to form with Grossmann the theological seminary faculty.

Loehe was also concerned that the students entering the Dubuque theological seminary should matriculate with adequate preparation. For this he wanted Grossmann to open a Latin school with Fritschel as instructor.

A group of emigrants was preparing to leave Neuendettelsau. This group included 11 heads of families and some wives and children. Before leaving, they formed a traveling congregation and called Fritschel to serve as their pastor. Based on this call, Pastor J. Meinel in Hamburg ordained Fritschel on April 23, 1854. The group then boarded ship and made a sixty-eight-day voyage, arriving in New York on June 30, 1854.

S. Fritschel

The group also included theological Candidate J. Michael Schueller, who hoped to be ordained and to engage in mission work, and a young man named Ferdinand Duerr expecting to study at the seminary. Others with them were colonists planning to settle at Saint Sebald or elsewhere in Iowa and Georg Prottengeier whose sister Margaretha lived in Detroit. Georg was to become Fritschel's lifelong friend and Margaretha his wife.

From New York the group traveled by rail through Canada bound for Detroit. In Canada, the train collided with some horses and was derailed. Four immigrants were killed. As group leader, Fritschel helped victims out of the wreckage, arranged for travel to shelter and medical aid, and dealt with railway officials about compensation for the dead and injured. Now it was necessary to divide the group. Schueller went on with those who were still well and arrived in Dubuque on July 11. Fritschel came on July 28.

Besides helping Grossmann create a theological seminary, Fritschel set about developing the teachers seminary into a Latin school or preparatory academy. For this he used a course of instruction modeled after that used by the Mission Institute at Neuendettelsau. By the fall of 1854 the teachers seminary was converted into a pre-theological academy. It would one day operate separately as Wartburg College, which claims the teachers seminary's 1852 founding date as its own. To this was added a theological department that became Wartburg Theological Seminary, which today recognizes 1854 as the date it began. For more than a decade after that, the preparatory school and the theological seminary operated under one roof.

The seminary was still owned and supported by the Society for Inner Missions Institute at Neuendettelsau. The cost of operation that first year in Dubuque was $626.19 besides the $100-per-year salary paid to Grossmann. Deindoerfer at Saint Sebald felt the school should save funds by moving to the developing colony, where the students might garden and raise their own food and cut their own firewood. Grossmann suggested to Loehe that the Dubuque location made the seminary a strategic center from which to do missionary work in the tri-state region. Loehe agreed and Deindoerfer reluctantly accepted that decision.

In February 1854, Grossmann wrote to Loehe that Deindoerfer, who was now directing mission work from Saint Sebald, had found evangelistic opportunities in Garnavillo (then known as Jacksonville) and there wanted to use one of Grossmann's students as a parish school teacher. Because Loehe knew the student, Grossmann asked him when he thought the student might graduate and be available to work with Deindoerfer.

CHAPTER 14

THE FOUNDING OF
THE IOWA SYNOD

L oehe advised those he sent to America that they should keep day books (diaries) and inform him of events he should know about. Many simply sent him copies of their day book entries. These copies in the Loehe Museum in Neuendettelsau are a rich source of American church history. George Fritschel appears to have drawn from these reports for his history, *Aus den Tagen der Vaeter.* The day book entries and accounts of the founding conference of the Iowa Synod that follow are drawn from Fritschel's research. Parenthetical additions are by the writer.

Sigmund Fritschel's daybook includes interesting first impressions of church life among the former Frankenhilfers in Iowa.

"Sunday, July 30 [1854], 7th after Trinity. Schueller preached in the morning on this Sunday's gospel. Church quite full. The complete liturgy [Loehe's *Agenda*] made a great impression on me as I heard it for the first time in America. Location: court house, a large auditorium about as big as the Martha Church in Nuremberg.

"Monday, August 14. On Saturday Kleinlein[49], who had gone to Dyersville during the week, came and told of an innkeeper in Elkport who wished that Deindoerfer might come once and preach there."

[Sunday, August 20] "The last time Deindoerfer was here we had agreed that he would come last week in order that the conference [to organize the Iowa Synod], long considered necessary, could take place. In case he could not leave Saint Sebald, we should go there, and Deindoerfer was to have met and taken us there from a tavern 21 miles from here [Dubuque]. But when the appointed day came [when Deindoerfer had not arrived at Dubuque], Grossmann's little Wilhelm, whom I found sick already when I arrived here, was so ill that

Grossmann didn't dare take a chance on going along. So Beckel and I had left without him.

"It was my first opportunity to look around the country a bit. The road to Deindoerfer's is already wide enough to use and learn to know the country. It is a pleasure to see the beautiful surroundings, the wide panorama one views with the constant change from hill to valley.

"But [along the way] one notes the scarcity of wood. There is plenty of woodland around Dubuque. [But then] there is prairie as far as one can see. We followed the road onto which we had been directed for about 20 miles. No one we asked knew of the '21 Mile House.'

"A house did stand 21 miles from Dubuque, but it was not the one we sought. It was not a tavern. Beckel, who speaks perfect English and can actually understand the Irish, came luckily to an understanding with the Irish lady of this house and learned that we were on the Delhi road. We had to go at right angles to get to the Strawberry Point road.

"It was a dangerous situation to go over the prairie as the sun was already down. There were many rattlesnakes in the area. One had already slipped by close to Beckel's feet. Still, we luckily found the road and hurried on it as fast as possible as it was becoming very dark.

"The day had been fearfully hot, and we had literally bathed in our sweat. The sudden coolness caused Beckel to develop a fever while we still could see no house anywhere. He became so weak he could hardly stay on his feet. At last we came to a house where we could change our clothes. Brother Beckel felt better as soon as he came into the house. But then we had to hear the unwelcome news that the house we were looking for was not on this road but on one lying ten miles farther to our right.

[Monday, August 21] "The next morning we had to go through the tall prairie grass, heavy with dew that wet us to the waist, to the other road. We encountered some very nice farms. One in particular that we entered was very neat and its Methodist owners were extremely cordial. The lady of the house came from German parents but had become so Americanized that her German speech was quite faulty. It is astonishing to one who has recently come into the land to see a wretched log cabin that is hardly equal to the poorest huts in New

Dettelsau and to be greeted there by ladies with the whitest skin and dressed in flowery and lacy dresses.

"It was about 10:00 a.m. when we arrived at the 21 Mile House. We were surprised that no one from Saint Sebald had been there to meet us. We did not want to return to Dubuque in the heat, so we waited until the afternoon. Fortunately, a wagon came along on which we rode to within seven miles of Dubuque. We completed our journey on foot and arrived after 9:00 P.M., tired but otherwise in good health.

[Tuesday], "August 22. This morning Amman arrived at 11:30 A.M. to tell us that he had reached the 21 Mile House yesterday two hours after we had left for Dubuque. He told us that Pastor Deindoerfer lay seriously ill and that they had even feared his death. This was the cause of Amman's late arrival at the 21 Mile House. Deindoerfer had been overtaken by a sudden rainstorm while hauling boards [from Clayton for the parsonage-church] and had to ride a whole day before he could dry his clothes.

"When Amman arrived at Dubuque, Grossmann's son Wilhelm was so sick it was evident that death was near. Amman stayed to await what would come. In the evening, while I was preaching at the court house, the child died. Much peace under heavy pain."

[During that week, Fritschel, Grossmann, and Schueller drove to Saint Sebald for Wilhelm's burial and to meet with Deindoerfer for the delayed formation of the Iowa Synod. Carrying Wilhelm's body to the location of the future colony was an act of faith similar to that of the Israelites bearing Joseph's bones to Canaan for burial.]

[Friday], "September 1. Returned this morning from Saint Sebald, where we had gone for the burial of our Wilhelm. As the conference decisions [concerning the new synod] will be sent out, I can think of nothing to write in my day book except the gracious protection afforded us on [Wednesday, August 23].

"We had left Dubuque late, and it was pitch dark as we rode through the thick woods, still several miles from the '21 Mile House.' It was so dark we had to lead the horses. When we were out of the woods, we let the horses lead a bit. Suddenly a bump. [The wagon stopped with a jolt], and I felt my face hit the tail and then the hind leg of one of the horses. Instinctively I crawled over the leather tug [connecting the horse to the wagon] into the grass and recovered myself. There was dead silence. The wagon did not move. The hind wheels stuck in a deep ditch which an irresponsible farmer must have dug a couple of days before to drain the road.

"Soon something moved. Grossmann lay under the wagon where the wheels would run over him. Only he and I had fallen out of the wagon. The persons in the back had been thrown into the front end. Except for bruises and scratches, no one was hurt. When we examined the wagon, we found the evener broken.... We made another one as well as we could and led the frightened horses on. At last we came to a farm house whose owner was friendly. He gave us linen cloth and salve for our wounds, that had begun to burn. Since he could not accommodate all of us, he roused two of his family to accompany us about four miles to the 21 Mile House where, praise God, we arrived at midnight.

"The next day we reached Saint Sebald. We found Brother Deindoerfer so weak that he could not speak. During the conference he had alternately good and bad days. On Saturday, August 26, we summarized all the discussion in written formulae.

"Sunday, August 27. We ordained Brother Schueller. The conference continued to occupy the days that followed."

This was a dramatic beginning for Fritschel and Schueller so soon after their arrival. Loehe had urged the former Frankenhilfers to organize their own synod. Grossmann and Deindoerfer knew they would not be welcome to join forces with the Missouri Synod in the forseeable future. Now that their numbers were growing, they decided to act on Loehe's advice. Beginning on August 24, 1854, in the

First Parsonage and church at St. Sebald, Iowa

half-finished parsonage at Saint Sebald, they organized the "Evangelical Lutheran Synod of Iowa and Other States." George Fritschel wrote, "No synod was ever brought to life under such wretched and discouraging circumstances." Deindoerfer participated in the organizational work from his bed.

G. J. Zeilinger wrote, "It was at this parsonage that four men, all strangers in a strange land, and yet not strangers nor foreigners, but 'fellow citizens with the saints, and members of the household of God,' met in solemn convocation August 24, 1854. And in this primitive and as yet unfinished house, called a church and a parsonage combined, there was founded that day the Evangelical Lutheran Synod of Iowa and Other States." [50]

Here four men of God gathered to come to grips with the common work that for the next seventy-six years would be conducted by the Iowa Synod. The charter members of the new synod and the only people present were Pastors Georg M. Grossmann, Johannes Deindoerfer, Sigmund Fritschel, and Candidate J. M. Schueller, who was ordained on that occasion. Only two pastors, Deindoerfer and Grossmann, had congregations, and these but a few families each. The other two, Fritschel and Schueller, were helpers of Deindoerfer in his sick bed and of Grossmann as he grieved over the child he had just laid to rest, the first burial in the Saint Sebald cemetery.

The first session on August 24 began with a song. Then Grossmann, as the oldest present, spoke of the purpose and goal of the synod. On bended knee they asked God's blessing and guidance.

No preparations had been made. Each spoke of whatever he wished. They abandoned the idea of adopting a formal constitution. They knew of the Missouri Synod's constitution, but they had no copy at hand and no one had any experience in drafting one. They decided instead to write a declaration of the reasons for and the objectives of the new synod. After these were discussed, Grossmann formulated a platform on which the new synod was to stand and from which it expected to confess the gospel in this country:

> "This synod subscribes to all the symbols [confessions] of the Evangelical Lutheran Church because it recognizes all the confessional decisions of such articles about which disputes arose before and during the time of the Reformation as being in agreement with the Word of God.

> "Since various positions have been taken within the Lutheran Church, this Synod adopts the one which, based upon our confessions, governed by the Word of God, strives for the ever higher development and greater fulfillment of the Lutheran Church.

> "In founding congregations, Synod cannot content herself with mere assent to her principles with regard to doctrine and life, but she demands probation and, therefore,

restablishes the catechumenate of the ancient church. The aim of her congregations should be to attain to apostolic life. Therefore, both official and brotherly discipline are to be exercised." (Translated from German by G. J. Zeilinger and edited by the writer.)

Fritschel: "This is the ground on which we place ourselves, the teachings of the Lutheran Church conforming to Scripture.... Our synod confesses all the Lutheran Confessions."

Grossmann: "Certainly. But we are in America where a large Lutheran church exists, the General Synod. It is Lutheran in name only. It confesses itself as Lutheran but its Lutheranism is said to be 'American.'

Fritschel: "They say, `We have learned a lot from neighboring churches.'"

Grossmann: "Yes. It is customary in this country to confess to the Lutheran Confessions without actually accepting all their parts. Often they mean that they take them 'in-so-far-as' they conform to God's Word. So it is good for us to say that we not only confess to the Lutheran Confessions (they all say that), but we should add why and how far we do it. It seems to me our duty to lay down a clear confession."

Schueller: "I agree with that. Therefore at my ordination next Sunday I will make my confession not only to Scripture but to all the Confessions as my own confession."

Grossmann: "That is the reason I have put the emphasis on our synod confessing the Lutheran Confessions because they are in agreement with the Word of God in contrast with the 'in-so-far-as' they agree with Scripture confessed by Lutherans-in-name-only. By comparing the Confessions with Scripture we have convinced ourselves that they agree entirely."

Deindoerfer: "With this we confess that we, exactly like the Missouri, the Buffalo and, I believe, the Tennessee Synods, stand fast and true to the Confessions of the fathers and do not deviate an inch from them in any teaching or belief. The Word of God that they confess, we also confess. We are Lutherans only because the Lutheran Church stands entirely and without qualification on the unfailing Word of God."

Grossmann: "To this is added the second paragraph: 'Since various positions have been taken within the Lutheran Church, this Synod adopts the one which, based upon our confessions, governed by the Word of God, strives for the ever higher development and ultimate perfection of the Lutheran Church.' Since we have added to our un-qualified belief in the Confessions that they are 'governed by the Word of God,' we thereby declare our separation from all unionists in Germany and from the unionistic (Lutheran) General Synod here." [51]

"But besides the unionistic trend in the General Synod, there is also another trend to which we do not subscribe."

Deindoerfer: "We tasted that peculiarity in Saginaw."

Fritschel: "How often in Germany and also here it was said orally and in writing, 'One must set himself at the feet of our elder teachers who have told us God's Word and hear them first, before one searches Scripture for himself.'"

Grossmann: "Certainly. In Germany many took that stand. It al-most seems to me that Grabau belongs to this trend. They always emphasize, 'So spoke Luther, so the church has spoken.' For them that is decisive and final."

Deindoerfer: "Our statement opposes that trend and speaks clearly that we feel that we work from a different position. We belong to those Lutherans who believe that there is a growth of knowledge for individual Christians as well as for the Church. We believe that in the future new questions may arise that never came up before. We recognize one correct way to answer these questions: 'Since various positions have been taken within the Lutheran Church, this Synod adopts the one which, based upon our confessions, governed by the Word of God, strives for the ever higher development and greater fulfillment [Vollendung] of the Lutheran Church.'"

Schueller: "How should one understand the last phrase 'greater fulfillment of the Lutheran Church'?"

Fritschel: "This says that there is a current, a trend, a large group of Lutherans who believe that there is a holy progress in the Lutheran Church. This progress enters the entire life of the church. It describes a forward motion on the road to knowledge. New questions that have never before been raised can and will arise. Then we have faith in the Savior that he will make his Word true today and will lead the church into all truth. He will give no other teachings, but will lead us deeper into the understanding and knowledge of the teachings of his Word that the church of the Reformation already possesses.

"In the same way there can also be progress in connection with theological study, liturgy, the constitution, congregational life and church work.... We count ourselves with those people....

"Of course, it might happen that one might read something else into our words. God himself couldn't make his Word so clear that mortals could not read other thoughts into it...."

It was agreed that the statement drafted by Grossmann would suffice for the present. Grossmann was also asked to prepare a model constitution for congregations that could be presented to a pastors' conference at the end of October. He was to base it on the Frankenhilf constitution that Loehe had prepared. (The Frankenhilf constitution is printed in the Appendix.)

A formal constitution was not adopted for ten years. In 1864 Sigmund Fritschel submitted one of two drafts received by the Iowa Synod convention, which it then adopted.

George Fritschel wrote, "So the Evangelical Lutheran Synod of Iowa stepped into being, poor and humble. She was small. One pardoned oneself when speaking of her as a synod in the presence of Missourians. The founders even forgot to elect officers."

Officers were chosen at the second synod convention in 1855. Grossmann was elected president of the Iowa synod and held that position thirty-nine years, after which he was succeeded by Deindoerfer. Fritschel was elected secretary. Over the years they gradually established offices, committees, conferences, and procedures.

With the infant church body established, Loehe offered to transfer to it the seminary and the $1,200 left in the Frankenhilf colonization fund at Saginaw (mostly in outstanding loans). At its pastors' conference December 6-7, 1854, the new Iowa Synod declined the offer. Relations with the St. Michael Church and its members of the Frankenhilf colony near Saginaw were such that the Iowa Synod would find it hard to liquidate the fund's assets there. And the synod's two young congregations at Saint Sebald and Dubuque could not carry the seminary operations even with help from Neuendettelsau. But when Loehe renewed his offer the following year, the young synod accepted the burden. The seminary then operated fully under the direction of the Evangelical Lutheran Synod of Iowa and Other States.

As soon as the Iowa Synod was born, the immigrant colonial structure under Amman's leadership evaporated. Amman seems not to have attended the birth of the synod that happened "two hundred paces" from his home. No lay delegates represented either Saint Sebald or Saint John of Dubuque at this meeting. The Iowa Synod was created and operated entirely under clergy control. This reflected the thinking of Loehe and his disciples, who believed leadership by pastors supervised by bishops to be the best tradition in the history of the church. It was this position that had caused the break with the Missouri Synod after Missouri's Saxon leaders insisted on "democratic, independent, congregational principles" in the Missouri Synod's constitution.

Nevertheless, Amman, the Weeges, Kleinleins, and others continued to provide strong lay leadership in the Saint Sebald congregation. Later they were also deeply involved in finding a new location for the seminary and underwriting the construction of the buildings at Saint Sebald.

The December 1854 conference of the infant synod had before it a paper from Pastor Roebbelen in Saginaw. It discussed two questions: "How do we stand toward Pastor Loehe?" and "How does Loehe stand toward us?" His presentation of the events in the Franken colonies was one-sided and the answers to his questions unclear. Roebbelen iinvited the Iowa men to reply to his paper. The pastors at the conference declined.

Loehe also received a copy of this paper. His comment:

"A rich material lies at my command, to which my friendly opponents at Saginaw have added their personal views. Out of this much light for our cause could be won and given. But to what purpose? Should I begin a fight with my brethren before the whole world and add another example of Lutheran incompatibility to the old and new examples that I abhor? Should the 'Father in Christ,' as they call me, start a war with the 'Sons of Christ,' as my friends call themselves? May there be peace between us. It is true that there are differences between us. But they are not of the significance that people overseas attribute to them. Differences have always existed within the Lutheran Church without, for that reason, terminating altar fellowship. The Spirit of truth can lead to harmony among those who place themselves subject to God's Word."

Why had Loehe with a heavy heart decided to give up the mission work in Saginaw and move it to Iowa? He could easily refute the false thoughts he had been charged with. But, "What does that help at present when we can no longer work effectively in Saginaw County and when, against our wishes, we are placed in opposition? The Lord will turn all to the best. We call to our friends in Saginaw from the bottom of our heart, 'Grow in thousand times thousands, and may your offspring occupy the gates of your enemies. But we are not your enemies. We are your friends.'"

Teachers Seminary

Grossmann was head of the seminary and pastor of the growing St. John Lutheran Church. The teachers seminary students had studied as one class. There is no record of the date when the class of teachers graduated in the spring of 1854. That fall, with the addition of a theological department, some graduates such as Karl Beckel and H. Weege who had taught school for a time returned to study for the ministry. The others did not return, and there is no record of where they served.

By the summer of 1854 the seminary staff was looking for a change of quarters. The house they were renting at Eagle Point was not in good condition, and the owner would neither repair it or sell it at a fair price. Grossmann and Fritschel decided that both the seminary and St. John Church needed a more suitable home.

Banker Jesup had drawn Grossmann's attention to a newer and larger house in the center of town. He bought it for $2,000—$1,000 down, the balance to be paid after one year at 10 percent interest. $1,100 would be due on October 20, 1855. Grossmann reported to Loehe and the German Friends the need to settle that balance when it came due.

As the time drew near for the final payment on the house, financial pressures mounted. Support from the German Friends in Neuendettelsau had declined as they heard from Missouri Synod leaders accusations that the Iowa Synod leaders had forsaken the Lutheran Confessions.

Grossmann tried to borrow money to meet the payment due, but he had no success. If the payment could not be made, the house together with the down payment would revert to the seller. Additional anxieties developed over the daily expenses for food and housekeeping. On one occasion a voluntary fast day was declared. Once the seminary was temporarily closed. Then an unexpected sum of money arrived from Russia, and the students returned to their labors.

But the $1,100 debt due on October 20 was still hanging over their heads. Grossmann pondered in his study on the evening of October 17. He had tried everything, and there was not a cent in the treasury. Yet he was quiet and relaxed. God had so often showed that he had journeyed to Iowa with them. Grossmann prayed and went to bed.

Later he wrote, "I placed the matter in God's hands and slept peacefully." In the morning there was a knock at the door, and student Weege came in. "Herr Inspector, I was at the post office. These letters were there for you."

Both letters were in Fr. Bauer's handwriting from Neuendettelsau. Both were addressed to "Rev. G. Grossmann, Rector of a German Lutheran Schoolmaster's Seminary and Lutheran Pastor, Dubuque, Iowa. North America. Via Liverpool. First Royal Mail Steamer."

He opened the first and found this letter:

"Neuendettelsau, Sept. 21, 1855

"Dear Brother:

"Herewith you receive as a matter of foresight a communication about a letter dated Sept. 20 that was sent to you together with a draft for $1,100.00. Should it get lost, I have out of foresight made a duplicate draft."

Grossmann did not read further. He opened the other letter with shaking hands. A draft for $1100.00 fell out of it. Not a cent more. The full amount. The backup letter and the letter with the draft had arrived together.

The second letter read:

"Neuendettelsau, Sept. 20, 1855.

"Dear Brother:

"Herewith you receive the wished for and necessary sum for the purchase of the seminary building, representing the second half, a draft for $1,100.00 with the request that you return a receipt immediately. Here you have a new evidence that we do not neglect the brothers in Iowa but follow their undertakings with greater sacrifice and personal care and responsibility than any previous undertaking. We have raised this sum with difficulty and had to borrow with interest as the first half is not yet paid. We hope the brethren will appreciate this service. We have done all that is possible, far beyond our resources. So, we are no longer in position to render support of this kind.

"In hearty brotherly love, your brother in the Lord,

"Fr. Bauer, for the Society."

Grossmann lifted his eyes to God with a heart too full for words.

Two hours later there was another knock at the door. It was Mr. Branscom, former owner of the new seminary house. He had come two hundred miles to collect his money. He wished to inquire if the payment would be made. "Certainly," was the reply. "We will have the payment for you tomorrow at the bank of Jesup and Company."

On October 20, 1855, the debt was paid. Mr. Jesup saw to it that the deed from Mr. and Mrs. John Branscom was completed. At 3:06 P.M. the second lot, 51 ½ by 150 feet, in block 481 was transferred to Grossmann's name.

Students and teachers spent the rest of October painting and whitewashing, building a cistern, and digging a cellar. The house had eight rooms on two floors. An addition was built on the front as worship space for St. John Church. A wooden addition was built at the rear. A separate structure was built as a stable.

The building housed Grossmann, his family, Fritschel, and at least eight students. When pastors or teachers arrived from Germany, they also stayed at the seminary until they were placed in parishes or mission stations. Mrs. Grossmann (Nanny) and a maid served as the kitchen staff.

On October 31 the new school year began.

The following spring, Beckel and Weege were expected to be assigned to pastorates and ordained, the first students to be graduated for the ministry at Wartburg Theological Seminary. The Iowa Synod required that all seminary examinations be held before the pastors of that body. In the spring of 1856, these were oral examinations in Bible history, world history, Latin, and Greek. The fact that theology was not included indicates that the six students were working only on college courses that semester. For the sake of efficiency, classes were combined as much as possible each semester for students at various levels. Two of the students were American, the rest had come from Germany.

Its new building was paid for. But Wartburg Seminary was still having difficulties with its current expenses. In 1855 the synod had become ten congregations. It established a treasury for the support of the preparatory school and seminary. The congregations were small and poverty-stricken, scarcely able to provide their pastors with enough to eat. The first year's income from the synod and from Germany was $120.23.

So, the seminary's first years at Dubuque were lean. The interest that had once been shown by the German Friends had cooled. The number of readers of reports of Loehe's missions in America had fallen from eight thousand to three thousand. Moreover, money contributed by the three thousand was needed at Neuendettelsau where the Missionary Institute had also been operating as a seminary. In addition, the conduct of the Missouri Synod had dampened much of the enthusiasm that once had supported the former Frankenhilfers. Finally, Loehe's battle against unionism in the Bavarian church had cost him many friends.

Loehe bore his losses in silence and loneliness.

In November 1856, Grossmann made a journey to Neuendettelsau and other Bavarian cities to remove misapprehensions that had arisen among the German Friends concerning the Iowa Synod and to strengthen the synod's bonds of fellowship with the mother church. While he was away, Pastor J. J. Schmidt took his place at the seminary. Grossmann returned to Dubuque April 30, 1857, with positive reports about the results of his trip. Grossmann believed that the German Friends now realized that they must more than ever support the young synod and its seminary. He expected that more money and more students would be sent to Iowa in the future.

In the meantime, the Dubuque seminary was suffering hardships. In the spring of 1855, there was nothing to eat at the seminary kitchen and no money to buy food. Grossmann wrote that the seminary family would have gone hungry but for contributions from Dubuque supporters for the purchase of coffee and black bread. During the 1855–1856 school year, the students took their meals at the homes of members of St. John congregation.

Because of this necessity, Sigmund Fritschel's Latin school boys were temporarily sent home, while he went to Menominee, Wisconsin, where he had earlier established congregations. He stayed with his new friend, Georg Prottengeier, who had bought a farm there with his sister Margaretha as his housekeeper. Sigmund earned his keep by helping them with the spring farm work.

Since the seminary could now afford only one teacher. Grossmann took over both the Latin school and the seminary classes. Fritschel then accepted a call from the church he had started at Platteville, Wisconsin, from where he could visit his other preaching places. He still made trips to Dubuque to guide his Latin school boys and the two theological students Beckel and Weege. He also relieved Grossmann when his duties as synod president kept him away.

CHAPTER 15

THE NEW SYNOD IN MISSION

Following his ordination at the organizational meeting of the Iowa Synod, J. Michael Schueller stayed at Saint Sebald to assist Deindoerfer, who was sick with typhoid fever. Deindoerfer's wife Katherina Elisabetha was expecting their first child. On September 3, their baby boy was stillborn. The following Sunday, Schueller conducted a graveside service with a meditation based on Mark 10:14.

During the time Schueller spent assisting Deindoerfer, he began serving a group of German Lutherans at Clayton Center. On July 4, 1855, Schueller and fifteen men and women *organized die Evangelisch-Lutherische Zionsgemeinde* (Zion Evangelical Lutheran Church). Two of these charter members were Mr. and Mrs. Peter Kleinlein. They came from the St. Sebald flock to help Schueller organize this mission church.

Pastors of the young synod were gathering German Lutherans into flocks wherever they could find them. Sigmund Fritschel continued to serve many of them. George Fritschel offers this story of Sigmund's mission work [52]:

One Saturday in October, Sigmund Fritschel with his robe and Loehe's *Agenda* set out on foot for Tete des Mortes (Death's Head), now known as Saint Donatus, sixteen miles south of Dubuque. Word of mouth had it that Lutherans there were reluctantly listening to a Reformed pastor and wished for a Lutheran. But the seminary had also received a letter from a certain Mr. Felderman telling them to stay away. Fritschel took with him student Christian Bauer as his companion and cantor.

They found Felderman's house. A stately old man answered the door and bade them enter. When they told him who they were, he asked, "Didn't you get my letter?"

"Yes, that is exactly why we came. We have heard that there are Lutherans in this area who wish for Lutheran worship services. So, we

140 • The Pilgrim Colony

do not understand why we are not wanted. We want to find out why we should not come."

The old man explained that he and his Lutheran neighbors had been afflicted with three pastors in succession who failed to preach and teach the gospel as the Lutherans had come to know it. One was Methodist, one tried to "convert" them, and the last claimed to be Lutheran but was such in name only.

Felderman proceeded to examine Fritschel's knowledge of the Lutheran catechism, his belief concerning the Sacraments of Baptism and Holy Communion and salvation by God's grace. He rejoiced over what he heard and welcomed his guests to conduct services at his home the next day. He had served in Napoleon's campaign into Russia. Late into the night he told of his war-time experiences.

Early the next day Felderman rode from farm to farm inviting people to gather at his home for a 10:00 worship service.

Men came from all directions, afoot, on horse or in wagons, singly or with wives and children. They carried tables out of the house to make room. They laid planks on chairs. Fritschel donned his robe and found a place near the kitchen stove.

Student Bauer spoke two lines of the hymn, "I will never leave my Jesus" and then sang it. The entire assembly began to sing with such enthusiasm that cantor Bauer was too astonished to lead them. They sang the entire song to the end.

As the professor started to preach, sweat ran down his body with the stove glowing three feet from him. Mrs. Felderman stirred the soup on the stove several times during the thirty-minute sermon.

After the service, the men assembled. They were satisfied because old Felderman told them that this pastor was a good Lutheran. There would be another worship in fourteen days and more people would come. Then they would discuss whether they could obtain a pastor of their own. He must teach school and he must know the English language.

There have been many as faithful as Felderman at Saint Donatus. Over the years a number of them have settled in other places and founded Lutheran churches there.

In the early 1860s Schueller served the Saint Donatus parish. Schueller also went to Andrew, Iowa, every four weeks to minister to scattered German Lutherans there. In 1863 he founded Salem Lutheran Church at Andrew.

Sigmund Fritschel also claimed the territory across the Missisippi from Dubuque for his own mission work. Soon he was serving groups at Menominee and Platteville, Wisconsin, and at Galena and Elizabeth, Illinois.

His missionary expeditions covered five to thirty miles on foot in all kinds of weather. Once on a trip to Platteville, he crossed the unbridged Mississippi in a boat rowed by a drunken boatman in a winter storm amid crashing ice floes. Before he reached Platteville, rain soaked him to the skin. The result was influenza that confined him in bed several days.

Fritschel's mission efforts were soon to be expanded. On September 14, 1855, an unannounced and unexpected guest came to see Grossmann: Pastor John Andrew Augustus Grabau, president of the Buffalo Synod. (See chapter 2 for an account of Grabau's dispute with the Missouri Synod.) Grabau had been directed by the Buffalo ministerium to visit the leaders of the new Iowa Synod and had come with three assignments:

1. To inquire as to the Iowa position on the Lutheran Confessions.

2. To ask the Iowa Synod to help develop a court of arbitration to settle the quarrels between synods.

3. To inquire if help could be obtained in furnishing pastors for a number of congregations for which Buffalo had no pastors available.

Grabau and Grossmann discussed articles published in *Der Lutheraner* criticizing the Buffalo and Iowa leaders. George Fritschel wrote this account of the event [53]:

Grossmann: "At our summer conference we discussed whether we would answer Sihler's and Wyneken's articles or not. Our resolution reads, 'Concerning an insulting article in *Der Lutheraner* authored by Dr. Sihler against Pastor Loehe and the Pastors Grossmann and Deindoerfer, the conference chooses to make no reply, for the Synod does not wish to give occasion for an open feud, and Dr. Sihler's slander speaks for itself.'"

Grabau: "I did not have that article in mind, for no man can possibly believe without further proof that Deindoerfer simply ran away from his congregation and took the bells and altar cloths along with him illegally.... I have the later articles in mind in which the entire tone gives rise to suspicions that here also an out-pouring of the 'old Adam,' who only indicates the worst, is at work."

Fritschel: "You probably refer to the article in *Der Lutheraner* of May 22, 1855, regarding the founding of [the Iowa] Synod and our fundamentals [*Grundsaetze*]."

Grabau: "Yes. Then also the articles by Pastor Fick of August 14 and 28 of this year, 'The Position of the Iowa Synod in Regard to the Symbolical Books of the Lutheran Church.'"

Grossmann: "I think we had better take both articles together. Both articles are based on what Pastor Loehe says about the founding of our synod. As Pastor Loehe wrote, he had before him our founding paragraphs and the minutes of the meeting at which they were drafted. Neither Professor Walther or Pastor Fick are acquainted with either of them. They draw conclusions from Loehe's report which neither could have arrived at had they known the exact wording...."

Fritschel: *Der Lutheraner* could have spared itself the six columns and no doubt would have done so if it had known our [founding] paragraphs."

Grabau: "That satisfies me entirely in regard to my first question. I see that you want to accept the Confessions exactly as has heretofore been done in the Lutheran Church and deny the 'in-so-far.'"

Fritschel: "Entirely so. That is expressed in our obligation formulation [*Verpflichtungsform*] which agrees word for word with that of Missouri. Here there is complete unity between us."

Grossmann: "May I again read my answer to you out of my report to Synod? 'Thereto we reply that at least it was not our intention to condition our position regarding the Symbols [Confessions]. What caused our Synod, exactly as it happened in the sentence under discussion, to express its position toward the Confessions was not seeking to do wrong under the guise of doing right, but the wish to express her convictions. Those convictions are, first, that among all Symbolical decisions there are none whose agreement with God's Word cannot be confirmed; secondly, that only what is Symbolical decision, that means any questioned teaching that the church has brought to light as Godly truth after battle, can make claim to Symbolical recognition.'" [54]

Grabau: "Now, dear brethren, I see from your sentences, and perceive from your words, that there can be no doubt that you wish, firmly and entirely, to stand on the Word of God and the Confessions. That answers my first question."

The other questions were discussed further. Grabau was given assurance that since students Beckel and Weege would soon take their examinations, there was a prospect of furnishing a pastor for Madison and the congregations in the area. They also declared themselves ready to support the organization of a church court. Grabau left much encouraged.

But candidate Heinrich Weege, age 20, son of the Kantor Weege and brother-in-law to Deindoerfer, became ill and died on October 2, 1855. He was buried at Dubuque. So, in 1856 Deindoerfer accepted the call to Madison, Wisconsin, Daniel Dietz came to Saint Sebald, and Karl Beckel went to serve at Cottage Grove, Wisconsin. [55]

In late September 1855 the Iowa Synod accepted Loehe's offer and took over the seminary. But it could support only one teacher, Georg Grossmann. So Fritschel resigned until conditions might improve, and accepted a pastoral call from the church he had been serving at Platteville.

Fritschel saw his temporary leave from the seminary as a possible opportunity to serve his (and Loehe's) first love, foreign missions. That autumn a missionary, Jacob J. Schmidt, came looking for a suitable Indian tribe to work among. Fritschel asked permission from the Platteville congregation to take time away and go with Schmidt to study the Indian language so that, in accordance with earlier plans, he could offer at the seminary a course of instruction for Indian missionaries. His brother Gottfried, still in Germany, was enthusiastic about this project and hoped to work with Indian missions himself. Sigmund accompanied Schmidt into Wisconsin, Michigan, and Toronto. But they failed to find an opportunity to stay with an Indian tribe and study their language.

When he returned to Platteville, Fritschel's interest in Menominee began to include more than just the congregations in that area. After more visits to the Prottengeier farm near Menominee, Margaretha Prottengeier said "Yes." On January 20, 1856, she married Sigmund at Dubuque.

Grabau's trust in Sigmund Fritschel now showed itself. He invited the Iowa Synod to loan Fritschel to do Buffalo Synod work in Michigan and Ohio. He accepted on a temporary basis until the seminary in Dubuque would be strong enough to support both him and Grossmann.

Fritschel began work in Detroit and extended his outreach to Marine City (Newport), Port Huron, and Saint Clair, Michigan, and Swan Creek near Toledo, Ohio. He was assisted by John Doerfler, whom

Loehe had sent in 1855 to study at the Dubuque seminary. In 1857 he replaced Fritschel at the Toledo congregation.

Doerfler's assistance to Fritschel began when Fritschel arranged for the seminary's senior class of two students to live with him during his two years in Detroit so that they could complete their theological studies under his supervision. (William H. Weiblen wrote in his *Life Together at Wartburg,* "It was the first experience of carrying on theological training at detached sites for which a century later Wartburg would be distinguished." [56]) Georg Grossmann continued teaching the other classes at Dubuque.

Grabau's friendly approach to the Iowa Synod did not last. In 1857 a controversy developed between the Iowa Synod and Missouri over *chiliasm* (the question of whether Revelation 20 teaches that Christ will return for a thousand-year reign on earth before the resurrection of all flesh). In this dispute, Grabau sided with Missouri. Fritschel resigned from the work that Grabau had assigned him in Michigan and returned to the seminary, by then relocated at Saint Sebald. Doerfler remained at Toledo, Ohio, but the Toledo congregation together with Marine City (Newport), Port Huron, and Saint Clair, Michigan, and Swan Creek near Toledo, withdrew from the Buffalo Synod and affiliated with Iowa. These churches became the nucleus of what later was organized as the Eastern District of the Iowa Synod.

Earlier, in 1856, the Iowa Synod decided to increase the seminary faculty once more to two professors. Instead of recalling Sigmund Fritschel from his Detroit congregations, the synod called his brother Gottfried L. Fritschel from Germany, where he had just completed studies at the University of Erlangen under the sponsorship of Loehe's Mission Institute. Sigmund had migrated on a sailing ship, but Gottfried traveled on a steamer, the Borussia. He brought with him their parents Martin and Katherina Fritschel and their younger brother Johann Friedrich. The family arrived at Dubuque on May 18, 1857. The synod promptly ordained Gottfried and installed him as Grossmann's associate at the seminary.

Gottfried L. Fritschel

Gottfried also brought with him from Neuendettelsau Pastor Johannes List, future pastor at Saint Sebald. List began work at Fort des Moines. He established a congregation there, and soon a number of congregations in that area looked to it as their mother church.

Four students from Neuendettelsau also accompanied Gottfried. This raised the Latin school and seminary enrollment to a new high of fourteen.

Gottfried had an advantage over Grossmann and his brother Sigmund in that he had learned English in Germany. He suggested opening an English division in the Latin school section. But such expansion had to be deferred. The costs of the institution were once more above the income, and the building was already too small for the faculty, staff, and students. Two deaconesses had arrived from Germany and lived at the seminary, one to teach St. John's parish school and one to direct the kitchen. In 1857 only one student still roomed at the seminary. Gottfried described conditions at the seminary in a letter to Neuendettelsau dated June 8-11, 1857 [57]:

"Dearly beloved Fathers in Christ...

"Above all, I must report the entire arrangement and our way of life at the seminary. Our small house is full of people from top to bottom. Every corner is occupied. As you know our seminary has eight rooms. A quiet roomy school room is on the first floor in which a large lecturer's chair is placed. It serves also as the dining room for the entire household and as a work room for the students. Next to it is the kitchen where our housekeeper Sister Katherina works. The other two rooms are occupied by Inspector Grossmann and his family.

"My room is on the second floor, from which the nearby bluffs covered with pretty greenery present a lovely picture.

"Until recently Friedrich Doerfler lived next to me with his family...before going to Wolcottsville to teach. The room is now released as a second workroom for the students. The two deaconess sisters live in the other room, and it is quite lively because of the youth of Sister Rosetta, who gives part of her teaching time here. The last room is occupied by a student who, though married, decided to dedicate himself to the Lord. He is a soul deeply loving Jesus whom I have come to value highly because of his deep piety.

"Since no rooms are free for a dormitory, our seminarians have about a 15 minute walk to the home of Johann Kleinlein [future head of the Kleinlein industries at Saint Sebald], at Eagle Point where he has prepared two rooms on the ground floor. The walk back and forth is always made together and is useful for the exchange of scholarly discussions.

"At 6:00 A.M. the seminary assembles for matins worship at the adjoining friendly church (Saint John Lutheran Church). A frame from which our two bells are hung (which Deindoerfer had been accused of stealing) is beside the door. Their iron tongues are our pride and joy. I think our church here is the only one that can ring in its worship with two bells. It sounds so festive in this bell-scarce region when the two together invite all for the meeting of the saints. The bells must help us missionaries. They are a call to lift up hearts for prayer.

"Our church is not large, but inside it is lovely.... Here I hold the matins and vespers....

"I would like to make you acquainted with our scholars. ...If you could see us all sit together so trusting and peaceful, and if you could observe the attention with which our students follow the instruction, particularly the young 15-16-year-old ones with their trusting eyes taking every word from my mouth, you would certainly be happy, as I am.... We also have a beautiful table companionship. We form quite a group that daily sits at the same table.

"Because our [Iowa Synod] congregations have a probation period before admitting persons as members, their memberships are quite small and can give little support to the seminary. So you can easily understand that it goes very sparingly [to feed] our large household when occasionally moneys are not received from Germany. (For the last fourteen days I have been the cashier.) Then Sister Katherina comes to me and will give me no rest until I give her five dollars. Then I have only twenty cents in the treasury. But that does not cause us anxiety. We know that our institution does not belong to us but to our beloved Lord Jesus. The rich Lord will provide for it. I also have the firm confidence that when I eventually lay down my job as cashier, I can make a happy jubilant speech on the question: 'Did you ever suffer want?' With all our loved ones over here, I will joyously and thankfully, with deeply reverent hearts, triumphantly give answer, 'Lord, never!'

"The past Pentecost and Trinity festivals were lovely and blessed days of joy in God and inner awakening for us. Brother Grossmann and I had intended on the first festival day to ride to Sherrill's Mount where I had been asked to conduct services. But it was impossible to get to this settlement ten to twelve miles away. I was unable to get a horse and buggy because of the heavy downpour of rain. So we stayed at home.

"That night I was ordained. Brother Grossmann ordained me, assisted by Brother Schmidt. Oh, how I feel, since the moment that God laid this holy, precious office on me, what a difference it makes to be in direct awareness of God's command and call, not only to speak to one's congregation but to act in carrying out the priestly office. It is encouraging to me to recall the festive moments that night when I, with bells ringing, under the prayers of a praying congregation, consecrated myself to the Lord with a joyous heart, made my commitment to the Confessions of the Church and took up the precious burden.

"On the past Sunday, on Trinity Festival, I began my office in my Charlesmount congregation. I preached early in Dubuque, and as we came out of the church at 12:30, a buggy stood before the door to take Brother Grossmann and me to the German settlement ten to twelve miles away. We had a quick bite to eat and packed our robes, *Agenda* etc., in a traveling bag, swung ourselves into the buggy, opened an umbrella against the hot sun, and rode as fast as our old nag Klapper would go through the dust clouds to Charlesmount.

"A number of my congregation live where the settlement begins. So we tarried with them, and after we had refreshed ourselves a bit, it was high time that we should get in and proceed to ride to the church, still three miles away. We climbed into the buggy. The members [we had been with] had previously hitched their wagons quite loaded with people, and we drove quickly to the church. Here and there single persons also joined the wagons following us, helping to increase our crowd.

"And so we came to the trim Evangelical stone church.... But now pay attention. We are in America, where it goes fairly American. Picture for yourself a single school house lawn around which numerous unhitched wagons stand. The oxen and horses graze free and peacefully nearby. One sees the mantillas and hats of the American farmer ladies through the open windows. We get down [out of the buggy], beat the finger-thick dust out of our clothes and go into the school house, decorated prettily by the congregation to celebrate the day. There are benches on both sides and at the rear. At the end of the room opposite the door stand two tables with just enough room between them for a chair. I must crowd myself between the two tables when I preach, with the chair before me as a pulpit. The table to my right serves as an altar. It is covered with a shiny white cloth. On it is a beautiful crucifix and candelabra...."

"It often happened that, as I preached, a wind arose outside and a dust cloud came through the door directly at the pastor, as though the demons of the wind wanted to stuff my mouth with dust.

"The congregation is very small, and my listeners include Methodists and Reformed. But the congregation has begun to grow. I am very pleased with it. I often perceive here in this land, above all things, how heaven-distant different the little Lutheran congregations are from the massive (European) churches. Here one perceives that faith and love in the heart builds the communion of the saints. One bows joyously under the living God."

(Then the letter discusses plans Gottfried has to work with other German Lutheran groups. He also reports rumors that the seminary may be moved to Kansas.)

From a later letter by Gottfried Fritschel: "A fourth preaching place, at which I conducted worship for the first time is the French Settlement nine miles from here....

"Sometimes the work days are torrid. For instance, last Sunday I preached three times, and it took about twenty miles of footwork to do it. I had stayed over night at the home of one of my members at Sherrill's Mount. Early Sunday morning it took me a forty-five-minute walk to the school house where I preached. I had to be on my way as soon as services were over. Then I had to wander for three hours in the glowing sun on a hot July day at midday, through woods and bluffs, over fields, prairies and streams, in unbroken haste to the French Settlement.

"The people were already gathered in the church when I arrived. I had no more than fifteen minutes rest and a chance to quench my thirst before I ascended the pulpit. It was about 4:30 P.M. at the end of the service. After a very few minutes, I must promptly start the trip back to Dubuque and hurry in order to get back in time to begin the worship service there. I literally had no time to eat throughout the day, let alone allow a meal to be prepared for me. It was already 7:45 when I arrived at Dubuque.

"The bells were ringing by the time I stopped puffing and changed clothes, and I must hasten to the church. This time I entered the pulpit in house shoes because my feet were worn sore on the American corduroy roads. I could not stand the boots any longer.

"Oh, and at what kind of places we preach—in churches, schools, houses, log cabins, in large and small farm house rooms, under trees and in the open field. I wish I could show you our last service at Rush Creek. As the farm house could not hold half of the people, we held services in the open, under some trees on a high hill. It made a unique impression on me to hear my dear Wuerttembergers under the open heaven with their melting, sentimental, slurring melodies, more slurs than syllables, with a number of women softly humming, while numerous strong base voices growled along, all with a spirit of deep devotion.

"I then began to preach, while my hair and robe fluttered in the wind, with my farmers seated before me on the logs rolled together for that purpose under the shade trees. Suddenly the clouds gathered, distant thunder rolled. Wind, announcing a storm and whipping my robe, made my voice almost inaudible. I then shortened my sermon and all hurried to corn crib, granary, barn and kitchen to avoid the downpour. I held Sunday school in the corn crib. At least you see that we obey the command of our Lord Jesus to preach what we have learned on the roof tops and the highways."

Elkport and the Lost Horse

From another report by Gottfried Fritschel to Loehe [58]:

Deindoerfer had learned that there were Germans in Elkport and that a German innkeeper in particular wanted a Lutheran worship service. Fritschel knew the general direction of Elkport about forty-three miles from Dubuque in the Volga River valley. He set out one Saturday on the seminary's horse, Prince. After riding twenty-five miles, he came to a woods with no house in sight. At twilight he came upon some men at a brook. Is this the right road to Elkport? No, sir! They directed him to the way. After five minutes the road disappeared into the trees. At a farm house nearby, he found a heavy-bearded man, dirty and unkempt. He recognized Fritschel as a German and asked, *"Hast du kein Kautobak?* (Have you no chewing tobacco?)"The farmer showed Fritschel the way, which had become a footpath.

It became darker, and Fritschel soon lost the trail. Then dogs appeared, and he rode toward a house. A German widow lived there with her son. She said he would be unable to find his way in the dark and must stay with them over night. They had also longed for a church. They would go to his church service at Elkport in the morning. The son took care of Fritschel's horse.

Because Fritschel had only seventy-five cents with him, at supper he took only a cup of coffee. His hosts made bed for him in the barn loft on corn husks. There he fed on the bread and sausage that Sister Katherina had packed.

When he awakened in the morning, he found his horse Prince in the stable, untied. The door was broken and lay on the ground. Prince walked out over the fallen door to his master. Where had the young man put the horse's bridle? [Fritschel makes no mention of a saddle, so he must have ridden bareback.] Finding some old rope nearby, Fritschel tied one end around the horse's neck and the other to a tree. He ran to the house to shake the young man awake. "Where is my bridle?"

Running out again, he saw the horse's tail disappear into the woods. Running, shouting, and searching were in vain.

"So I gave up searching, considered the horse lost, and wondered how I could repay the seminary $140."

He got exact directions to Elkport and arrived in plenty of time for services.

"That Sunday the innkeeper was my host and host to the entire congregation. He pleased me very much. It was a pleasure as I entered to see this honorable elderly person with a long white beard seated by the fireplace, so deeply concentrated on a Bible opened over his knees that he did not observe my entry. Afterward he brought forth a large sermon book by Rambach, a book so tattered it was hardly legible. What bright joy shone in the eyes of my host when I promised, God willing, to come every two weeks....

"I preached standing by the fireplace in the drawing room. It was full. And I was told that more would come to future services. The valleys that run together around Elkport are settled by Germans. I found many people there who are longing for salvation.

"Another group of real Americans there have very stunted impressions of religious teachings. How could it be otherwise when, for years, they have been deprived of pastoral care. But most of these were attentive to the preaching and concentrated on my words. All expressed joy that they will be provided with God's Word regularly. All, even those who I feared were not deeply interested in spiritual needs, denied interest in the detested Methodist pastors. However, many former Methodists, longing for the familiar services of their tradition, could not overcome the desire to visit Methodist services occasionally."

But what about the horse? The people promised Fritschel that they would advertise its loss. And so in open places and at cross roads, signs were placed telling that the Lutheran pastor had lost his horse. "If it is found, notify the innkeeper."

Fritschel had to make his way back to Dubuque on foot. Four days passed with no news of the horse. Fritschel sat writing beggar notes to his friends in Germany, asking for help to replace the horse to the seminary.

Student Conrad Ide came in. "Professor, I have heard that an Irishman at Strawberry Point has found a runaway horse. Should I go and see if it is Prince?"

"Certainly, if you will be so kind."

The rumor was correct. When student Ide appeared at the Irishman's farm yard, the horse neighed in recognition. The Irishman said that the riderless horse had come running down the road with a rope around its neck. He had had much trouble capturing him.

The horse easily accepted the bridle. But as the student expressed his thanks and prepared to ride away, the Irishman called, "Wait! You forgot to pay me."

Ide dismounted. Pay? He had not thought of that. He had only fifty cents in his pocket. "How much do you want?"

"$2.50 for feed."

The horse looked hungry and was not even brushed. "Didn't you know that you had a runaway horse?"

"No. The horse does not leave this barnyard until you pay me $2.50."

"I have fifty cents. I will give it to you. If you are not satisfied, we will go to the justice of the peace, and then you may pay me."

"Don't talk silly. I captured the horse and took care of it."

"Certainly, you captured the horse on the open road as it was on its way home. You fed it dry hay. Nothing else. Who gives you the right to stop a horse on the open road? We have lost the use of the horse all those days, and it is right that you should pay us."

The Irishman looked in amazement at the student who had not lost his head and who had so skillfully used his own story against him. He swore an oath and said, "Give me the money and get out of my barnyard!"

So Prince came home, healthy, happy, and hungry. Fritschel's begging letters went into the waste basket.

The best of the story was that by posting notices, it became known everywhere around that a Lutheran pastor was preaching in Elkport. Now no other group would think of organizing a congregation there and calling a pastor.

Fritschel wrote, "My horse that I got back after four days did a greater service for me and the cause than if it had carried me six miles farther to Elkport. So everything must serve the children of God for the best."

CHAPTER 16

THE SEMINARY
REJOINS THE COLONY

Since Grossmann was still in Germany, the synod delayed its spring conference in 1857. As soon as Grossmann returned, the synod gathered at Saint Sebald. [59] Peter Kleinlein, the budding industrialist at Saint Sebald, was also present.

Grossmann's report: "In Germany, it became clear to me that despite the greatest effort that could be made, Neuendettelsau can give us little support, for these reasons:

1. The first missionary fervor in Germany has disappeared.

2. Missouri's break with Loehe has estranged many from American missionary work.

3. The American mission has become a Bavarian matter, a cause of Loehe's alone. Loehe's position in Germany has become isolated.

4. The Bavarian group is taken to task about maintaining our seminary and the deaconess institution there.

5. It is often said, 'The Americans can now help themselves and no longer need our aid.'"

Deindoerfer: "We must earnestly keep in mind the idea of relocating the seminary. We must reduce our expenses if we don't want to become bankrupt. It is impossible to maintain the institution, let alone expand it, where every pound of flour, every radish, every stick of wood costs us dearly.

Gottfried Fritschel: "Last year we considered relocating the seminary in Kansas, where a strong stream of settlers has spread. Our faithful traveling salesman Peter Kleinlein proposed to buy a large tract of land, large enough for a colony and so carry out Loehe's plan. But today it is no longer possible. Now one can obtain only 160 acres, and that only if one builds and lives on it. Government land is no longer for sale, and we cannot bring fifty to sixty families together at one time. Besides, many brethren will have no part in a relocation at such a distance."

Grossmann:"But we must also consider an expansion.The friends in Germany have promised to send students to study with us from year to year as they did to the seminary at Fort Wayne.We don't have enough sleeping room now for our students. What would happen if my young colleague [Gottfried Fritschel, who lived at the seminary] found a lady who would accept him, as he has need? The Word applies also to him: 'It is not good that a man should be alone.' Real estate in Dubuque sells by the front foot."

Deindoerfer: "Irrespective of that, we must go into the country. Then vegetables, flour and meat can be grown and heating wood can be cut free."

Schueller:"Two places are under consideration.The vicinity of Clayton and Saint Sebald.The ease of travel to the outside speaks for Clayton. It is on the Mississippi where one can easily travel north and south.

Dietz:"The cheap price of good land and the nearness of congregations of the better people argues for Saint Sebald.These congregations will grow if the seminary goes there."

The situation was discussed at length.The Dubuque leaders explored the Saint Sebald area.A 120-acre farm with half of the harvest included was for sale at $2,100.00. Sixty acres were under cultivation, sixty acres were woodland. The lay of the rugged land at the north edge of the prairie was attractive.To the south, the land sloped from the building site on a hill that could be seen from a long distance over the prairie.

As Fritschel said, several locations had been considered earlier in Iowa, Minnesota, and Kansas. In 1964 Else Prottengeier recorded family recollections of this search.A Saint Sebald committee consisting of her grandfather Georg Prottengeier, Karl Gottlob Amman, and Amman's future son-in-law Georg Schuchmann embarked on an expedition as far as Kansas to search for a seminary location. On the way they considered Ames, Iowa. Else wrote, "It was a dry summer and crops didn't look good. They arrived on Saturday night, payday for the Indians. It was a wild, noisy night. They didn't think it a good place to build a seminary."

Eleanora (Guetzlaff) Deguisne wrote in her *Glimpses of the Early Days of the Prottengeier Family* that the committee traveled as far as

Kansas because it was "settled by large numbers of German immigrants and [was] becoming famed for its fertile soil.... On their return they reported the country too wild. It was not a fit place to go. Indians were still roaming the plains."

Grossmann now agreed to Deindoerfer's suggestion of three years earlier that the school should be placed with the Saint Sebald colony, as had been the original plan back at Saginaw. This was their recommendation to the synod.

The Iowa Synod agreed to locate the Latin or preparatory school and the seminary on the available Saint Sebald area farm surrounded by the Lutheran colony. Hoping to take advantage of a rise in real estate values, the synod decided to sell the Dubuque property. The seminary property at Dubuque was worth at least seven thousand dollars. But banker Jesup advised Grossmann to hold the property a year, after which he thought it would bring eight or ten thousand dollars. Since Peter Kleinlein was eager to advance the money to establish the seminary at Saint Sebald, Grossmann accepted Jesup's advice. That fall (1857) there was a national financial crisis and the soap bubble of land speculation in Dubuque burst. Up to 36 percent interest was demanded for loans. Nearly all the banks in Dubuque went bankrupt. Now the seminary property could not be sold. Saint John Lutheran Church continued to use it as its parsonage and after some years it was sold by the congregation.

At the delayed spring conference of 1857, Grossmann had presented a plan for the building to be erected on the new site: "I have drawn up on paper my idea of a seminary building that I will present. Naturally we will be required to build of wood since that will go faster and we can build larger.

"I would build a 32 x 48 feet two-story frame structure with a large attic to serve as a dormitory. On both first and second floors, I have a hall going the entire length of the building. In order to lose no space to inside stairs, I have a two-story veranda surrounding the house which includes steps on the east and west ends. I have provided for a cellar under the entire structure.

"There are eight rooms on the first floor, five for the families of two professors, a kitchen, dining hall and a servants room. There are six rooms on the second floor, including a large lecture hall and students' workshop, a small lecture room, and four additional rooms for which use can easily be found."

Grossmann's plan was studied thoroughly and improvements were suggested. The space would be generous compared to the eight crowded rooms in Dubuque. It was agreed that the new seminary quarters would be built on a high point with a view of the level land to the south.

The proposed site for the seminary lay about two miles west of the church Deindoerfer was pastoring at Saint Sebald.

Peter Kleinlein loaned the money to buy the farm for the synod and advanced the funds for the construction of the seminary building. The deed to the property was placed in the name of his brother Johannes Leonhard Kleinlein. Peter Kleinlein was at the same time building in his valley to the east a large complex that included a brewery, a flour mill, and a cheese factory.

An abstract of title shows that Kleinlein bought forty acres on July 1, 1857, for $500 and an adjoining eighty acres on July 29, 1857, for $3,500—all in the Northwest quarter of Section 5, Township 91. Two years later (June 2, 1859), Kleinlein conveyed title to the property to the Fritschel brothers' father Martin H. Fritschel for $4,160 (probably $4,000 plus accrued interest). The difference between this amount and the $2,100 price of the land indicates that it cost $1,900 to construct the seminary building.

Martin and Katherine Fritschel held title for the seminary until April 9, 1867, when the seminary paid them the token sum of $1,400 for two forty-acre tracts, on one of which stood the seminary structure. This was a significant gift to the seminary by the parents of the Fritschel brothers who by then constituted the seminary faculty. On that date, April 9, 1867, Wartburg Seminary was incorporated with its "principal place of business to be St. Sebald, Clayton County, Iowa." The original seminary trustees were Sigmund and Gottfried Fritschel, Michael Eder, Karl Gottlob Amman, P. Bredow, Johannes Deindoerfer, and S. Klineworth.

At the end of the spring term of 1857, two students were graduated in Dubuque and assigned to mission congregations. Again the senior class of two were sent to Detroit to study with Sigmund Fritschel.

Grossmann and the older theological students moved into the small log cabin on the seminary's farm at Saint Sebald to build their new home. These apprentice builders were Moritz Braeuninger (a cabinet maker), Brandt, Kluge, Christian Kraenzlein, and Seyler. In addition Conrad Ide appeared, having left studying and ministering with Sigmund Fritschel at Marine City, Michigan.

Ground was broken for the seminary building on a knoll just west of the farmstead that was developed later by Andreas Schmidt and his successors.The stones for the foundation and cellar were quarried and cut nearby. Most of the lumber was brought from Volga or Clayton with a team of oxen. Guided by a carpenter, Grossmann and his students worked from early morning until late at night. The construction took all summer.

Gottfried Fritschel wrote, "We naturally had to suspend instructions a number of weeks and give 'building vacations' in order to complete the building as soon and as economically as possible. Our dear seminarians worked like heroes, and we thank them alone that we could celebrate the dedication promptly. We cannot acknowledge enough the self-sacrifice, self-denial, and willingness with which they conducted themselves under the unfamiliar heavy work and toil and countless inconveniences. It was a joy to watch the busy hands dragging stones, preparing mortar, sawing, hammering, nailing, lathing, painting, doing cabinet work, and well-digging.What they started went well because a spirit of joy, love, and unity went with it. One could see that their work was an offering laid on the altar of Jesus. Their goal was to build a house for the beloved Lord Jesus."

During that construction period in the summer of 1857, the younger boys in the preparatory school at Dubuque continued their studies under the sole care of Gottfried Fritschel. In October Gottfried Fritschel and the preparatory school moved from Dubuque into the new building.

All the space was needed, for it had to include a chapel, class rooms and a students' dormitory. As planned, the building also supplied housing for the professors, for their families and for a deaconess housemother. The students lived on the upper floors; the faculty and staff on the lower.Almost at once Grossmann added to the building the space needed by the kitchen and dining room.

On Reformation Day, October 31, 1857, the new building was dedicated. Almost all the pastors of the young Iowa Synod attended the celebration.The day began with a Reformation Festival Eucharist in the little Saint Sebald parsonage-church by the spring two miles to the east. Then all participants hurried to "the Wartburg" for dinner and the afternoon dedication.The new building scarcely held the crowd who gathered from all directions.

Inspector Grossmann delivered the dedicatory sermon and prayers. In the evening a discourse was conducted about the work of the Reformation. Then the seminary was considered to be under way.

People were calling the institution "the Wartburg," because many thought the surrounding hills resembled the Thuringian countryside in Germany, home of the Wartburg Castle (*warte, burg* means "wait, castle") where Martin Luther translated the New Testament. Gottfried Fritschel wrote, "We had agreed among ourselves to denote by that name that we should wait and be quiet before our God who helps us. Our God, the merciful, grant that streams of blessing go out into the entire surrounding country from our lofty 'burg'; that hosts of evangelists go out with the pure gospel on their lips; that many joy-enriched, blessing-bringing soldiers of our dear church go out from our Wartburg in all directions."

The classes opened with eleven students. After three months there were 16, and the facilities were already crowded. As head of the seminary, Grossmann still carried the title "Inspector." During that first school year, Gottfried Fritschel was the sole professor.

The Wartburg and the home of the Gottfried Fritchels

CHAPTER 17

LIFE AT THE WARTBURG

G ottfried Fritschel's son George, born at Saint Sebald's semi-nary, described life on the Wartburg, where the rugged hills of Saint Sebald met the rolling prairie south and west [60]:

"It was a quiet and serene life in beautiful Saint Sebald and at the new Wartburg. There was no friction between students and professors. No one disturbed the work. Yet, in our day we can hardly picture their primitive conditions. There were none of the conveniences considered indispens-able in such institutions today. There was no bathroom, no wash stand with hot and cold water. A student went four miles to the Maquoketa River to bathe. [Or to Ensign Creek a mile to the north. In winter he squatted in a galvanized wash tub.] The students did not live in pairs in rooms warmed by centralized furnace heat. They lived in their class-room, where they learned and studied until bedtime. Then they climbed to the attic under the roof, where they almost froze in winter and almost roasted in summer. One did not dare to make much noise in the lecture room, for the pro-fessors lived directly below and could suddenly appear on the scene unannounced.

"The meals were plain. Day after day they drank wheat juice, wheat coffee that was given a bitter taste by adding chicory. The students spread molasses or pumpkin butter on their bread."

The wood necessary for the large household was cut from the seminary forest. Friends furnished a "buzz" saw powered by a horse and treadmill with which the huge oak trees were sawed to fire-wood lengths for heaters and for splitting to cook-stove size.

When the crops ripened, classes were suspended so that stu-dents and professors could become harvest hands. Young livestock was raised on the farm, and the students did the butchering. In the summer fresh meat was bought only during harvest. Otherwise the meat served in summer had been smoked, salt cured or canned in winter at the seminary. In winter, fresh meat was on the table more often because sausages, roasts, steaks and chops could be kept frozen in an outdoor wooden box.

Students assisted with the daily chores, feeding the livestock, filling the kerosene lamps, bringing in firewood, and hauling water. Water came from a spring in the farm's forest about one-half mile away. Some years later a well was drilled and rain water cisterns were built on the site.

John Jacob Hoeger, age twenty-seven, was hired to run the farm. Hoeger was born September 15, 1827, at Niederoberbach near Heruden, Bavaria. After a few years of managing the farm, the seminary rented the farm to Hoeger, who then was responsible for furnishing the seminary with vegetables, meat, and teams of horses for transportation. From that time on, the students were paid by Hoeger for their farm labor.

On November 5, 1873, when he was forty-six years old, he married thirty-four-year-old Maria Margareta Wilhelmina Hoeflinger, a deasoness from Nuremberg, Bavaria. Margareta was ordained June 24, 1862, in the mother house at Augsburg, and in 1866 she served on the battlefields of the war between Austria-Bavaria and Prussia. The newly married couple moved with the seminary in 1874 to Mendota, Illinois, where Hoeger served as house master until the seminary moved to Dubuque in 1889.

One of Hoeger's assistants at the seminary at St. Sebald was Johannes Andreas Schmidt, whose descendants include pillars of today's St. Sebald congregation. When the seminary moved to Mendota, Schmidt bought the farm, having sold cordwood to accumulate the down payment. The Wartburg Seminary trustees named on the warranty deed were G. M. Eder, John Deindoerfer, Georg Grossmann, John Wittig, and H. Michaelson.

When the seminary arrived at Saint Sebald, there were staff changes. Saint Sebald's Pastor Deindoerfer had accepted a call to Ohio in 1856. Saint Sebald called Pastor Daniel Dietz. In 1857 Grossmann arrived with the seminary and would serve as Saint Sebald's pastor along with his missionary efforts, his duties as professor, and his work as president of the Iowa Synod. Dietz replaced Grossmann at St. John in Dubuque. In August 1858, Professor Sigmund Fritschel was recalled from Detroit to his chair at the seminary. The two Fritschel brothers were reunited and continued on the faculty all the sixteen years that the Wartburg continued at Saint Sebald. Sigmund and Margaretha Fritschel now had a son Gottfried.

With Sigmund Fitschel back on the faculty, Grossmann now withdrew from teaching theology and taught only music. He continued as head of the seminary, and served as pastor of the Saint Sebald congregation until the seminary moved to Mendota.

Gottfried Fritschel had left Loehe's tutelage with an understanding that when he was ready for marriage, Loehe would assist him as a matchmaker. In his report to Loehe in January 1858, Gottfried reminded Loehe of this provision and announced that he was now ready. He asked Loehe to submit his proposal to a Neuendettelsau deaconess. Loehe presented the offer of marriage to Elise Koeberle, a woman from a prominent church family. Elise accepted and arrived at the Wartburg that summer. They were married by Sigmund Fritschel at Saint Sebald on August 29, 1858.

The two Fritschel families lived at the seminary, each family with two rooms. A residence was soon built near the seminary for Gottfried and his bride. Sigmund and his family stayed in the seminary building where he carried the title housefather (*Hausvater*).

George Fritschel wrote,

"After 1861 the seminary household was directed by the never-to-be-forgotten Aunt Augusta von Schwartz [see chapter 19], the former maid of honor of the Kaiser's Minister von Gamalaya in Russia. When Sigmund Fritschel had left on his fund-raising trip in Germany, he had been asked to bring back a housekeeper. Then he wrote from Europe that he would bring a maiden lady back with him. Upon reading this letter, his brother [Gottfried] held his head and went about the room mumbling, 'Sigmund is crazy, Sigmund is crazy to bring a noble lady back to us here in our wilderness.'

"Sigmund had tried to talk the little lady out of coming, but to no avail. When he painted in the darkest colors the primitive conditions and poor circumstances [at the seminary], he only got this calm answer, 'You have fully explained all this to me, and I have considered it thoroughly. I have decided to undertake this work and thereby serve the

Lord Jesus. My relatives here no longer require my help. There [at the seminary] I can continue to work for the Lord.'

"She became the 'Students' Mother' in the fullest sense of the word. She worked selflessly and devotedly and was happy in those poor circumstances. Later when she took time off to visit in Russia, her friends and relatives could not persuade her to stay. She had to return to her dear seminary, her dear professors, her dear Iowa Synod." *(The refectory at Wartburg Theological Seminary carries her name.)*

"The circumstances were indeed poor. There is a synodical resolution in an old copy of the minutes that the salary of the professors should consist of free housing, living necessities [board], and $100.00 per year.... When the wife of one of the professors used $1.00 worth of sugar in one month making plum sauce for the winter, the question was raised, 'Isn't that too much?'...

"The greatest hardship felt by the professors and students was their inablilty to purchase needed books. But they studied what they had all the more intently, and God provided that they could borrow the rest.

"[Martin Fritschel], the father of the two Professors Fritschel, lived at the seminary with his small friendly wife Katherina or *Grossmutterle* (Little Grandma). With the younger brother [Gottfried Fritschel] lived his mother-in-law 'Frau Pastor Koeberle,' widow of a pastor in Bavaria. Her beautiful stories from the Bible and from fairy-tale books pleased the growing children of both families.... When she ran out of stories she made some up herself."

On Sundays and holidays the faculty and students worshiped at Saint Sebald. Grossmann usually preached at least an hour, but his sermons were said to be appreciated for their special warmth. Often he asked one of the professors to preach when they were not away at a mission congregation. The service followed the full liturgy of the Loehe *Agenda*.

Fritschel:

"The congregation did not have an organ in the years that the seminary was there. The old Kantor Weege led the singing.... It always interested us young ones when he solemnly rose, struck the tuning fork, and then loudly began the hymn....

"As the church was only one end of the parsonage until 1867, the bell hung in the gable end. After the church was built, about a dozen young poplar trees stood before the front door. It seemed that a tree had grown between each window. It smelled so woodsy.

At noon [on Sunday] every student, or two together, had a host [from the Saint Sebald congregation] assigned with whom to have dinner. Their hostesses also did the student's laundry and mending."

One hundred paces from the church, the example for this hospitality was set by Karl Gottlob and Christina Amman and continued by their daughter Anna and her husband George Schuchmann. Their guests included seminary students and worshipers who had come long distances from the prairies to the west and who needed food before they began the long trip home by wagon or horseback.

Fritschel: "In the afternoon, the whole congregation took part in Bible study [*Christenlehre*]. One returned home to the quiet of the seminary only in late afternoon of evening."

The students walked the two miles to church. The women and children took the wagon. Spring wagons and spring seats were unknown in the colony. In winter the bobsled box was filled with straw and then packed full of passengers.

George Fritschel remembers,

"One time so much snow fell that we were isolated from the outer world for two weeks. Then the Sebalders brought a herd of oxen together and with them broke a road from the seminary to the church. With the huge snow drifts, it easily happened that when we rode over the fences, one sled runner would strike the rail fence and tip the whole load of people into the snow. Only once or twice were any lacerations caused by this.

"Once, lacking a cutter [a sleigh with a seat and one set of runners], Grossmann hitched up a rocking chair. He called to Mrs. Emma Koeberle, 'I have come to take you for a sleigh ride.' But she would not trust herself to the fragile vehicle.

"The country between the seminary and the church was all forested. The students set out for the church going northward past the seminary spring into the valley past the Prottengeier farm, and thus approached the church from the north. In spring and summer, it was a wonderful promenade.

"Timber wolves lived in the stone crevices of the hills. They loved to make themselves heard at night. If hog houses were not well-built, the wolves broke in and feasted on young pigs. One Saint Sebalder lost many pigs this way. When this misfortune became known, students volunteered to watch the seminary pigs and shoot any thieving animals. Even the professors undertook a night watch from the hay loft. But no animals showed up while the professors lay in wait. But it was claimed that during the long watch learned conversations were held....

"At first there were rattlesnakes in profusion.... Still as near as I can remember, no one was bitten....

"There were splendid people in the settlement. They were the fruits of the German Awakening Movement and therefore firmly grounded Christians. Their intimate association with each other and with the students and professors gave the congregation a character of its own. One felt good among them. There was the old Kantor Weege, father-in-law of Pastor Deindoerfer, who had been a teacher in Hesse and then came to Saginaw with Grossmann as a leader of the colonists. There was Mr. Amman, the original founder of Frankenhilf, a faithful Swabian from Memmingen, true as gold and utterly selfless, also a true Israelite without deceit....There were the Huebschs, Peblers, Prottengeiers, Schuchmanns, and many others."

With a faculty of three (the Fritschel brothers and Grossmann), an increasing number of students, and a farm to supply their food, the future of the seminary seemed bright.

Since Grossmann lived two miles away at the Saint Sebald parsonage, the Fritschel brothers were responsible for managing the seminary and for supervising the farm management. The keeping of books and accounts added a wearisome chore. But they developed a warm spiritual atmosphere at the seminary. The feeling of fellowship and brotherhood at Saint Sebald's Wartburg remained stronger in the later memories of the students than the hardships of cramped quarters and spartan living.

Besides their teaching duties, the Fritschel brothers were burdened with writing, editorships, and membership on demanding synodical committees—especially the Ausschuss, the executive committee of the Iowa Synod on which they served with Grossmann and Deindoerfer. Since 1854, a "directorate" consisting of the faculty had been in charge of curriculum and internal affairs and reported to the synod concerning these responsibilities. Because the ministerium had grown too large to meet and consider these reports and administrative details, the synod executive committee, or Ausschuss, was established around 1860. The directorate now reported to this body. Housefather Sigmund Fritschel usually prepared a draft of the curriculum schedule and then submitted it to the Ausschuss for approval with or without changes.

The growing ministerium also could no longer conduct student examinations in person. A committee on examinations was appointed to this task.

In 1861 the synod elected for the seminary a "commission of management." This was a precursor of a board of regents. It helped with supervision of finances, renting of the farm, and advised the housefather on questions of building and repairs.

In 1860 there were seven students in the preparatory school and seven in the theological seminary. During the Civil War, the student enrollment ran between ten and fifteen.

In 1860 boys were admitted to the preparatory division after confirmation, when they were about fourteen years old. In 1864 the synod ruled that entrance requirements be confirmation age and the ability to read and write both German and English.

Preparatory studies normally ran four years. Three years were given to theological work. But this varied. Some students came poorly prepared and needed a total of eight years of training. Others had been given preliminary instruction by their pastors and needed only six years to pass through both divisions.

With a faculty of three and limited space, the preparatory and seminary divisions did not operate as entirely separate organizations.

In 1858–1859 the preparatory division offered English, German, Latin, Greek, Hebrew, dialectics, history, and music. Classes were combined as much as possible. In religious studies, joint classes from the Latin school and the seminary were arranged. Some courses had to be offered in alternate years.

In 1860 it was announced that while the Latin school offered preparatory instruction for seminary students, it would also enroll youths who did not plan to enter the ministry. This announcement was made in the synod's *Kirchenblatt* (church paper) and in a Lutheran Year Book that had national circulation. In 1864 the *Kirchenblatt* stated that nontheological students need not study Latin and Greek. In the three years that followed, four such students were enrolled.

In 1864 the synod convention decided that the preparatory division was to be a five-year course designed to correspond to the German *Gymnasium*, similar to today's high school and junior college. It stressed the subjects of Christianity, German, English, Latin, and Greek. It also offered history, geography, arithmetic, algebra, geometry, logic, rhetoric, and music (both vocal and instrumental). The seminary level included courses in catechetics, dogmatics, exegesis, homiletics, symbolics, biblical history, church history, and pastoral theology.

The preparatory school did not supply all the students who entered the seminary. Some came from Germany ready to study theology. Others enrolled in more mature years and were given as little preparatory work as they could get by with. But normally the preparatory school laid the foundation for well-educated pastors.

The Fritschel brothers were still in the early years of adulthood. In 1858 Sigmund was twenty-five and Gottfried was twenty-two. Almost all of their fellow pastors were also young adults. Many responsibilities fell on the Fritschels, partly because they were located at the headquarters of the Iowa Synod where synod president Georg Grossmann was a pastor. It was also because of their training and skills that the Fritschels were involved in the historic decisions. They made mistakes, but their leadership abilities grew as they worked with the challenges. To the end of their careers they remained powerful leaders with extraordinary vision.

The burdens became heavier as the synod spread over wider territory. The synod still had no constitution. In the early years when decisions had to be made, a pastoral conference was called. But as the membership spread far and wide, frequent conferences were not practical. Then decisions were made by the Ausschuss or the Indian Mission Committee.

As members of the Ausschuss, Grossmann, Deindoerfer, and the Fritschel brothers laid out the business to come before the synodical conventions. They also handled the duties that later would be assigned to a salaried president: the calling of pastors to congregations, pastoral transfers, visitations, complaints, and the investigation of disputes. Matters that required travel were usually dealt with by President Grossmann, but he reported to and was counseled by the Ausschuss.

The Colony as a Center of Mission

Under the leadership of the Fritschels and the Saint Sebald pastors the colony and its seminary fulfilled Loehe's dream that it serve as a center of mission work. Organized in 1854 by four pastors and two congregations, by 1855 the gospel was being preached at sixteen places by pastors of the Iowa synod. The professors continued to plant congregations in the towns and villages surrounding the colony. One of Gottfried Fritschel's early foundings was the church at Elkport that he had first begun to serve from Dubuque. (See chapter 15.) From Saint Sebald it was nearer, sixteen miles as the crow flies, but twenty to twenty-five miles through rugged hills and winding creek and river valleys. Once a month Gottfried left Saint Sebald on Saturday morning and rode his horse until night to reach Elkport for the Sunday worship.

As stated Schueller had organized worship at Clayton Center. Soon other worship centers were started by students and professors at National, Guttenberg, McGregor (all in Iowa), and Prairie du Chien, Wisconsin.

Turning west to Fayette County, Iowa, the Saint Sebald colony expanded its outreach to rural West Union, Immanuel at Lawler (Crane Creek), Eldorado, and Fort Atkinson. This work began when Pastor Moritz Braeuniger graduated from the Saint Sebald seminary in 1858. He served a small group worshiping in private homes in West Union.

The West Union services attracted German Lutheran immigrants from nearby Eldorado. But Peter Schatz and John Trapp expressed a wish to have worship services in Eldorado. The difficulty with coming to West Union, they explained, was that no one wanted to stay home to tend their cattle. Because no fences had yet been built, they had to tie their cattle behind their wagons and bring them six miles to church. While the farmers were inside worshiping God, the cows stood outside eating grain that had to be brought along to keep them quiet.

When that same year Pastor Braeuninger joined Pastor John Jakob Schmidt on a missionary expedition to the Indians in Montana, Pastor Johannes Deindoerfer came from Madison, Wisconsin, and took up the work Braeuninger had begun. He preached alternately at West Union and in a two-point parish at Eldorado and Fort Atkinson.

Other Lutheran settlers came long distances on horse back or by horse and buggy from Fayette County to Saint Sebald for worship and education. Their children of confirmation age boarded with Saint Sebald families and attended its Christian day school until they were confirmed.

But one-room public schools became more convenient gathering places for the Fayette County Lutherans. About 1860 Pastor Georg Grossmann began conducting worship services northeast of Arlington at the one-room "Meisgeier School," located northeast of Brush Creek (later named Arlington). The leader of this group was Hermann Meisgeier. When Grossmann left in 1874, Pastor G. H. Fuehr continued pastoring these families until 1891, when five families organized as Saint John Lutheran Church at Brush Creek, worshiping there in the Church of Christ. Later these Lutherans worshiped at the Garden Prairie church of the United Brethren until 1911, when they erected their own church in Arlington.

Fuehr also traveled more than fifteen miles to minister to families first at a school near Aurora and then at the Union Church three miles north of Aurora. Families from this group later organized Saint Paul Lutheran Church of Aurora and Saint Peter Lutheran Church of Lamont.

Fuehr led worship in a third Fayette County school at Garden Prairie, a center that never made the road maps (four miles west of Highway 187 and three miles north of Highway 3). A United Brethren Church was built there in 1877, but only a cemetery remains.

The Saint Sebald seminary students also were active evangelists. G. J. Zeilinger [61] reports that an abandoned Missouri Synod congregation at Maxfield in Bremer County was discovered by student A. Sack. This congregation became a center of missionary activity that was responsible for Iowa Synod dominance in Bremer County.

The pastors did not think of their mission work as out of the ordinary. Every pastor was trained to think of himself as a missionary. From whatever place God called him to work, he looked for people to gather into congregations, his own or new ones that he could organize. His church would soon be surrounded by a number of affiliated charges.

It was all in a day's work to drive their teams over the Iowa prairies to preach at three or more different places and to come home late at night. "They would not be dismayed either if some nights they lost the road and had to wait until the new morning dawned before they could pick their way out of sloughs and swamps." [62] They also for the sake of conscience studied by kerosene lamps late at night preparing sermons and studying the doctrinal questions that their synod was debating.

In 1860 the Iowa Synod convention met at Madison, Wisconsin. In only six years, the synod had grown to include twenty-five pastors, twenty-eight congregations, and more than twelve preaching places. By its tenth anniversary in 1864, the synod numbered forty-one pastors, professors, and missionaries with more than fifty congregations distributed over seven states. [63]

Pastors attending the 1860 Synod Convention at Madison

Lutheran Social Service Begins

Early in 1863, at Saint Donatus, a Civil War widow brought a child in need of shelter to J. Michael Schueller, then pastor of Salem Church at Andrew, Iowa. Schueller and his wife accepted the child into their home and gave it the care they would have given their own. In a few months another child was brought to the parsonage. By early 1864, the Schuellers were caring for seven orphans.

That spring Schueller asked his congregation to help create an orphans' home. They agreed. That fall (1864) they dedicated a new three-story, 30 x60 foot building at Andrew. The home was named "Asylum for Orphaned and Destitute Children."

In 1900 the orphanage was moved to Waverly. Today it continues its service as Bremwood Lutheran Children's Home. In 2004 Bremwood served one hundred twenty children in residential care. It has through all its history received firm support from Saint Sebald.

CHAPTER 18

The Mission to the Indians

A Native American mission to the West on the model of Friedrich A. Craemer's effort in Michigan was one of Loehe's hopes when the Frankenhilf colony moved to Saint Sebald.

Neither of the Fritschel brothers was free to serve personally as a missionary, but the Wartburg at Saint Sebald became Loehe's staging point for expeditions that others undertook. Over a period of several years, eight to ten men came from Germany to serve as Indian missionaries. Several received further training at the Saint Sebald seminary. All were ordained and commissioned there. Sigmund Fritschel was a member of the special "Indian Mission Committee" that managed the outreach to Native Americans. These duties, shared by Gottfried Fritschel, involved complex negotiations, heavy correspondence, and many worries.

In 1856, while plans were under way to move the seminary to Saint Sebald, Pastor John Jakob Schmidt was sent from Neuendettelsau to serve as the Iowa Synod's first missionary to the Indians. Schmidt visited Grand Portage on the north shore of Lake Superior and found Roman Catholic mission work well underway.

In 1857 at Detroit, Schmidt met Mr. A. Redfield, government agent for the Crow tribe along the Yellowstone and Big Horn Rivers near what is now the city of Billings, Montana, in the area of today's Crow Indian Reservation. Redfield agreed to take missionaries with him to "Crowland" if they had no family and would live a primitive way of life.

In the meantime, Moritz Braeuninger from Germany graduated from the Saint Sebald seminary and was working at West Union. Eager to work among the Indians, he gladly accepted Schmidt's invitation to join him. In the spring of 1858, Schmidt and Braeuninger joined Redfield's party in Saint Louis. On Pentecost Sunday, May 23, they left

Saint Louis on the government steamboat *Twilight* and headed up the Missouri River to deliver government supplies to Indians on the northern plains as agreed in the 1851 Treaty of Fort Laramie.

The Treaty of Fort Laramie guaranteed the Indians hunting and fishing rights and freedom from white settlements on the lands reserved for them. They were also promised annual provisions, domestic animals, and farm tools. The treaty was signed by the the Arriakaras, Arapahoes, Assiniboines, Cheyennes, Crows, many of Dakota tribes, Gros-Ventes, and Mandans.

Instantly, many whites dismissed the treaty. They invited white settlers into the Indian territories by opening trails and constructing forts to protect the newcomers. This was the setting into which Schmidt and Braeuninger were venturing to bring the gospel.

On June 23, the boat arrived at Fort Union, a fur-trading center where the Yellowstone joins the Missouri near today's Williston, North Dakota. Redfield suggested that Schmidt and Braeuninger might return in 1859 to begin a mission near Fort Union. But enthusiasm for this project died. Schmidt wrote in his journal, "Not only did we have to see the crying injustices committed to the Indians, but also the changing of the fort to a house of drunks and whores."

Charles P. Lutz comments in his book *Church Roots*, "The experience at Fort Union was an almost overwhelming moral jolt for the two gentle men of God. They were most eager to move on to the yet unspoiled Crows to carry out their mission. They were more than ready to depart on July 7, 1858, for their next destination, Fort Sarpy, some 300 miles upstream on the Yellowstone. It took 37 days to make the trip, their headway slowed by low water, requiring constant cordelling (pulling the boat with rope from the shore by men or horses)." [64]

On August 12, Schmidt and Braeuninger arrived in Montana at Fort Sarpy, a collection of seven fortified houses along the Yellowstone River.

The missionaries found life intolerable among the military degenerates at the fort, who were, Lutz writes, "if anything more depraved" than those at Fort Union. The distribution of annuities to certain Indians was made, but in a way that left the missionaries convinced they were being defrauded. Not all the Indians arrived to claim their goods; the remainder was to be placed in storage for later delivery. At one point Schmidt was invited by Redfield to certify that the goods were properly delivered to the Indians. Schmidt declined, despite his knowledge that honest whites were in short supply at Sarpy, because he felt it would compromise their mission.

The two missionaries decided leave Sarpy and live among the 1,500 yet unspoiled Crow Indians in a camp of 160 tents nearby. Chief Dachbizaschuch (Head of a Bear) gave them lodging in his own tepee and let them use his own horses. For two months the two missionaries traveled with the Crow nomads, learning their language and sharing their hardships. They traveled southwest to the Bighorn River, then southeast to the Tongue River through the region where General George Custer would face the Sioux in his last battle.

(Today the Sioux tease other tribes for not having been at the battle of the Little Big Horn. The Crows were traditional enemies of the Sioux. They joke that they served as Custer's scouts in order to bring Custer where the Sioux could get at him.)

In the fall, part of the Crow tribe brought Braeuninger and Schmidt into what is now Wyoming along the east side of the Bighorn Mountains to Deer Creek on the North Platte River in order to smoke the peace pipe with a hostile tribe. An Indian agency station was located there near the present town of Glenrock on what became the Oregon Trail.

By now, the missionaries had learned the Crow language well enough so that Braeuninger could compose a small dictionary. They began to share their faith in conversation with the tribal leaders. They decided, however, to return to Iowa for the winter and to raise funds for a permanent mission among the the Crows in 1859.

The missionaries set out for home, arriving at Saint Sebald on November 25. They reported, "Only reluctantly did they [the natives] let us depart, for they would rather have persuaded us to stay. A thousand times they asked us if we would really return when the winter had passed and the grass grew again. Some even offered to accompany us to Iowa, which offer we had to decline."

As their encouraging report spread, money for Native American missions came in from both Iowa and Buffalo Synod congregations, from the Central Mission Society of Bavaria, and from the Mission Society of Luebeck.

Once again Wilhelm Loehe decided to found a colony, this time among the Crow Indians at Deer Creek. In early 1859, the Nuremberg *Missionsblatt* published Schmidt's appeal for gifts for the Indian mission. Schmidt presented with his appeal the program he hoped to pursue—one that today may seem both idealistic and naive. Schmutterer and Lutz tell the plan in *Church Roots.* [65] :

> 1. The traders must be removed from the region if missionaries are to accomplish anything. The church itself should provide people to manage honest trade for the Indians.

> 2. We should set up a farm in a fertile area, with agricultural experts who can teach the Indians how to settle and cultivate the land.

> 3. A church and a school building should be built, along with houses of log construction. A small colony should be developed and additional Lutheran families should be settled there. To build the settlement, Schmidt felt "at least 12 devoted young men are needed."

Collecting and sending funds from from overseas occupied precious time. Finally, by July 1859, enough money had been gathered for the expanded mission effort to begin. On July 5, Missionaries Schmidt, Braeuninger, and Ferdinand Doederlein, with Wartburg student Theodore Seyler and Saint Sebald farmers Beck and Bunge set out again for Deer Creek.

> "They took the overland route with heavy, well-equipped wagons, using first horses and then oxen to cross Iowa and into Nebraska. Following the Platte via Kearney and Fort Laramie, they arrived in late fall 1859 at Deer Creek. Most of their supplies and funds were consumed on the long journey. Their major disappointment was the discovery that their beloved Crows were not in the vicinity, nor had they come to Deer Creek in the spring, as agreed. To add to the group's misery, Schmidt who had been ailing most of the trip decided to return to Iowa and missionary Doederlein accompanied him. They said they would return early in the spring of 1860 with more men and goods.

Neither the ailing Schmidt nor Doederlein returned. "Doederlein soon thereafter joined the Missouri Synod. Schmidt married Margarethe Lutz [a great-great-aunt of author Lutz] and accepted a call to an Iowa Synod congregation in Detroit. He died there in 1912." (Note 9, p. 213.)

> "The group at Deer Creek, now under Braeuninger's leadership, was almost without financial resources. Fortu-

nately, Captain W. F. Raynolds of the U. S. Army Corps of Engineers, who was wintering at Deer Creek, provided some employment for the mission workers through the long winter, for which they received food, lodging and some money. They celebrated Christmas by decorating a spruce tree with candles. Captain Raynolds read the Christmas gospel in English and Braeuninger in German. Local Indians were present and one of Raynold's officers explained the meaning of Christmas in the Indian tongue. Captain Raynolds played the flute and Braeuninger the violin to accompany Christmas carols." [66]

Advised by Captain Reynolds, Braeuninger and the others pushed on in the spring of 1860 and established a mission station in northern Wyoming on the bank of the Powder River, a branch of the Yellowstone. They chose a location that they thought to be central for their work among the Crows; but it turned out to be on the boundary between the Crows and Teton Sioux Indians who were unfriendly to both Crows and whites. The mission group built a log house, a cellar and planted a garden. Soon natives began to visit them.

Then farmer Bunge resigned from the mission to return to Iowa. Braeuninger went with him as far as Deer Creek to get more supplies. Braeuninger sent with Bunge back to Saint Sebald an encouraging report and a pencil sketch of their sta-
tion. Then he headed
north toward the
Powder River station.
As he went, on July 21,
Ogalala Sioux, angry
because whites had
settled along the Pow-
der River, ambushed
him. Friendly natives

Mission station near the Powder River

reported to the other missionaries that Braeuninger had been shot in the back. Then, as the wounded man rose, his assassins killed him with blows, cut his face, and threw his body in the swollen river.

In grief the remaining missionaries, Theodore Seyler, and Beck retreated to Deer Creek where they were reinforced by the arrival of missionaries Krebs and Flachenecker. They sent word of the tragedy to Saint Sebald and waited for orders from the Iowa Synod mission board.

In September of 1860, the board met and decided to locate the mission base at Deer Creek for work in central Wyoming among the Cheyennes and their friends the Arapahoes. The board agreed to send Pastor Christian Kessler to join the four missionaries there.

In October Krebs wrote to Saint Sebald that they had located their new station 1 ½ miles from the trading post along Deer Creek south of the Platte River. They expected to build there the next spring. In the spring of 1861 they built the station of logs as they had planned.

Krebs and Flachenecker had been sent with the expectation that when they arrived, Braeuninger would ordain them. When Kessler arrived in the spring of 1861, he immediately ordained them to the ministry.

"In May 1861, Kessler, Krebs and Seyler left Deer Creek looking for Indians. They headed north and seemed drawn to the Powder River location. At the site of the station, now in ashes, they camped for several days. Finding no Indians, they returned to Deer Creek, hoping Indians might be there. Finally in August, Cheyennes came. Flachenecker and Kessler were allowed to travel with them; in four weeks they learned the basics of their language." [67]

Kessler and Krebs lived with the Cheyennes in their wigwams and began to conduct worship services among them. Krebs also gained the confidence of the Arapahoes.

"During 1862, tensions between whites and Indians were high at all points along the frontier. Civil War fighting back East had led to reduced garrisons at the frontier forts. The uprising of Sioux (Dakota) around New Ulm in southwest Minnesota encouraged Indians elsewhere to take up arms. Many stage stations along the Oregon-Mormon Trail west of Fort Laramie were raided and burned. Flackenecker, Krebs, and Beck moved (50 miles east) to the safer Fort Laramie for several weeks in the summer of 1862, while Kessler and Seyler returned to Iowa for supplies.; when they journeyed back to Wyoming in the spring of 1863, another seminary graduate, Franz Matter, was with them." [68]

Through most of 1861-63, preaching services were held for Indians near the mission station at Deer Creek. Eventually, some of the Cheyennes learned to pray the Lord's Prayer in their own language.

Three orphaned Cheyenne boys were entrusted to Krebs and

Flachenecker for Christian instruction. They taught them Bible history, the catechism, reading, writing, arithmetic, and the German language. On Christmas Day 1863, the oldest boy, Muchsianoe (Brown Moccasin), was baptized at the Deer Creek mission station and renamed Friederich Sigmund Christopher after his sponsors, one of whom was Sigmund Fritschel. The following Easter (1864) Ekois (Little Bone) was baptized and named Paulus, after Iowa Pastor Paul Bredow. He was about fourteen years old. The youngest was baptized later and named Gottfried after the other Fritschel brother.

Indian boys

By now the Civil War demanded all available troops, and whites in the Northwest were left insufficiently protected. In September 1864, the friendly Cheyennes warned the missionaries that the Sioux were about to attack their Deer Creek station and the military post. They urged them to leave in four days and to take the three Indian boys with them.

The missionaries again sought protection at Fort Laramie. They conducted a worship together on September 25. Leaving Flachenecker and Matter at Fort Laramie, the rest joined an ox train that left for Iowa the next day. On October 20, they reached security at Fort Kearney, Nebraska. Their journey led to Nebraska City, Ottumwa (Iowa), and north to the synod's new orphans' home at Andrew. They arrived in Dubuque November 30.

In January 1865, Flachenecher and Matter returned from Fort Laramie. For the first time since 1858, there were no Iowa Synod missionaries among the Indians.

Krebs took the Indian boys to the seminary at Saint Sebald where he began to train them to serve as missionaries to their people. But lacking immunity to the white man's diseases, two of the boys contracted tuberculosis. Gottfried, the youngest, died on August 2 and Paulus, the second youngest, on December 15, 1865. They are buried in the Saint Sebald cemetery. In 1929 a large flint boulder bearing a bronze memorial tablet was placed at their double grave through the efforts of Professor George Fritschel. John Georg Weger and Glenn Chappell provided the stone and placed it on the site. This marks the

Bronze memorial

only visible remains of the Iowa Synod's and Loehe's missions to the Native Americans. Translated from the German, the plaque reads "Here two baptized Indians rest in God—GOTTFRIED died August 2, 1865; PAULUS died December 15, 1865." The plaque also carries the names of the eight missionaries and the martyrdom of Braeuninger.

In 1864 federal troops were still occupied with the Civil War. Fear of Indian uprisings brought volunteer troops from the western states and territories to the Missouri, Platte, and Arkansas river valleys. In October 1864, two Cheyenne leaders, Black Kettle and White Antelope, agreed to an armistice and took their people into a peaceful camp at Sand Creek in Colorado. But all hope of further Iowa Synod mission work among the Cheyennes was destroyed on November 29, when Colonel J. M. Chivington and a force of Colorado militia fell on the Sand Creek encampment and massacred 133 Cheyenne men, women, and children. The surprise assault scattered the Cheyennes and stirred the entire central plains into new warfare.

In 1866, with the Civil War concluded, peace with the Indians was expected. Missionaries Krebs and Matter, with Friederich, the oldest of the Indian boys, tried again to reach the Indians of the Northwest. They traveled in a farm wagon pulled by four mules through Des Moines and Omaha and up the Platte River Valley. But while they were on their way, new fighting broke out. They had to halt at Fort McPherson east of what is now North Platte, Nebraska. They waited at the fort eight months and returned to Iowa the next spring.

At Wartburg Seminary, Krebs and Matter were told that further mission work must wait until the Indians had been conquered and settled on reservations. Matter said later, "Our mission among the Indians was buried when we left Fort McPherson."

That summer the Iowa Synod met at Toledo and declared Indian mission work "temporarily" abandoned. The synod asked Krebs to continue to watch for an opportunity to resume work among the Cheyennes. But no such occasion ever appeared. Continued invasion into native lands by the U.S. military and occupation of those lands by the whites, with the resultant Indian uprisings, prevented further mission efforts.

In 1885 the remaining funds held for missions to Native Americans were sent back to Neuendettelsau for use in mission work among the Papuans of New Guinea. This formally closed the Indian work commissioned from Wartburg Seminary at Saint Sebald.

After 1867, Friederich, the oldest Indian boy, left the seminary and fell into troubled ways. He died in his youth, but knowledge of where he is buried has been lost. Zeilinger wrote, "Those who knew him believe God's grace helped also this wandering sheep to reach home." [69]

"The Powder River Station is long forgotten, its exact site unknown today.... In [1863] John M. Bozeman pioneered a trail north from the North Platte into Montana. The Bozeman Trail crossed the Powder River just a couple miles downsteam from the area where the mission station stood. In 1865, a military post, Fort Reno, was built where the Bozeman Trail crossed the Powder. It was abandoned and burned three years later. A monument is all that marks its location today.

"The critical reader can detect many reasons for the failure of the Iowa Synod's efforts among the Western Indians. One could blame the involved chain of command from Bavaria via Iowa to the frontier; the haphazard planning, lack of funds, and inexperience of the synod's mission board; the faulty logistics and exhausting travel routes to the frontier; the inter-tribal conflicts among the Indians; the dishonesty of many whites with whom the Indians dealt; the routine violation of treaties by whites in general; the untimely outbreak of the Civil War and the concomitant withdrawals of military forces in the West; and finally, the inexperience, isolation and naivete of the German-speaking missionaries operating in a twice-foreign environment. The collusion of all these forces brought about the collapse of the Iowa Synod's hopeful, visionary enterprise among the Indians of the western plains.

"Still, the effort was in many ways a remarkable one. A people came across the ocean with the gospel. Even before arriving in the New World, they had the compelling vision that it must be shared with the native peoples of their adopted land. Uprooted by a theological dispute they did not desire in one place, they moved on to root themselves in another, carrying the vision with them. Even as they organized a new church, they planned with meager resources to seek native Americans with whom they might live the gospel. When there were too few trained leaders to care for their own people settling in the farmlands of the Midwest, they deployed many of their best for the mission in the West. After disappointments, even the death of one of their top men, they did not quit. For seven more years they stayed with their vision. And when at last they did suspend the effort, the remaining rsources were directed to another alien culture, the Papuans of New Guinea, where it would be 13 long years before the first Baptism!" [70]

Church Roots author Gerhard M. Schmutterer made several trips to areas where the Saint Sebald missionaries directed their efforts. He visited the location of Fort Union near Williston, North Dakota; the territory around Glenrock, Wyoming, where Deer Creek station was built; and Fort Laramie. He searched without success for the site of the burned-out mission station on the Powder River between Sussex, Wyoming, and the monument marking where Fort Reno stood.

Fund-raising and Cost Accounting

Meanwhile financial troubles had arisen for the seminary at Saint Sebald. When real estate values crashed in the panic of 1857, the Dubuque property was lost. (See chapter 16.) The Saint Sebald property was not paid for, and the synod could not even pay the interest on the debt. At the 1860 synod in Madison, the seventeen pastors attending the convention (on Gottfried Fritschel's motion) commissioned Sigmund Fritschel to go on a fund-raising trip to Europe. The pastors would solicit contributions in their parishes and from the well-established Lutheran churches of other synods in the eastern states.

Very little money was raised in the synod parishes and no approach was made at all in the eastern states. So, to Sigmund Fritschel's grief, the entire burden fell on his shoulders. The pastors scraped up enough money to pay his steamship fare with the cheapest accommodations. In July 1860, he left for Neuendettelsau to make arrangements and to secure introductions to European officials and churches.

At Neuendettelsau, Pfarrer Loehe gave him credentials to speak at mission festivals in Germany and Russia. At Saint Petersburg, the Czar himself gave Fritschel permission to speak in the churches there and in Moscow.

It was at Saint Petersburg that Fritschel met noblewoman Augusta von Schwartz. (See chapter 17.) Hearing of the needs of the seminary, she renounced home, friends, and comfort to go to Saint Sebald and serve her Lord as stewardess and mother to the students at Wartburg.

Another Russian noble woman won to the Iowa Synod by Fritschel was the widow of General von Helffreich. She was not wealthy, but she sold her jewels to establish the Iowa Synod's first publishing house at the seminary.

To save money to give to the Wartburg, Frau von Helffreich omitted a course from her family's dinner. She would accept no birthday gifts but linen and woolen goods to send to the seminary. She raised thousands of rubles to erect a house near the seminary for Sigmund Fritschel and his family. [71]

Fritschel visited also in the churches of Germany and the Netherlands. The synod had hoped that Fritschel's efforts would yield enough to pay its entire debt and its accumulated interest plus his own expenses. But in October 1861, he returned to report that he had not raised enough money to pay all the seminary's obligations. He had, however, made many friends in Europe for the Iowa Synod.

Fritschel's work did reduce the debt enough so that everfaithful Neuendettelsau could take over the balance and gradually erase it. Sigmund's contributors in Russia continued to gather funds and send them to Saint Sebald over the next ten years for special purposes such as building a home for Gottfried Fritschel and to endow the salary of a seminary teacher.

Fritschel had also made contacts in Germany with two organizations that began to send students to the Saint Sebald seminary. Twice in the next ten years he revisited Europe to nurture these relationships. This additional manpower greatly increased the synod's rate of expansion.

While Fritschel was fund-raising in Europe, the 1860 synod convention made new efforts at budget calculations and cost accounting. Students were for the first time asked to pay toward the cost of their room, board, and tuition. The seminary's annual operating costs came to $60 per student. Each student was assigned a share of the operations deficit (costs less contributions). During the summer, students could work on the seminary farm and earn funds toward their bill. By 1864 the share charged to students had reached $20 per year.

The 1864 convention drafted rules of discipline and specified costs. Christian conduct and obedience to house rules were required. The penalty was dismissal. The charge for room, board, and laundry was $1.50 per week for a forty-eight-week school year. The tuition charge was set at $1.00 per month. Students in financial straits were asked to pay a minimum of $15 a year. However, most students seem to have been so lacking in funds that little was collected from them.

In 1860 the synod had set faculty salaries at $100 per year, plus an additional $100 if synod income was adequate. This was raised to $300 in 1864. But because student tuition was not paid, even the minimum faculty salaries were not always met. Salaries were augmented with free housing, meat and flour, firewood and $12 to fuel kerosene lamps. The only non-faculty staff was housemother Augusta von Schwartz, who did the kitchen and laundry duties.

To further communications between the synod and its lay members, the synod established a church paper at its 1856 convention. In January 1858 the first number of the *Kirchenblatt* was published by the Saint Sebald seminary. Problems with local printers were relieved when Frau von Helffreich in Russia sold her jewels to underwrite the cost of establishing a printshop at the seminary.

Gottfried Fritschel learned the necessary printing skills while on vacation that summer by volunteering as apprentice to a printer in Madison. He shared what he had learned with seminary students who then prepared the pages for the press. Gottfried served as editor and publisher of the *Kirchenblatt*. After the seminary left Saint Sebald in 1874, the *Kirchenblatt* was printed elsewhere until the Wartburg Press was established at Waverly. [72]

CHAPTER 19

IOWA-MISSOURI COLLOQUY
NUMBER ONE

In 1867 the Iowa Synod met at Toledo, Ohio. Always conscious of its schism with Missouri, Iowa considered again the question, "What is necessary for unity in the Church?" A number of theses were adopted including, "There has never been an absolute doctrinal unity in the Church, and it ought not be made a condition of church-fellowship." Since, as Deindoerfer recorded, "Many pastors of the synod were strongly inclined toward Missouri," Iowa decided to ask the Missouri Synod for a colloquy to discuss the doctrinal differences between them.[73]

Missouri cheerfully granted this request, and the meeting took place in Milwaukee November 13-18. Iowa was represented by its President Georg Grossmann, Professors Sigmund and Gottfried Fritschel, and a lay delegate, F. R. Becker; Missouri by President C. F. W. Walther; Dr. Wilhelm Sihler, president of Concordia College, Fort Wayne; Pastor J. A. Huegli, later president of the Northern District; Pastor Chr. B. Hochstetter, who had just transferred from the Buffalo Synod; and lay delegates K. Koch, C. Wassermann, F. R. Stutz, and J. Bierlein.

The delegates discussed the attitude of both synods toward the Lutheran Confessions, "open questions," and eschatology (doctrine of the last things). Agreement was not achieved. Iowa would not agree with Missouri that doctrines on the observance of Sunday (whether or not God has commanded a certain day for the day of rest), on the question of the Antichrist, and on the first resurrection (Revelation 20) must be classed as articles of faith. For the term "open questions" the Iowans were willing to substitute "problems." The two sides agreed that there *are* open questions or problems, questions that are not clearly settled or even considered in Scripture. But they did not agree as to *what* could be counted among such problems.

True to its principle, Iowa was ready to enter into church fellowship with Missouri because it considered the doctrines on which they could not agree to be open questions that ought not be divisive. Missouri, true to its principle, held that some of the differences involved such weighty matters of doctrine that church fellowship with Iowa was impossible.

CHAPTER 20

WARTBURG COLLEGE
AT GALENA

The writer has relied heavily on Gerhard Ottersburg's Wartburg College, 1852-1952: A Centennial History, *for the material in this chapter, editing and condensing pages 29 to 35.*

After the Civil War, enrollmen grew and in 1868, Wartburg at Saint Sebald boasted thirty students, fifteen in the preparatory division and fifteen in the seminary. Seven came from the Synod of Illinois and Adjacent States. Illinois had established church fellowship with Iowa, and had permission to send students to Wartburg. The faculty was still only Sigmund and Gottfried Fritschel with Grossmann teaching music.

Thirty students severely crowded the Saint Sebald facility. Housing that many students of different ages in one building under primitive conditions intensified discipline problems. Expecting continued growth, the synod was forced in 1868 to reconsider a proposal brought before it by the Ausschuss in 1861, namely, to establish a separate preparatory school. It was either that or build another dormitory.

In September 1868 a special convention of the Iowa Synod met at Madison. J. Klindworth, pastor of a strong congregation in Galena, Illinois, put before the synod a resolution to convert the Saint Sebald preparatory school into a college and to locate it in a former Catholic convent that was for sale at Galena. Klindworth argued that it would ease discipline problems to separate the younger students from the older and that the town environment was better than Saint Sebald's isolation. Grossmann, the Fritschels, and some pastors opposed this move and preferred to erect a new building at Saint Sebald so that classes could continue to be shared.

Then a member of the Synod of Illinois proposed that the college or seminary or both be moved to Beardstown, Illinois, a community that would provide generous support. Since nearly 25 percent of the present enrollment was from the Synod of Illinois, and since Iowa wished to strengthen relationships between the two synods, a committee was created to negotiate possible developments from this suggestion with Illinois.[74]

To ease the immediate problem, Iowa resolved to convert the preparatory school into a college and to locate it provisionally at Galena, renting the convent building until the Synod of Illinois had been consulted. But Klindworth persuaded a local group to *buy* the building in behalf of the synod for $2,500. The college now had a brick structure 62 x 27, with two stories, an attic, and a cellar. The grounds was only a narrow yard with an unheated building that served as a lavatory.[75]

Klindworth was named rector. Pastor F. Lutz, a Saint Sebald graduate, served as the only teacher and the housefather. A few months later, candidate A. Preller came to assist Lutz. Those three men formed the staff through all the time the college was at Galena.[76]

Classes at Galena began November 1, 1868, with twenty-one students, ten of them from Saint Sebald. Five came from Galena and were not pretheological students. [77]

But that year the usual seven students from the Synod of Illinois and Adjacent States did not appear, because Illinois had begun negotiating church fellowship with the Missouri Synod. In 1872 the twenty-six congregations of the Synod of Illinois helped Missouri organize the Synodical Conferencre. On May 24, 1880, at Quincy, Illinois, the Illinois Synod merged with the Missouri Synod. Its developing relationships with Missouri forced Illinois to break its fellowship with the Iowa Synod. This also ended the discussion of sharing the college that Iowa had placed provisionally at Galena.

The synod named the school the "College at Galena." ("Wartburg" designated only the seminary while the college was at Galena.) The curriculum was still based on the six-year pattern of the German *Gymnasium* or preparatory school. The subjects taught the first year after the college opened were religion, Latin, German, English, history, geography, natural history, arithmetic, writing, drawing, singing, and music. The committee on examinations, with Klindworth added to it, served the College at Galena and Wartburg at Saint Sebald.[78]

By the end of the first year the five local Galena students had all withdrawn or had been expelled. Klindworth said the non-Lutheran public was repelled by the German Lutheran character of the college. Most of the courses were taught in German. The German-born teachers found English difficult. Furthermore, Loehe's life-style regimen placed behavior restrictions that the public found annoying. Even the Lutheran youths found the rules too difficult, as the troubles at Saint Sebald had made clear. Klindworth complained that the students who had transferred from Saint Sebald were difficult to handle. The bad habits they had formed in the crowded Saint Sebald facility were hard to erase.[79]

Student life continued to be cramped and uncomfortable at Galena. Personal cleanliness was limited in the winter because of the unheated washhouse. There was but a single classroom that also served as dining room. A refectory was added shortly before the college moved away. Students not meeting with an instructor used one part of the classroom for study periods while one or two classes gathered with their instructors in other parts. The heavy schedule burdened both students and teachers. One year Lutz carried thirty-two hours of class per week and Preller twenty-nine. Klindworth taught five hours.[80]

Galena enrollments never reached the numbers Klindworth expected. Most years there were seventeen or eighteen students. The high was twenty-six in 1871. After that withdrawals were heavy. In 1873 only three of the six class levels had students enrolled. Lutz used the *Kirchenblatt* to advertise for new students. He also pleaded with the students to enroll at the opening of the school term. The tendency of students to straggle in during the course of the year had been and continued to be a problem at the college for many years.[81]

The college suffered financial problems all seven of its years at Galena. Beginning in 1868 the synod ordered special appeals for higher education support in all its approximately 150 congregations. Klindworth and a Pastor Hoerlein visited selected parishes. But the results of all these efforts were minimal. The pastors of the congregations were themselves underpaid (an average of less than $300 per year), and the laity seemed to have little interest in institutions of higher education. Debts mounted at both the Saint Sebald seminary and at the Galena college. By the time the synod met in 1871, debts totalled $7,000.[82]

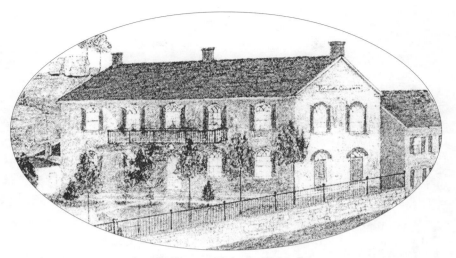

College at Galena, Illinois

CHAPTER 21

THE WARTBURGS MOVE TO MENDOTA

S eminary graduates usually established mission congregations on their own without subsidy from the synod. The 1871 convention decided that this justified using mission festival offerings for the $6,000 annual operating costs of the college and seminary. The synod looked to friends in Germany to retire the seminary debt. It asked the synod pastors to pay off the college debt. But the pastors pledged only $2,000 toward the college's $3,000 debt, and not all pledges were kept. Mission offerings fell short of needs, and so debt retirement funds were used for current operating costs.

Wartburg Seminary Moves to Mendota

In 1873 the Iowa Synod met at Davenport, Iowa. It decided that its geographical growth required dividing the synod into eastern and western districts.

It also faced housing problems that had intensified as the enrollment at Saint Sebald's Wartburg Seminary continued to grow. It was in the midst of the 1873 national financial panic that the convention heard that Saint Sebald would need another dormitory. Pastor William A. Passavant, founder of deaconess work in America, presented an offer to secure for the synod at low cost a 40 x 50 foot, four-story building vacated by a defunct college at Mendota, Illinois. The convention authorized the Ausschuss to investigate and take appropriate action.

The Ausschuss decided that the seminary should be moved to Mendota, the fourth location of the seminary in twenty-two years. The first move had been made to end conflict with the Missouri Synod. The second had been caused by financial stress. The move to Mendota was forced by the seminary's growth.

On May 18, 1874, the seminary community left Saint Sebald and took a special railway car from Strawberry Point to Mendota. On June 21 the new Wartburg location was dedicated. A remarkable era came to a close in the story of the Saint Sebald colony. [83]

When the Fritschels and Wartburg Seminary moved to Mendota, Illinois, the seminary again served as a nursery for new congregations. The missionary zeal of the Fritschels and their students brought into being a number of rapidly growing parishes in northern Illinois.

The seminary's enrollment kept growing. The Fritschels found relief from their heavy teaching loads with assistant teachers. Mendota Pastor F. B. Richter began to assist in 1876, serving later as full time professor until 1894 when he became president of Wartburg College at Clinton. The Fritschel brothers stayed involved with managing the synod and serving on the Ausschuss.

The financial stress it had experienced at Saint Sebald followed the seminary to Mendota. Added to the previous deficit and debts were the cost of moving the seminary, the purchase of the Mendota facility, new faculty housing expenses, and the cost of food previously grown on the Saint Sebald farm.

The college at Galena and the seminary were competing for support. There had been disputes over the division of income and bookkeeping systems. Now rumors floated that the college might also be moved to Mendota to a residence on the seminary property. By 1874 Galena college Rector J. Klindworth was voicing hostility on the part of the college faculty toward Grossmann and the Fritschels.

Klindworth also led a group of Iowa Synod pastors who supported the Missouri Synod's positions in the doctrinal controversies that were increasing between the leaders of Iowa (Deindoerfer, Grossmann, and the Fritschels) and Missouri. The same issues were at dispute within the Iowa Synod itself: the Church and the ministry, the Antichrist, chiliasm (1,000-year reign of Christ on earth), the Confessions, open questions, Sunday, usury, justification, predestination, and conversion.

In 1876, the year after the seminary moved to Mendota, the Fritschel brothers founded and edited a theological journal, the *Kirchliche Zeitschrift*. Its writings defended Loehe's open questions position within the Iowa Synod and among all Lutherans. It engaged actively in what became a fifty-year debate on election and conversion. Without this journal's challenge, the powerful Missouri Synod might have established rigid doctrinal conformity among all Lutherans, at least in the Midwest. But the Iowa Synod insisted that faithfulness in fundamental teachings should be the basis for growth of understanding.[84]

The Pains of Schism

Theological controversies continued between the Iowa Synod and the Missouri Synod. Missouri held to unbending definitions of its teachings and an insistence on the complete inerrancy of Scripture even on questions of science, history, and mathematics. Wilhelm Loehe and the Iowa Synod still permitted Iowa pastors and congregations to regard as "open questions" doctrines not essential to the faith on which Christians often differ. Iowa thus kept its distinction between binding and nonbinding doctrines in the Lutheran Confessions.

"Because Iowa's doctrinal position was not as narrow as Missouri's, the two synods feuded for decades over Iowa's 'open questions' theory, which asserted that on some doctrines scriptural utterances permitted some variety of interpretation which should not disrupt church fellowship." [85]

Missouri rejected this principle. The synod insisted on complete agreement concerning every doctrine based on Scripture as a prerequisite for fellowship with Iowa or any other synod, for fear of disloyalty to the Word of God by tolerating two opinions at once. Missouri described the principle of "open questions" as "a most dangerous (because a most subtle and disguised) unionistic poison, driving congregations into the grasp of skepticism and infidelity."

When the Iowa Synod met at Davenport, Iowa, in 1873, its Northern Iowa Conference asked the synod to state its position toward the Missouri Synod, especially for pastors who were new in the synod and not acquainted with the course of the controversies. As a result Iowa adopted twenty-one theses on its doctrinal differences with the Missouri Synod that became known as the Davenport Theses, indicating on what points the two synods had approached agreement and on what points they still differed. Deindoerfer wrote, "With this declaration the result of the Milwaukee colloquy [see chapter 19] was accepted by Synod." [86]

Following this convention, serious protests were voiced by pastors in the Iowa Synod who were dissatisfied with Iowa's continued separation from Missouri. They saw the Davenport Theses as the basis for closer fellowship and asked that this be pursued by alliance with Missouri along with Ohio, Wisconsin, Minnesota, and Illinois.

On the other hand, the Iowa Synod pastors who had come from Neuendettelsau saw the Davenport Theses as a surrender of Loehe's theology to Missouri Synod views. Inspector Friedrich Bauer, head of the Neuendettelsau seminary, urged Iowa's Neuendettelsau supporters to seek to restore Iowa's "original position" and to repudiate the Davenport Theses.

The split developed into a war of essays and personalities. "In its earnest endeavor to make peace with Missouri, Iowa almost lost its friends in Germany while it reaped discord in its own ranks" [87]

"In 1873 Synod numbered 100 pastors though quite a few had severed their connection with the synod during the past few years." [88]

Continuing attacks from Missouri leaders questioning the soundness of positions taken by the Fritschels and Grossmann were echoed by Rector J. Klindworth's group, who also expressed dissatisfaction with the way the Fritschels handled administrative affairs for the synod and the seminary. Klindworth was charged with developing organized opposition in the synod.

The College Moves to Mendota

A special Iowa Synod convention was called at Madison in the spring of 1875 to deal with the problems of the college and seminary. Most of the time, however, was spent in debate on doctrinal issues between the Fritschel and Klindworth groups. The synod needed to state again its position against Missouri. It did so in its "Madison Theses" of eight paragraphs in which Iowa made it clear that essentially it had not left its original doctrines. The synod upheld the Fritschels and endorsed their positions.

It was known among the delegates that Klindworth had during the previous year suggested that his group might secede from the synod and take the college along to convert it into a seminary. Suspicions were voiced at the convention that Klindworth might now act upon this idea. The hour for adjournment was near.

The convention had no information on the financial situation at Galena, but the delegates suspected the Galena faculty of disloyalty. Without much debate, the convention voted to transfer the college provisionally to Mendota. It appointed a committee to close out the college's affairs at Galena and to sell its property.

Klindworth then led an exodus of twenty Iowa pastors who later joined the Wisconsin Synod. However, these and previous defections were more than made up for by Wartburg Seminary graduates and pastors who came from Germany. In 1873 alone eighteen pastors arrived from Neuendettelsau, Hesse, and other German sources.

The Galena college property was sold some years later at a substantial loss. The college debts that remained were taken over by the synod.

The Galena college faculty was gone. Instructor A. Preller had left with Klindworth's secession. F. Lutz was suspended from the clergy roster and later reinstated. Eventually he was reappointed to the college faculty. That fall (1875) the Galena college students were transferred to the Mendota campus.

Iowa continued to give its witness as doctrinal controversies persisted. But the synod's focus stayed on the missionary goals Loehe had envisioned for his *Nothelfers*. During the next twenty years (1875–1895) the synod's membership trebled to 334 pastors, 40 parish school teachers, 534 congregations, 149 preaching places, and 106,349 baptized members.

1879 was the year of Iowa's twenty-fifth anniversary. Loehe had died Jan. 2, 1872, but the synod remembered its birth under his nurturing care. At its synodical meeting theses were adopted stating the purpose of its organization and in a general way restating its doctrinal position.

Thesis No. 10 recites the story of the debate on "open questions":

"The occasion for the formation of the Evangelical Lutheran Church of Iowa was given by the intolerance of the Missouri Synod. In the controversy with reference to some parts of the doctrine of the Church and the ministerial office, Pastor Loehe had voiced certain opinions which were not in accord with certain theses of the Missouri Synod. Although Loehe's opinions were not contrary to the faith of the Church and to her Confessions, yet the Missouri Synod could not bear with him and his men. Later certain divergent opinions in eschatological (last things) doctrines were also made a matter of controversy.

"As a result our Synod was from its very beginning persuaded to make a distinction between such articles in the Confessions of the Evangelical Lutheran Church as are necessary articles of faith [*Glaubenslehren*] and such other doctrines [Lehrpunkten] as are not doctrines necessary for salvation. And our Synod has considered it one of her duties very earnestly and emphatically to teach as an important truth…that there are doctrines, even doctrines of the Bible, concerning which members of our Church may hold different views and convictions without thereby being compelled to refuse each other Church fellowship; and that these are the very doctrines for the sake of which the Missourians adjudge us to be heretical. In such matters unity should indeed be sought; but it is not absolutely required as in the doctrines of faith." [89]

In 1922 Professor John H. C. Fritz of Concordia Seminary, Saint Louis, referred in his history to Iowa's Open Questions principle as "that peculiar tendency which permits a churchman to consider as an open question what the Bible teaches, but what has not been symbolically defined by the Lutheran Church." [90]

Fritz continued, "Iowa desired to be Lutheran; but while it was not willing to grant as wide a berth for Lutheranism as was found with the Eastern synods, it regarded the Lutheranism of the Missouri Synod as much too narrow." [91]

The 1931 "Brief Statement of the Doctrinal Position of the Missouri Synod" declares:

> "Those questions in the domain of Christian doctrine may be termed open questions which Scriptures answers either not at all or not clearly. Since neither individuals nor the Church as a whole are permitted to develop or augment the Christian doctrine, but are rather ordered and commanded by God to continue in the doctrine of the apostles, 2 Thess. 2:15; Acts 2:42, open questions must remain open questions. Not to be included in the number of open questions are the following: the doctrine of the Church and the Ministry, of Sunday, of Chiliasm, and of Antichrist, these doctrines being clearly defined in Scripture." [92]

CHAPTER 22

IOWA AND THE
EASTERN SYNODS

The General Synod, a collection of synodical groups in the eastern states, was organized on October 22, 1820. By 1860 it included two-thirds of the Lutherans in America (864 of 1313 pastors, 164,000 of 235,000 communicants). But the Midwest Lutherans such as Buffalo, Iowa, Ohio, Minnesota, Wisconsin, Illinois, Norwegian, and Missouri Synods stayed aloof, believing many General Synod leaders lacking in commitment to Scripture and to the Lutheran Confessions.

When the Civil War divided the North from the South, southern synods were unable to send delegates through the army lines to the 1862 convention of the General Synod. On May 20-26, 1863, at Concord, North Carolina, five southern synods met and signed a constitution for the "General Synod of the Evangelical Lutheran Church in the Confederate States of America." After the war confessional disputes in the north led the southern group to continue as a separate body. Its membership fluctuated. On June 23-28, 1886, at Roanoke, Virginia, eight synods adopted the Confessions of the Book of Concord at the first convention of The United Synod of the Evangelical Lutheran Church in the South.

In May 1866, the Ministerium of Pennsylvania, led by Dr. Charles Porterfield Krauth, voted to leave the General Synod and to call all (especially the Midwest) synods that confess the Unaltered Augsburg Confession to organize a new general body organized on distinctive Lutheran principles. On December 11-14, 1866, thirteen synods sent delegates to consider this invitation at Reading, Pennsylvania. A new body was planned under the name "The General Council of the Evangelical Lutheran Church in North America."

After this preliminary organization, the General Council held its first convention in Trinity Lutheran Church, Fort Wayne, Indiana, November 20-26, 1867. The following synods, having adopted the "Fundamental Principles of Faith and Church Polity," agreed upon at the Reading Convention, sent delegates: Ministerium of Pennsylvania, New York Ministerium, Canada Synod, Synod of Illinois, Michigan Synod, Minnesota Synod, English Synod of Ohio, English District Synod of Ohio, Swedish Augustana Synod, Wisconsin Synod, Pittsburgh Synod, and the First Evangelical Lutheran Synod of Texas.

Pulpit and Altar Fellowship

The Iowa Synod had sent the Fritschels prepared to unite with the General Council. But Iowa first wanted the Council to declare its position concerning pulpit and altar fellowship with members of other denominations and altar fellowship with members of secret societies. Because the Council was unprepared to deal with these questions, the delegates of the Iowa Synod adopted a semi-official relation to the Council with the right to speak on the floor but not to vote.

By 1872 similar dissatisfaction with the Council's inaction on these questions and also the question of chiliasm caused Wisconsin, Minnesota, Illinois. and the English District of Ohio to leave the Council. Michigan left in 1887, Texas in 1894. The goal of the General Council was a gradual growth toward genuine Lutheran practice. The Western synods wanted to adopt immediately solid disciplinary rules for which the older Eastern synods were not yet ready.

At the General Council's Lancaster, Ohio, convention in 1870, in response to a question from the Minnesota Synod on pulpit and altar fellowship, President C. P. Krauth had declared, "The rule is Lutheran pulpits for Lutheran ministers; Lutheran altars for Lutheran communicants."

The Iowa Synod came to the next convention at Akron, Ohio, in 1872 asking the General Council to give Krauth's personal declaration official action. The Council adopted the following statement:

> "1. The rule is: Lutheran pulpits are for Lutheran ministers only. Lutheran altars are for Lutheran communicants only.
>
> "2. The exceptions to this rule belong to the sphere of privilege, not of right.
>
> "3. The determination of the exceptions is to be made

in consonance with these principles by the conscientious judgment of the pastors as the cases arise."

This statement should have become known as the Akron Rule of 1872. But because it became the subject of further review and comment at the Galesburg, Illinois, convention in 1875, historians have popularly referred to it as the "Galesburg Rule." It resulted in a stricter practice among the synods of the General Council.

Although Iowa was not a full member of the General Council, President C. P. Krauth explicitly gave Iowa credit for the Council's progress toward conservative Lutheranism. This credit was almost entirely owing to the Fritschel brothers who led Iowa's delegations to the Council's meetings.

From 1867 on Iowa had a consultative relationship with the General Council. After 1872 Ohio wanted no part of the Council.

Later, Iowa consulted with Ohio on the possibility of establishing pulpit and altar fellowship. Ohio steadfastly refused to join Iowa in full fellowship until Iowa decided to leave the council in 1917.

The Fritschel brothers, Grossmann, and Deindoerfer represented the Iowa Synod in many intersynodical efforts. The Fritschels felt that Iowa's position toward the General Council was rather rigid. But they never were able to get their synod to go beyond an associate membership that allowed sharing in action and discussion without vote.

The brothers developed personal relationships with all the synodical leaders of the eastern states. They received calls to teaching positions that would have paid far more than Wartburg Seminary could match, but they declined. Sigmund Fritschel was a leading member of the Council's Committee on Church Forms. The *Kirchliche Zeitschrift*, the theological journal of Wartburg Seminary and the Iowa Synod edited by the Fritschels, had a large readership among Council members.

Iowa cooperated in many ways with the Council. It laid aside a German hymn book that it was about to publish and helped prepare one for the Council. Sigmund Fritschel then served on the General Council's committee that, after years of research, published in 1877 a German hymnal, the *Kirchenbuch fuer Evangelisch Lutherische Gemeinden* (Churchbook for Evangelical Lutheran Congregations) that became popular. The *Kirchenbuch* was adopted by Iowa and reprinted in 1902 under its own copyright by Wartburg Publishing House.

The Missouri Synod had declined membership in the General Council. In 1868 Wisconsin withdrew, followed in 1870 by Minnesota and Illinois, in 1872 by the English District Synod of Ohio, and in 1887 by Michigan. All left because the General Council was not able to declare its position concerning pulpit and altar fellowship with members of other denominations and altar fellowship with members of secret societies.

The Synodical Conference

In 1871 Ohio invited the synods outside the Council to consider federation. Delegates from Missouri, Ohio, Wisconsin, and the Norwegian Synod met in Chicago. They considered forming a "Synodical Conference." They met again later in the year at Fort Wayne, Indiana, along with delegates from Minnesota and Illinois, to plan for the synodical conference. The Evangelical Lutheran Synodical Conference of North America was organized July 10-16, 1872, at Milwaukee. C. F. W. Walther was elected president.

During the time of Ohio's membership in the Synodical Conference, it ordered its Capital University at Columbus Ohio, to confer upon Walther the degree of Doctor of Divinity.

CHAPTER 23

THE PREDESTINATION CONTROVERSY

From about 1870 to 1920, the Iowa Synod was caught up in a new controversy that raged among all U.S. Lutherans, including the Scandinavians, over predestination.

According to J. L. Neve, "It is an undecided question just at what time Walther adopted the theory of predestination which he later propounded. But it is certain that he arrived at his conclusions, not through the study of Scripture, but rather through the old dogmaticians [early Lutheran theologians]. This he himself admitted later. The matter was not presented publicly until in 1868, when, at the meeting of the Wisconsin District, Pastor [J. A.] Huegli set forth Walther's doctrine. On that occasion Walther expressed himself much more strongly than is indicated in the minutes of the synod. The slight objections referred to in the minutes were made by [Norwegian Synod] Professor F.A. Schmidt, a colleague of Walther's at Concordia Seminary in St. Louis.

"Professor S. Fritschel, passing through the city, attended the meeting, and reported the details of this doctrinal discussion to his brother (Gottfried), who continually observed the development." [93]

Iowa's involvement with Missouri's predestination debate developed on the questions: Does dissimilar conduct in natural man over against the converting and saving grace of God account for the fact that some are converted and saved while others remain unconverted and perish? Or does man's conversion and salvation depend solely upon God? In 1872 Gottfried Fritschel wrote a document that insisted that dissimilar conduct by men is the reason some are saved and some are lost. Gottfried charged Missouri with crypto-Calvinism (incorporating Calvinist theology, in this case Calvin's doctrine of double-predestination, teaching that God predestines both the saved and the lost to their fates). Walther replied in an article in Missouri's *Lehre und Wehre*: "Is It Really Lutheran Doctrine That Man's Salvation, in the Last Analysis, Depends on His Free Self-determination?"

Through Gottfried Fritschel, the Iowa Synod accused C. F. W. Walther and the Missouri Synod of teaching [like Jean Calvin] that if salvation is entirely an act of God's grace, then God chooses some to be saved and some to be damned. Missouri accused Fritschel and the Iowa Synod of teaching salvation by works because they said that Christians are saved by believing.

The controversy spread when Professor Friedrich August Schmidt, Concordia Seminary chair. charged his Missouri Synod with crypto-Calvinism for rejecting the theory "that not the mercy of God and the most holy merit of Christ, but also in *us* there is a cause why God has elected us unto eternal life." [94] Professor Schmidt sounded an alarm in January 1880 by publishing a new monthly organ, *Altes und Neues,* opposing Walther's views on predestination.

"Instantly universal attention was drawn to the controversy between Schmidt and Walther. Within the Norwegian Synod, whose ministers had been trained largely by Schmidt and Walther, a division took place. In almost every Norwegian congregation the issue was taken up and vigorously debated." [95]

On September 29, 1880, a public conference met at Chicago with 500 Missouri pastors present, but the conference failed to agree. A colloquy was held at Milwaukee January 5-10, 1881, between Missouri and Ohio representatives. On the fifth day the Ohio delegates ended the discussion and withdrew.

Walther proposed that the controversy should not be continued any longer in public. But Professor Schmidt declared that he had been commanded by God to wage this war. Walther replied, "Since you desire war, you shall have war."

Missouri called a general meeting of the pastors of the Synodical Conference at Chicago September 29-October 5, 1881, followed by a second pastors' meeting in 1882 at Fort Wayne. At the latter, Walther was opposed by two Missourians Pastor H. A. Allwardt of Lebanon, Wisconsin, and F. W. Stellhorn, professor at Fort Wayne College. After a brief discussion, the Missouri delegates caucussed and adopted Walther's thirteen theses. Only five voted against the theses.

Walther's opponents responded by meeting at Blue Island, Illinois, where they organized and left the Missouri Synod. They united with the Ohio Synod as its Northwestern District. Among them was Stellhorn, who became a professor at Ohio's Capital University and Seminary at Columbus, Ohio.

The Minnesota and Wisconsin Synods took sides with Missouri. This caused them also to lose several pastors to Ohio.

In 1882 the Norwegian Synod sent Professor Schmidt as a delegate to the Synodical Conference convention in Chicago. Missouri delegates protested against seating Schmidt unless he repented of meeting with pastors and congregations that had left Synodical Conference synods. Schmidt was not seated and was not permitted to speak and justify his actions. Later Missouri expressed regret over some scenes that took place at this conference.

Besides Schmidt and Stellhorn, the chief opponents of Missouri's predestination doctrine were Ohio's H. A. Allwardt, Matthias Loy, and A. C. Ernst of its Saint Paul Seminary. At its 1881 convention in Wheeling, WV, Ohio entered a protest against Missouri's "heresy" and declared allegiance to the old Lutheran doctrine of salvation "in view of faith" (*intuitu fidei*). At the same convention, Ohio voted to leave the Synodical Conference because Misssouri (with Loy and Stellhorn in mind) had instructed its delegates not to sit together and deliberate in any session "with such as have publicly decried us as Calvinists" and "not to recognize any synod which as a synod has raised the same accusation of Calvinism against us."

The Saint Sebald Theses

Meeting at Saint Sebald in 1881, the Iowa Synod also adopted what became known as the "Theses of Saint Sebald" against Missouri's "new" doctrines on predestination and election. In 1882 Iowa reinforced this position at Dubuque, where a series of theses by Sigmund Fritschel was studied and ordered printed; a similar tract by Gottfried Fritschel was ordered published as well.

Until this time, Iowa had insisted that the doctrinal differences between Missouri and Iowa were not of a serious nature. But now Iowa accused Missouri of fundamental error and heresy that were sufficent cause for their continued separation. Sigmund Fritschel declared in his third thesis: "The Lutheran Church has always considered it a Calvinistic error...to speak of election has having been made without reference to the conduct of man, merely in accordance with the pleasure of [God's] divine will without respect to faith that he foresaw. According to the doctrine of the Lutheran Church, God in his eternal, divine counsel has decreed that he would save no one except those who would know Christ, His Son, and truly believe in him."

In rejecting the idea that God saves us "in view of our faith," the Missourians wanted to safeguard the doctrine that we are saved by grace alone and that faith cannot be something that we produce and so are saved by something we do. Luther's explanation to the Third Article of the Apostles' Creed: "I cannot by my own understanding or effort believe in Jesus Christ my Lord or come to him. But the Holy Spirit has called me through the gospel, enlightened me with his gifts, and sanctified and kept me in true faith."

On the question, "Why is it that some are saved and others not, though the same grace is offered to all?" Missouri replied, "Scripture repeatedly states both: that salvation depends entirely upon the grace of God, and that all men are alike dead in trespasses and sins, *but does not solve the mystery.*" By leaving this mystery unsolved, the Missourians claimed to follow both Scripture and the Confessions.

The battle continued for decades and was not brought to any clear conclusion, except that voiced by Johannes Deindoerfer in his *Geschichte der Iowa Synode:* "Although in former years the difference between us and the Missouri Synod did not stand in the way of church fellowship, the difference now existing in the doctrine of election is of such a nature that there can no longer be any church fellowship." [96]

In 1922 Concordia Seminary Professor John H. C. Fritz, writing in *Ebenezer,* summarized the controversies by contrasting Iowa's willingness to leave unsettled arguments as "open questions" with Missouri's position that God's Word is plain enough for us to know what he wants us to believe and teach.

> "The Missouri Synod believes that...no certain day of the week has been set aside for worship, but that according to the Lutheran Catechism, we should 'gladly hear and learn the Word of God,' the time of so doing being left to the choice of the Church; that the prophecies of the Bible, especially 2 Thess. 2, clearly designate the Pope to be the Antichrist, and that we are not to look for any particular person of the future in whom the characteristic marks of the Antichrist shall be found; that the Bible forbids us to believe

that there will be any bodily resurrection preceding that of the general resurrection on Judgment Day, for this would contradict such clear passages of the Bible as clearly tell us that the only warning of the Lord's coming are the general signs which shall precede it, and that therefore we should expect his return for the final judgment at any moment.

"As to the doctrine of election, we believe that the Scriptures clearly teach that, although God earnestly desires the salvation of all men and for this purpose has his Gospel preached to them, he has from eternity (not because he foresaw that some would believe and others not, all being by nature under like condemnation, but solely because of his good will and pleasure and grace in Christ) elected such as should be saved; and that in the course of time he converts and saves these by his Gospel, such work of conversion and bringing to Christ being solely the work of God and in no part the work of man.

"We do not teach, either in so many words or by implication, the Calvinistic error that God has elected some to eternal damnation. Those who are saved are saved only by the grace of God; those who are lost are lost solely by their own fault." [97]

Convinced of its doctrinal purity, for a number of years the Western District of the Missouri Synod discussed the theme: "Only through the doctrine of the Lutheran Church is God alone given all glory, an irrefutable proof that its doctrine is the only one." (*Ebenezer*, p. 408.)

(Obviously neither Missouri Synod members nor their opponents should be bound today by extreme statements made by their ancestors on both sides in the heat of controversy.)

The Norwegian Lutherans

The Norwegian Synod from its beginning sent its theological students to Concordia Seminary, Saint Louis. They established a Norwegian professorship there filled by Laur. Larsen (1859–1861) and F. A. Schmidt (1872–1876), the expenses paid from a fund collected for the eventual erection of a college for the Norwegian Synod. In 1875 O. Asperheim was appointed Norwegian professor at Missouri's seminary in Springfield, Illinois. By the time the Norwegian Synod established its own seminary, 127 candidates for ordination in that synod had graduated from Concordia. Each new class of graduates brought with it from Saint Louis the spirit of Walther and the sound Lutheranism of his teaching.

In 1876 both professorships were ended because of the predestinarian controversy and Luther Seminary was opened in Madison, Wisconsin. The Norwegian Synod's first institution was Luther College established in 1861 in Wisconsin and moved to Decorah, Iowa, in 1862.

Hoping to maintain unity among its own pastors, the Norwegian Synod left the Synodical Conference in 1883. Walther viewed this action with deep sorrow. In 1887 Schmidt led about a third of the Norwegian Synod into a schismatic association called the Anti-Missourian Brotherhood, but not a synodical corporation.

On June 13, 1890, through negotiations with other Norwegian synods, this Brotherhood helped form the United Norwegian Synod. The Anti-Missourian Brotherhood had been operating a seminary at Saint Olaf College, Northfield, Minnesota. When the United Norwegian Synod was formed, to supply its pastors this seminary was merged with Augustana Seminary of Beloit, Wisconsin, and elements of Augsburg Seminary of Minneapolis under the name of Luther Seminary at St. Anthony Park, Saint Paul, Minnesota.

On June 7, 1917, the United Norwegian Synod joined with the Norwegian Synod and the Hauge Synod to form the Norwegian Lutheran Church of North America, later named the Evangelical Lutheran Church. A dissident group then formed the Lutheran Free Church, with its Augsburg College and Seminary located in Minneapolis.

CHAPTER 24

THE MERGER OF THE IOWA, OHIO, AND BUFFALO SYNODS

Even though Loehe had broken his relations with the Ohio Synod because of his missionaries' experiences in the early years, the Fritschels kept alive an interest in closer fellowship between the Iowa and Ohio bodies. The two synods developed bonds partly through joint opposition to the Missouri Synod and also because their synodical lines overlapped. The Fritschels and the Ohio theologians began talking about doctrinal unity at Richmond, Indiana, in 1883.

In July 1893, a colloquy was held in Michigan City, Indiana, by Ohio representatives and Iowa's Sigmund Fritschel, W. Proehl, Friederich Richter, Th. Meier, H. Doermann, and others. Six theses were drafted, but they were not accepted by the two synods.

Another colloquy was held at Toledo, Ohio, in 1909 at which the Michigan City theses were revised. These "Toledo Theses" were adopted by both synods and served as the basis of a joint declaration of fellowship in 1918. Shortly after this a joint committee was named to discuss a merger of the two bodies. In 1925 the Buffalo Synod sent a delegation to a meeting of this committee.

The Toledo Theses summarized the doctrinal positions of the two synods on points at controversy with the Missouri Synod after fifty years of debate:

> Thesis I. The Church...is the communion of true believers as it is begotten through the means of grace and as by their use it edifies itself....According to its real essence the Church is...invisible....Common participation in the means of grace is the necessary form of the Church's appearance and the infallible mark of its existence.

Thesis II. The Office of the Ministry rests upon a special command of the Lord, valid throughout all time, and consists in the right and power conferred by special call to administer the means of grace publicly and by commission of the congregation. The call (to the pastorate) is a right of the congregation within whose bounds the minister is to discharge the office.

Thesis III. A binding subscription to the Confessions (of the Church) pertains only to the doctrines of faith therein set forth, and to these without exception...the doctrine of Sunday is not to be excluded....

Thesis IV. All doctrines revealed clearly and plainly in the Word of God are...dogmatically fixed as true and binding upon the conscience, whether they have been symbolically settled or not....There is...no authority whatever of departing from any truths clearly revealed by Scripture, be their contents considered fundamental or non-fundamental....Full agreement in all articles of faith constitutes the irremissible condition of church fellowship. Persistent error in an article of faith must under all circumstances lead to separation. Perfect agreement in all fundamental doctrines, though not attainable on earth, is nevertheless an end desirable and one we should labor to attain. Those who knowingly, obdurately, and persistently contradict the divine Word in any of its utterances whatsoever thereby overthrow the organic foundation (of the faith) and are therefore to be excluded from church fellowship.

Thesis V. Any chiliasm which conceives the kingdom of Christ to be something external, earthly, and after the manner of the kingdoms of the world, and which teaches a resurrection of all believers before the Day of Judgment shall come, is a doctrine directly contrary to the analogy of faith and is to be rejected as such....The belief that the reign of Christ and his saints referred to in Revelation 20 is an event belonging to the future, as also that the resurrection there spoken of is to be understood as a bodily resurrection of some believers unto life everlasting, is an opinion which, though not incompatible with the analogy of faith, cannot be strictly proved from Scripture, no more than the spiritual interpretation of said passages can be said to be the true one.

Thesis VI. The error of Missouri on predestination we find to consist in this, that thereby the universal gracious will of God and his decree of election are so separated as to exclude one another and that thus two contradictory wills are affirmed of God....Concerning conversion...we confess that, viewed as the placing or planting of a new spiritual life, conversion does not depend to any extent whatsoever on any cooperation...but that it is wholly and solely the work of the Holy Ghost....We deny that the Holy Ghost works conversion according to a mere pleasure of his elective will or despite the most willful resistance...but we hold that by such stubborn resistance both conversion and eternal election are hindered. [98]

On August 10, 1930 Iowa merged with the Buffalo and Ohio synods to form the American Lutheran Church. The merger negotiations were not free of difficulties. In 1926 a problem arose over a statement in the confessional paragraph of the first draft of the constitution that Scripture is without error. The statement had originated in the confessional paragraph of the National Lutheran Council organized September 6, 1918. The first president of that council was Dr. Hans Gerhard Stub, president of the Norwegian Lutheran Church of North America, organized the previous year. Stub insisted that the council adopt the Norwegian Lutheran Church of North America's confessional statement upholding belief in "the inerrancy of the scriptures." In 1926, Ohio Synod representatives on the Iowa, Ohio, Buffalo merger commission wanted to include in their constitution for the American Lutheran Church this insistence on the "inerrancy of the scriptures."

Dr. Michael Reu of Wartburg Seminary led the Iowa delegation. Reu reminded the commission that it was insistence on scriptural inerrancy that had led to the rigid doctrinal stance of the Missouri Synod on so many issues. The commission agreed to follow Iowa Synod policy and leave the inerrancy of the scriptures an open question. The constitution of the American Lutheran Church was adopted in 1930 without a statement affirming the inerrancy of Scripture.

In 1960, the joint union committee that prepared the constitution for The American Lutheran Church yielded to the demands of the

Stub's theological heirs in the Norwegian Evangelical Lutheran Church and inserted an inerrancy of the scriptures statement into that new body's constitution.

In 1986 the Commission for a New Lutheran Church omitted the inerrancy statement when it wrote the constitution for the Evangelical Lutheran Church in America, formed in 1988. Wilhelm Loehe, the Fritschels, and J. Michael Reu would have rejoiced.

Dr. Conrad G. Prottengeier, whose father Pastor Christoph Prottengeier trained at Wartburg Seminary at Saint Sebald, served as the last president of the Iowa Synod. He was elected second vice president of the newly merged American Lutheran Church. From 1932 until his death in 1949, he served on the ALC's Commission for Worship and Church Art.

In its seventy-seven-year history, the Iowa Synod grew from two congregations to more than 1,060. It served the gospel through its Wartburg Theological Seminary at Dubuque; colleges at Clinton and Waverly, Iowa, at Sterling Nebraska, and Eureka, South Dakota; hospitals in Milwaukee and Minneapolis; children's homes in Muscatine and Waverly, Iowa, and Toledo, Ohio; the Wartburg Hospice in Minneapolis for young men and women away from home; and the flourishing Wartburg Publishing House.

CHAPTER 25

THE COLLEGE(S) AT MENDOTA, ANDREW, CLINTON, & WAVERLY

The writer has relied heavily on Gerhard Ottersburg's Wartburg College, 1852-1952:A Centennial History, *for the material in this chapter, editing and condensing pages 43-79.*

T he number of Wartburg College students who were loyal enough to transfer from Galena to Mendota is not on record. A year later the college enrollment at Mendota was more than twenty. The residence in which they were housed served as the college home as long as the college remained at Mendota. Pastor J.A. List resigned as pastor at Saint Sebald to live with the students as housefather. The college students went to the seminary building only for meals and for chapel. Because of the synod's financial pressures, the students lived on a spartan diet.

The Mendota years were in many ways the time during which Sigmund and Gottfried Fritschel matured to their full potential. They led the Iowa Synod's on-going theological dialog with Missouri. Most of their positions were detailed in the *Kirchliche Zeitschrift*.

The number of candidates preparing for the ministry increased. Between 1876 and 1879, forty-eight graduates were presented for ordination. In 1875, Friederich Richter, former student of Wartburg Seminary at Saint Sebald, who later served as president of the Iowa Synod and from 1901 to 1926 edited the *Kirchenblatt*, joined the faculty. William Proehl, who later became president of the seminary, served as an instructor from 1882 to 1884.

The Fritschel brothers gave part of their time to the college and were assisted by young instructor E. Knappe. List taught little and was soon replaced by Professor H. Thilo, a classical scholar with a gift for teaching.[99]

Later Thilo was replaced by Professor Christian Otto Kraushaar, whose gifts made him one of the outstanding leaders in the college's history. For a number of years he edited the *Kirchenblatt*. He served as president of the college from 1900 to 1907 when he retired.[100]

The second generation of Fritschels, John and Maximilian (sons of Sigmund) and George and Herman (sons of Gottfried), were preparing to teach. Sigmund Fritschel's third son, John, graduated from the college with the class of 1878. He completed his training at the seminary and accepted a call as teacher on the college faculty at Mendota. After a leave for graduate study in Germany, he taught fifty years at Wartburg College in Waverly and Clinton, serving as Clinton's president from 1907 to 1919.

From the start of its stay at Mendota, the college's pattern of a six-year *Gymnasium* was replaced by a four-year course of study. The school emphasized the Latin, Greek, and Hebrew languages as before. Student life was still regimented. Sports were only intramural. Enrollment for the last three years at Mendota was recorded as nineteen, fourteen, and seventeen. Sons of Iowa's first pastors began to appear in the lists of graduates. Gerhard Ottersberg estimated that one-third of the students came from parsonages. Graduating classes ranged from two to six. All but two of the graduates at Mendota became pastors. [101]

A pastor who kept records of his son's expenses at Mendota for five years in the college and seminary, paid $200 tuition and $459.62 for clothing, books, travel, medical care, and personal expense.[102]

Wartburg Seminary, Mendota, Illinois

When the seminary moved to Mendota, a board of regents was appointed to supervise the financial affairs of the college and the seminary. The faculty continued to serve as the directorate that designed the curriculum. The college had no head other than the housefather. The synod's examination commission continued to conduct the examinations and the electoral commission still chose the teachers.[103]

While the college stayed small and struggled, the seminary grew rapidly, and its building was soon overcrowded. The synod's connections in Germany continued to produce a large flow of seminary students. Some had to rent rooms from Mendota families. As long as there was an ample supply of seminary students, the synod felt no urgency to strengthen the college.

As the Iowa Synod began to expand rapidly in the 1870s, it recognized the need for a stronger college. Because it could not grow well at Mendota, and since the seminary needed the college facilities to expand, a movement developed to again separate the college from the seminary. The need for parish school teachers finally brought this about.

Teacher training was the purpose for which Loehe and Grossmann had founded the Frankenhilf school in 1852. Parochial schools were a basic part of Loehe's ideal pattern for congregations in which God's Holy Spirit would be able to create and build strong faith. Under necessity, normal education had been dropped in favor of theological study when the colony arrived at Dubuque. But demand for parish school teachers had never died. Iowa Synod pastors faithfully founded schools and carried the teaching burden five days a week along with their pastoral work and preaching. When congregations became strong enough to support both pastors and teachers, the pastors gave the school over to qualified men and devoted more time to other duties. The synod suggested that local pastors train capable girls to teach in their schools until a normal school could be established once more.[104]

In 1868, the year that the Saint Sebald preparatory school moved to Galena, the synod approved a plan offered by Johannes Deindoerfer, then pastoring at Toledo, Ohio, that he and another pastor there would privately train small groups of teachers and offer them practice-teaching in Toledo parish schools. Deindoerfer trained a few men, but lack of money forced him to close the undertaking.

In 1878 Georg Grossmann with F. Eichler as his assistant reopened teacher training with six students in the orphanage that J. Michael Schueller had established at Andrew, Iowa. Studies were equivalent to the first three years of high school. Classes at the orphanage school provided practice-teaching for the seminary students.[105]

The teachers seminary wanted to add a second class in 1879 but lacked space at the orphanage. The synod convention that year recognized the school and provided a board of trustees to secure a charter for it and to supervise its development. Waverly offered to raise four thousand dollars to construct a permanent home for a normal training school. That September, Grossmann rented a hotel in Waverly for his six first-year students, a second class of six, and several local students who wanted a general education.

Two city blocks were acquired for the campus east of where Grossmann Hall was later erected. "Old Main" was built in 1882 at a cost of eight thousand dollars. Grossmann raised additional funds, but in 1882 he had to report a debt of more than two thousand dollars. Grossmann personally paid the balance. The synod took over the teachers seminary which immediately occupied the building. Later funds were privately raised to reimburse Grossmann in part.[106]

From 1882 to 1885, forty-four students were admitted. Nineteen students pursued the normal course and eight were graduated as teachers. The rest were admitted to classes in general education, and their presence helped make ends meet. The normal course was three years. The first class graduated in 1881.[107]

In 1884 the minimum age for entrance at the teachers seminary was set at sixteen; later it was lowered to age fourteen for its preparatory department. Membership in a Lutheran church and a testimonial from a pastor were also required for entrance.

The new school building had no central heating, light, water, or sewer. Dormitory rooms and class rooms were heated with stoves and lighted with kerosene lamps as in Mendota. Grossmann taught and served as synod president. Eichler taught and pastored the local congregation. These two constituted the entire faculty.[108]

After ten years at Mendota, the seminary needed to expand again. In September 1885, the Iowa Synod transferred Wartburg College from Mendota to Waverly to operate with the normal school. The lower classes of the two schools were combined. The upper classes took certain subjects together, but otherwise had separate curricula. The general college course was extended to five years (three academy and two college level). An instructor was added to those already serving—the two professors who came from Mendota and the two already at Waverly.[109]

Grossmann headed the school with the title "director." The rest of the faculty consisted of F. Lutz from the former Galena staff; Christian Otto Kraushaar from Mendota, who also served as housefather and supervisor; John Fritschel, who had completed studies in Germany; and A. Bartels, an alumnus of the college at Mendota. Later August Engelbrecht, a graduate of the normal school, joined the faculty.

The Waverly college, like the theological seminary at Saint Sebald, adopted the name *Wartburg.*[110]

The constitution adopted in 1891 authorized the board of trustees to adopt rules for the discipline and operation of the combined school.The synodical electoral commission or the convention selected the faculty. Constitutionally, the faculty had only the power to issue degrees. In practice, it set the curriculum, the calendar, and the rules of conduct and discipline.[111]

During the first year forty-nine students enrolled. The average for 1885-1894 was more than sixty.[112]

Old Main housed the student body, classrooms, the housefather, and another teacher.The general student dormitory was the attic with fifty wooden bedsteads. Students paid a charge for springs and mattresses. Four ropes were installed as fire escapes.The second and third floors contained classrooms equipped each with a stove, lamps, teachers' desks and chairs, and double schoolroom desks for the students.A telephone was installed in 1885.The first floor housed teachers.[113]

The basement contained the kitchen, dining room, and a washroom with a barrel that had to be filled daily as a reservoir. Gymnasium equipment was on the lawn for physical training classes when weather permitted. The campus was surrounded by a barbed wire fence. Students were not to leave campus without permission during the week.[114]

Discipline infractions were frequent—making noise or failing to meet work requirements such as janitorial duties, looking after the campus, or keeping a garden. Other offenses included slipping through the fence at night to go downtown or to take a girl for a walk. Hardly a year passed without dismissals.[114]5

The "outfly" (a picnic day in response to spontaneous student demonstrations) may have originated at that time. Faculty minutes show an outing to have been granted October 6, 1892.[116]

Enrollment expanded. Reacting to the demand of local students, a business course was begun in 1888.That year the synod authorized the erection of another building to house the kitchen, dining room, and members of the staff.A generous donor, Mr. F. Schack, provided the funds, and North Hall was built adjacent to Old Main on the north. Schack also gave funds for a laboratory and other equipment. He bought three blocks north and south of the eastern campus block and gave them to the college. This more than doubled the campus; it remained this size until 1946. Schack's generosity helped maintain the sound financial condition of the college during this time, even though the teaching staff grew to seven and salaries were substantially increased.[116]7

Even with the new North Hall, in only four years facilities again became crowded. It was reported to the synod that Old Main should not house more than forty-five students, though it then had sixty-five. A new dormitory was needed, large enough for another one hundred. The housing needs again raised the question of separating the general college and the normal school.[118]

The seminary moved to Dubuque in 1889 and the Mendota campus had been sold. But offers from various cities brought the possibility of a new college campus and an adequate modern building. In 1894 the general college and the preparatory department were installed in Clinton, Iowa, as Wartburg College, while the normal training school stayed in Waverly as Wartburg Normal School offering studies on the high school level. Grossmann and August Engelbrecht remained in Waverly to teach the normal school of nine students.

That same year (1894) Grossmann was forced to retire because of failing health. Except for an interval from 1875 to 1878 when he had taken leave because of ill health, Grossmann had served the school since its beginning in 1852. In 1893 Grossmann had retired as president of the Iowa Synod, a position he had held from its organization in 1854. He died on Tuesday, August 24, 1897, on the anniversary of the Iowa Synod's founding. His last words were, "God be with us and our Synod."

Engelbrecht was alone at the Waverly normal school until F. Lutz, who had taught at Galena, was called to the presidency. The normal school inherited the enlarged Waverly campus and buildings, half of the library (about five hundred volumes). The nine students were divided into three classes. Electric lights were installed in 1894. A year later the campus was connected to the Waverly water mains. Next the fence came down and cement sidewalks

George M. Grossmann

were laid. In 1900 the president's home was erected. In 1907 the campus was connected to the city sewer system and a steam heating plant was installed.[119]

These improvements were hardly in place when the number of synod parochial schools began to decline because of improvements in the public school system. This resulted in low enrollment at the teacher's seminary. In 1896 the synod had added a preparatory department to replace the one that had gone to Clinton with the general college. After 1900 this department had two classes corresponding to grades seven and eight in the public school. It peaked between 1914 and 1920 with thirty to fifty-three students. The seventh grade was dropped in 1921, the eighth in 1926.[120]

In 1896 the synod also transferred the pretheological department from Wartburg Seminary in Dubuque to Waverly. Dating back to Saint Sebald days, this was a course for second-career men who wished to enter the seminary and were given a minimum of preparatory work instead of a college course. This work had been burdening the theological faculty. It was transferred to Wartburg Normal School with provision for a two-year course with English as the chief language for instruction. In 1917 this program was increased to three years. Usually this department enrolled more than twenty men.[121]

In 1882, with the erection of Old Main, a department had been added called the "Academy," a Waverly-resident class of eight and an evening class of eight. At first it had its own teacher and was conducted separately from the other departments. In 1893 a second year was added to it; in 1905 a third year. The fourth year was added in 1913, and in 1915 it was accredited by the state as a four-year high school. It grew from eight students to a high of seventy-two in 1920 and then declined.[122]

The department of music (vocal, instrumental, and theoretical) became permanently established in 1911. It served members of other departments, and even local grade school children took lessons there. It usually listed more than fifty students. The high point was 149 in 1925.[123]

Coeducation began at the teachers seminary in 1896 with the admission of women to the Academy. They were then admitted to the business department and in 1907 to the normal school. By 1912 almost all students in the normal department were women.[124]

Normal training had been the original purposes of the school. After 1913 it had offered a four-year course on the high school level. Its graduating teachers increasingly were hired by public schools. Since standards were rising, in 1920 the school got synod permission (over objections from Wartburg College at Clinton) to open a two-year college course in teacher training. On that basis, the school adopted the name Wartburg Normal *College*.[125]

In 1922 the junior college courses were opened to students in liberal arts, pretheological students and others. In 1925 the junior college was accredited by the State Board of Examiners and in 1927 by the Iowa Intercollegiate Standing Committee.[126]

Director (president) F. Lutz resigned in 1905. G. Bergstraesser presided until 1909. That year August Engelbrecht began a presidency that lasted until the closing of Wartburg Normal College in 1933. Generations of students affectionately referred to him as "Brick." During his first twenty years the faculty increased from three to nine members.[127]

Increasing enrollment of women created a need for a girl's dormitory. In 1913 Wartburg Hall was built for girls, and in 1920 the men's dormitory Grossmann Hall was erected. That same year a small gymnasium was added, later converted to the Little Theater.[128]

A new administration building named Luther Hall was built in 1926 with classrooms and a library. This made Old Main available for the music department, bookstore, mailroom, and student newspaper—all of which occupied it for many years.[129]

After 1925, enrollments declined. The preparatory department was dying and the Academy was dwindling. The junior college was growing, but it was competing with the normal school.[130]

When the Iowa Synod merged into the American Lutheran Church (ALC) in 1930, the Great Depression required severe budget cutbacks. The question arose: Was it time once more to combine the two institutions that were separated in 1894, Wartburg College at Clinton and Wartburg Normal College at Waverly? [131]

Gerhard Ottersberg wrote:

> "Arguments favoring Waverly stressed the plant facilities available there, which, if not adequate in the long run, were considerably better than those in Clinton, and which would not be readily salable if vacated. Waverly's location in the midst of numerous Lutheran congregations also received stress. Advocates of Clinton pointed out that the campus there was fully adequate, over against a cramped site at Waverly which could be expanded only at great cost. The advantages of location in a city of moderate size and the centrality of location in respect to the entire area to be

served were other arguments strongly urged. In order to assure better building facilities, a tentative offer of the city of Clinton to provide funds for the construction of a science hall was obtained." [132]

In 1932, the ALC convention voted to merge the college and the normal school at Clinton. The merged school began its first year in September 1933. A new board of regents for the merged institution elected O. L. Proel president and chose twenty-one faculty members from the Clinton staff and three from among the Waverly teachers. Only three students transferred to Clinton from Waverly. The enrollment stayed at 192. [133]

Forced by the economic depression, the 1932 convention voted to merge the former Iowa Synod Dakota District's two year junior college at Eureka, South Dakota, with the former Ohio Synod's junior college (Saint Paul Luther) at Saint Paul, Minnesota. Saint Paul Luther College had previously combined with the Ohio Synod's Lutheran Seminary that closed at Afton, Minnesota. [134]

The Waverly campus stood empty for two years.

In October 1934, the ALC convention met at Waverly and made difficult decisions that caused much disappointment and aroused resentments that lasted many years. The Clinton buildings were to be sold and the merged Wartburg College was to be moved to Waverly. The depression having worsened, the church closed Saint Paul Luther College and Seminary at Saint Paul, Minnesota. Luther College was to be merged with Wartburg College, and Luther Seminary with Wartburg Seminary, now at Dubuque. [135]

A new board of regents appointed E. J. Braulick president of the college, with a faculty of 18. Eight of them came from Clinton and four from the faculty in Saint Paul. [136]

In 1935 Wartburg College reopened in Waverly with 188 students. There the pilgrim school remains. In 1942 Hebron Junior College at Hebron, Nebraska, was closed and merged with Wartburg. All the midwestern schools of the American Lutheran Church were now consolidated into what was to become a strong school. Wartburg College has since developed into one of the top liberal arts colleges in the nation.

CHAPTER 26

WARTBURG THEOLOGICAL SEMINARY MOVES BACK TO DUBUQUE

In 1888 George John Fritschel was called as assistant professor at Wartburg Seminary in Mendota. He was well prepared, having done graduate studies at the German Universities of Rostock, Erlangen, and Leipzig.

After 1885, when the college separated from the seminary, the seminary had the entire Mendota property for its own use. But even so it soon became inadequate for its growing enrollment.

When word spread that the seminary was looking for more adequate quarters, a number of cities offered incentives for the institution to move to their location, including Saint Paul, Minnesota.

In 1888, prodded by Pastor Heinrich Luz, pastor of Dubuque's Saint John Lutheran Church, the city of Dubuque offered to the Iowa Synod for its seminary facility the Emerson Estate at the end of Fremont Avenue. This included thirty-one acres of land and a 43 x 46 foot two-story building with an 41x43 annex. The synod accepted the gift and spent many thousands of dollars to remodel and enlarge the building with a chapel. It dedicated its new seminary (debt free) September 15, 1889.

Wartburg Seminary, Dubuque, Iowa

Just prior to the dedication, on July 13, Gottfried Fritschel died of cancer following a long illness. This sad event ended thirty-two years of the rich association of the brothers Sigmund and Gottfried Fritschel.

The Fritschel brothers had served together in harmony as pioneers of the Lutheran church in midwest America. The Fritschel brothers had crossed the ocean as young men to found a synod, a college, and a seminary. They instructed generations of future pastors who like them gathered the unchurched and built the kingdom of God. They followed the guidance of Loehe, and from its beginnings they gave impetus to the movement toward a united Lutheran church in America.

> "Professors Senior and Junior Fritschel were so united in the way they thought that they often remarked that they could tell what the other was going to say before he spoke. It wasn't as though they didn't experience the normal sibling rivalry in their youth or come to differences of opinion in their maturity. They simply had come to be open and honest with each other and were both thoroughly convinced that the Holy Spirit enabled them to support and strengthen one another for their common task. Together they had the highest reverence for their calling as teachers....

> "President J. Haas of Muehlenberg College summed it up well when he wrote: 'Again one of our great leaders has gone from us....Great in insight and conception of the truth, powerful in the doctrine of our Lutheran Church. Holding true middle ground, equally remote from leveling liberalism and narrow party spirit, he stands strong before our mental eye. Great in self-sacrificing faithfulness, in sincere surrender to his Savior, we felt the spirit and love of a Loehe.' It was estimated that at the time of his death, over 400 students had been influenced by his ministry." [137]

Sigmund Fritschel had served as president of the seminary since Grossmann's retirement in 1875. Now as he grieved for his brother, he alone directed the seminary's return to Dubuque.

At the same time that the seminary building was being prepared, two brick residences were built for faculty use at 445 and 465 Wartburg Place. Sigmund Fritschel and his family moved into the house at 445 Wartburg Place.

"The Dubuque to which Wartburg returned in 1889 was a busier and larger manufacturing, trade, medical and educational center than it was when the move was made to St. Sebald some 30 years before. When the dedication services were held September 15, a special train ran from downtown to the Wartburg bringing the many people from the community who joined to welcome Wartburg back to Dubuque.

"With the return to Dubuque a period of faculty changes and gradual curricular expansion began....This was the period when the second generation of Fritschels assumed leadership and when the prodigious scholarly achievements of J. Michael Reu would blossom." [138]

In 1892 George Fritschel was called as professor to the Evangelical Lutheran College of the Texas Synod at Brenham, Texas.

Largely due to George Fritschel's influence, the Evangelical Lutheran Synod of Texas joined the Iowa Synod in 1896 and increased the size of the Iowa Synod to about six hundred congregations with almost four hundred pastors. With the Texas Synod merger, the Iowa Synod inherited the Brenham school (which continued several decades as an academy) and Texas Lutheran College at Seguin, Texas.

By 1910 Synod President F. B. Richter reported to the synod that Wartburg Theological Seminary had again become overcrowded. In 1913 at Oshkosh, Wisconsin, the Iowa Synod resolved to build a new seminary and to complete it in time for the four hundredth anniversary of Luther's posting of his Ninety-five Theses in 1517. Located on a new site a block north of the old Wartburg, most of the structure was built of limestone quarried on the seminary property a block southwest of the old seminary building.

William Weiblen wrote:

"Of all historic events in the life of Wartburg Seminary during the early years of the twentieth century the construction of the buildings which are still the pride of the seminary and the community stands out. Lloyd Svensby (former president of Luther Seminary in Saint Paul) said the first time he was on campus, 'It's nice to be on a campus that was designed to be a theological seminary....'

"The well-respected firm of Perkins and Fellows from Chicago was engaged....The first sketch showed a typical early 20th century red brick building with classrooms, offices and chapel on the ground floor with dormitories in the floors above. It is reported that Hermann Fritschel...said 'For a Lutheran Seminary by the name of Wartburg, you ought to be able to come up with a more appropriate plan than a red brick box.' It is also reported that then Perkins and Fellows dispatched one of their architects to Eisenach, Germany, to study the Wartburg Castle. Whether in fact it happened that way may be disputed, but there is no doubt that the architects made a thorough study of the Wartburg and its towers. Out of their efforts came the very efficient and aesthetically pleasing design with the dimensions of one of the several towers of the Eisenach Wartburg as the central and organizing focus.

"The contract was let and construction began in 1914. The cornerstone was laid in a festive synodical celebration on Luther's birthday, November 10, 1914. A quarry for native Galena limestone was opened on the campus, and during the next two years the beautiful new Wartburg grew stone by [carefully selected and formed] stone. Mrs. Hedwig Reu Salzmann recalls watching the process of one team of horses hauling the huge blocks of limestone up to the inner court-yard where the stone masons carefully shaped each piece of stone. It was, she said, a genuine work of art. The new Wartburg was ready for dedication September 13 and 14, 1916. The total cost was $228,768.00, including furnishings. There was even a central vacuuming system for the entire well-integrated unit. The space on which the new buildings were constructed was, like the original Emerson Estate, purchased by supportive people from the Dubuque community and presented to Wartburg as an on-going expressing of support....

"The synod-wide reformation quadricentennial ingathering for building this beautiful new facility not only raised sufficient funds to cover the cost, but also provided additional funds for construction at the colleges in Clinton and Waverly....It was a great day when the little synod, which in its infancy on several occasions was on the brink of total financial collapse, could hear President Max Fritschel announce on the day of dedication that all the bills had been paid.

"The student body which moved into the new buildings was composed of 50 young men, practically all of whom came from congregations of the synod, since the stream of candidates coming from Neuendettelsau had now come to an end. For them each day began with 'Quiet Half-hour' from 6:30 a.m. to 7:00 a.m., immediately followed by breakfast. After Matins at 7:30, classes (each 50 minutes beginning on the hour) started at 8:00 a.m. Usually students were busy

with classes all morning. The afternoons were reserved for study, recreation and necessary seminary chores. All students had to take their turn at lawn care, snow shoveling, etc." [139]

In 1924, led by Dr. M. Reu, the Wartburg League (youth of the Iowa Synod) raised the money to place in the seminary quadrangle a statue of Martin Luther copied after the original monument in Worms, Germany.

The progress of Wartburg Theological Seminary over the years can be noted from the size of its faculty. It began as a teachers seminary in Michigan in July 1852 with Georg M. Grossmann as teacher. In 1859 at Saint Sebald, the faculty for the seminary and Latin school consisted of Grossmann and the brothers Sigmund and Gottfried

Fritschel. In 1879 the seminary at Mendota was taught by the Fritschel brothers. Gottfried Fritschel died just as the seminary was about to return to Dubuque. There the faculty was Sigmund, Gottfried's son Hermann, and William Proehl. Hermann taught four years and was succeeded in 1893 by Sigmund's son Maximilian, popularly known as "Max."

Hermann Fritschel next served parishes and then turned to hospital administration in Milwaukee. For more than forty years he was director of the Passavant Institutions. Gottfried Fritschel's son Gottlob served as pastor and later as superintendent of the Lutheran Orphanage, now Bremwood, at Waverly. Gottfried's son Paul served Wartburg Publishing House all his career.

In 1899 the teachers were Sigmund Fritschel and his son Max, Dr. William Proehl, and Dr. Johann Michael Reu. Sigmund retired that year because of heart disease. He had taught forty-five years at the Wartburg.

Konrad Sigmund Fritschel died April 26, 1900, at the age of sixty-six. Weiblen wrote, "The love and respect in which he was held was attested by the fact that it was impossible to find a church large enough to hold the throng who came together from community, Synod, and the wider Lutheran Church to thank God for his life and ministry." [140]

Professor William Proehl succeeded Sigmund Fritschel as president in 1900. He served until his unexpected death in 1905. After an interim term in 1906 served by Maximilian Fritschel, the presidency was conferred on J. Michael Reu.

About 1900 the first American-trained Ph.D. W. J. Sadler was called to the faculty with the title "English Professor." The German language and culture were not being downplayed, but the Iowa Synod was entering more fully into the culture where it lived and worked.

In the early years, the only library available for the students was the personal libraries of Sigmund and Gottfried Fritschel. Weiblen: "The oral tradition from the Fritschel family is that Loehe himself helped in the original collection of most of the volumes consisting primarily of exegetical and doctrinal works from the classical period of Lutheranism in the 17th century. In their holdings the seminary today possesses a rare book collection of inexplicable value." [141]

In 1909 the Wartburg Seminary faculty members were Max and George Fritschel (son of Gottfried), J. M. Reu, and George Zeilinger. In

1929 the faculty was the same with the addition of Julius Bodensieck. By 1939 it had grown to six, by 1949 to nine, by 1959 to fourteen, and by 1969 to fifteen. In 1989 the faculty numbered twenty-five with a student body of 223.

In 1936 George Fritschel was forced to retire because of a paralyzing stroke. It was the first time in seventy-five years there were not two Fritschels on the active faculty.

Some Wartburg Seminary policy changes that had been under consideration in the 1920s were adopted after the Iowa Synod merged with Ohio and Buffalo. The standard requirement for admission to the seminary was now graduation from a four-year liberal arts college. Loehe's program for training emergency pastors (*Nothelfers*) with lesser qualifications was no longer needed. The dominant need now was for pastors with a scholarly theological education. This was the goal of the man who succeeded the Fritschels as Wartburg Seminary's outstanding president and teacher: Johann Michael Reu.

CHAPTER 27

THE ERA OF THE REV.
DR. JOHANN MICHAEL REU

A new phase in the life of Wartburg Seminary and of the Iowa Synod began with Johann Michael Reu's academic career at Dubuuque. John H. Becker wrote the essay "The Genius of Wartburg Seminary," "A genius is one who represents the ideals and trends of his age (or group) in the fullest measure. In this sense we call Johann Michael Reu THE GENIUS OF WARTBURG SEMINARY." [142]

Johann Michael Reu was born November 16, 1869, in the village of Diebach in Mittelfranken, Bavaria, five miles west of Nuremberg and twennty miles from Wilhelm Loehe's church in Neuendettelsau. It was the heart of the Frankish country, the source of Loehe's four colonies near Saginaw, Michigan. Michael was the tenth and last child of master mason and contractor Johann Friedrich Reu and Margarete Henkelmann. Michael's father died when he was age two. All his life he was addressed by his friends as "Michael" or "Mike."

Like Samuel's mother Hannah, Reu's mother prayed her youngest son into the ministry. (Once she left the house at about 2:00 A.M. to walk seven or eight hours to Neuendettelsau to hear Wilhelm Loehe preach. She never forgot that sermon as long as she lived.) Her pastor, Pfarrer Bopp, recognized the genius in her son. He gave young Michael private instruction in Latin and Greek and perhaps Hebrew. At his suggestion, Michael was sent to the village school and then to the Latin school at nearby Oettingen.

There was no money for the German academy and university. So Bopp suggested that Margarete's son attend Loehe's Mission Institute, where Michael could train to serve God in America. Michael felt certain that God had called him to serve, if not in Germany, then in America.

Margarete was then age sixty. The years spent raising ten children had taken their toll. But she went to Rothenberg to take a position with distant relatives as their housekeeper. Her wages helped Michael pursue his studies when in 1886 at age seventeen he entered Loehe's seminary in Neuendettelsau.

Michael Reu was not quite twenty when he was ordained in 1889. He was called to Mendota, Illinois, as assistant to Pastor F. B. Richter, a future president of the Iowa Synod. A year later Reu accepted a call to Immanuel Congregation in Rock Falls, Illinois, where he pastored nine years until his call to Wartburg Seminary.

On his twenty-third birthday, Pastor Reu married Marie Wilhelmine Schmitthenner (who regularly used the name Wilhelmine), guest of a Pastor Schmitthenner in New York. They had met when Reu stopped at the pastor's home (perhaps at Loehe's suggestion) on his way from Neuendettelsau to Mendota. Wilhelmine was the granddaughter of the educator of the German emperor Frederick III. She could trace her family through a line of scholars and pastors back to 1600.

Reu's dream was to become a teacher of theology. When the aging Sigmund Fritschel, president of the seminary, was felled by his last illness and had to give up his classes, Michael Reu was chosen to fill the vacant chair. He moved to Dubuque in 1899.

Reu was given the highest responsibility in the school, the classes in systematic theology. This meant intensive study preparing for every class until late at night. The Reus moved into Sigmund Fritschel's house. It was near the seminary, a brick building with no bathroom. Three children had been born at Rock Falls and the fourth was born in this house at Dubuque. The light in Reu's study was seen by students at 5:00 A.M., and it was still burning when the last student went to bed. Over the years, in addition to dogmatics, he taught homiletics, catechetics, and exegesis.

In 1901 and 1903 he sent his first two manuscripts to Germany for publication, commentaries on the Old Testament lesson series of Thomasius. In 1904, partly at Reu's expense, the first volume of his nine-volume *Sources of Christian Education in Germany* appeared in Germany. It was a history of the Lutheran catechisms published there between 1530 and 1600.

That same year Reu took over as editor of *Kirchliche Zeitschrift*, the theological journal that had been co-edited by the Fritschel brothers since it began in 1875. Reu edited this journal until his death thirty-nine years later. He filled its columns with challenging and instructive material eagerly read by pastors not only of Iowa but of other synods.

For many it was the only theological nourishment they had. Dr. Julius Bodensieck reported that Reu reviewed for this journal 3,631 books, almost two a week or a hundred a year. Pastors who were too poor to buy books kept in touch with current publications through Reu's reviews.

A. Pilger wrote of Reu in the *Zeitschrift's* memorial issue: "Usually his copy [for the *Zeitschrift*] was sent in at the last moment, printers and presses waiting impatiently. How could it be otherwise? He was so overburdened with work, and his contributors often did not keep their promise, so that in the last hour he had to write something himself or at least find something printable, perhaps his last sermon, or a conference paper, or a suitable article in a foreign magazine." [143]

In the *Zeitschrift* Reu supplied sermon outlines for the coming Sundays. Once he was asked whether these homiletical outlines could be dropped. He said, "Then we would lose half of our subscribers." He foresaw that when he died, the *Zeitschrift* would also expire. At the end, its subscription list had dwindled to about 350.

Pastors wrote to Reu asking for help with a paper they had to prepare for a conference. He sent long letters in reply and often packages of works from his or the seminary's library.

Reu had a photographic memory. A legend reports that if a student needed to find the source for a quotation, Reu could say, "Go to my study. On the third shelf on the north side of the room, four volumes from the right, you'll find the book. Look on page 308, the second sentence of the third paragraph." One of his personal satisfactions was his inerrant memory of train schedules.

In 1906 the second volume of his *Sources* appeared, covering both catechisms and Bible histories and the whole scope of the church's instruction that were published in Germany between 1530 and 1600. For this 800-page volume, Reu consulted forty-two libraries. Twelve hundred catechisms were traced, discovered, and copied. He listed one hundred editions of the most widely known biblical history of that period. This German-American professor achieved from a distance of four thousand miles what no German scholar in that field with these resources at their very door had thought of attempting.

In America there were only two libraries where Reu was able to find material for his *Sources*, those of Wartburg and Concordia seminaries. He made eight trips to Germany to explore libraries and archives for yellowed manuscripts and books.

Proof of Reu's world recognition as a theological scholar came in 1914 when the theological faculty of the University of Leipzig, one of the oldest and most famous universities in Europe, elected Reu for its vacant chair of practical theology. But because in 1902 Reu had become an American citizen, the German state refused to approve Reu's appointment to that chair.

In 1910 the University of Erlangen, twenty miles from Reu's birthplace, recognized his labors as a research scholar by granting him its highest academic honor, the degree of *Doctor Theologiae*. This dignity could be conferred only by unanimous vote of the theological faculty of a university. Reu was the only German-American who had ever been so honored.

Critics complained that Reu remained "forever German," forgetting that Reu became a U.S. citizen during his thirteenth year in America.

Reu was now recognized as the greatest scholar that the Lutheran church in America had produced. He was sometimes described as a leader. But he was not. He was a teacher and a scholar. He was continuously asked to speak—at mission festivals, anniversaries, dedications, funerals, conferences—and out of his goodness, if it was possible, he went. He could not say "no." This forced him to spend many nights with little or no sleep, since it was his rigid rule never to miss a class.

Dr. Julius Bodensieck described how Reu's textbooks and theological articles developed out of similar requests at the seminary. Reu would be assigned to teach a certain subject. Soon he wrote a syllabus for the course of study. The next year he wrote a detailed script. After another revision, it became a book ready for the printer.

That was the origin of one of his finest works, *Catechetics or Theory and Practice of Religous Instruction*. It was written at first in German in 1915. This edition had a number of printings as it was used in three Lutheran seminaries, including that of the Wisconsin Synod. The English version in 1918 included a lecture, "The Significance of Luther's Small Catechism," that Reu delivered at the Second Lutheran World Convention at Copenhagen that met in 1929 to observe the four hundredth anniversary of Luther's Small Catechism. Countless books appeared in Germany that anniversary year, but Reu's book was recognized for its excellence in sixty favorable reviews.

As important as Reu's *Catechetics* was as a seminary textbook for training pastors to become teachers, Reu's *Homiletics* was just as important for training future preachers. The *Homiletics* text was published in 1922, subtitled, *A Manual of the Theory and Practice of Preaching*. In it Reu described the sermon as an organic part of the service of the worshiping congregation and as an oration. Ninety pages were dedicated to the sermon's content. One hundred seventy pages told the student how to draw the subject matter from the Bible text, how to organize it into a speech, and how to preach it.

Shortly before the second Lutheran World Convention, Kaiser Press in Munich published Reu's *D. Martin Luther's Kleiner Katechismus, Seine Entstehung, Seine Verbreitung und Seine Bedeutung* [Dr. Martin Luther's Small Catechism. Its Origin, Its Distribution and its Use]. In May 1929, Wartburg Publishing House produced an English edition. Reu inscribed the book "To Wilhelmine Schmitthenner-Reu, life companion for thirty-seven years, whose knowledge of Swedish enabled me to make use of the Scandinavian literature."

Dr. Reu

Reu's had genuine love and respect for his helpmeet. From the beginning she easily adapted to new surroundings. At Rock Falls Wilhelmine taught French in the local high school to help Reu's small salary stretch. She furthered his every enterprise. At home she made Michael the axis around which the household revolved, noiselessly, without a hitch. Nothing was given priority over him and his work. His children loved and revered him, knowing how precious was the time he took from his labors on a Saturday to stroll with them by the picturesque scenery along the Fremont Avenue ridge, his Germanically trained vocal organs vainly trying to name Dutchman's breeches, trillium, spring beauty, and wild geranium as they moved among the wild flowers.

From 1917 to 1930, Reu served on the Executive Board of the Iowa Synod. From 1910 to 1930 he was chairman of its Board of

Education and chairman of the Board of Sunday Schools and Young People's Societies.

In 1930 Reu observed the our hundredth anniversary of the Augsburg Confession with his book *The Augsburg Confession: A Collection of Sources with an Historical Introduction*, published by Wartburg Publishing House. That was the year the Iowa Synod merged into the American Lutheran Church. The book was the final volume off the press that had published Reu's works for nearly thirty years.

In his later years, Reu served on the Commission on Lutheran Unity and attended its meeting on September 16, 1943, twenty-eight days before he died. He served on the Intersynodical Committee on the Translation of Luther's Small Catechism. He was a delegate to all three meetings of the Lutheran World Convention—at Eisenach in 1943, at Copenhagen in 1929, and he chaired its Committee on Resolutions in 1935.

In 1930 Reu was sixty-one years old. He still worked from early morning until late at night. No grey showed in his dark curly hair. Students referred to him as "Mike," not in disrespect but with affection. Everyone who knew Reu knew of his great heart. He lent money to students in need. He contributed to almost every worthy cause.

Reu's relief efforts for European sufferers after the first World War raised nearly $1 million from Iowa Synod congregations, a huge sum in those days. In 1919 he urged the Executive Board of the Iowa Synod to take a part in meeting the hunger distress in defeated Germany. A committee of Reu, Dr. Herman L. Fritschel, and Pastor August Engelbrecht was appointed with Reu in charge. Reu and Fritschel had large circles of friends in Germany who handled the distribution of the cash, food, and clothing collected by the Iowa Synod. The committee even found a way to bring relief to Lutheran colonies in southern Russia, in the Volga district, and the Ukraine. Iowa Synod congregations in the Dakotas where German-Russian immigrants had settled rose up as one person to send relief. They formed their own relief organization to carry on this work together with the Iowa Synod committee. The European relief work lasted from 1920 to 1926.

This relief work of the Iowa Synod was the most extensive and successful charity service ever undertaken by that body. At that time it stood out as unique among the synods of America. Reu was its resolute and tireless leader.

In July, August, and September 1922, Reu was sent by the synod to Germany to give material support and to strengthen confessional Lutheran Free Churches against the inroads of the state church. The free churches were organized independent of the state much like the synods in America: Neuendettelsau in Bavaria, the Breslau Synod in Prussia, free churches in Hessen, Hannover, and Hamburg. Some wanted help to form a confessional seminary in affiliation with the Iowa Synod. In Hamburg a college for boys was desired. Pastors in Eisenach asked to become a district of the Iowa Synod.

During this postwar stress the Lutheran foreign mission institutes of Germany needed help to save their work: Leipzig for East Africa; the Neuendettelsau and Rhenish missions for New Guinea. When Neuendettelsau came into desperate financial straits, the Iowa Synod readily gave to supply the need. The victorious Allies cut the German empire off from its colonies in Africa, Brazil, and New Guinea. The Iowa Synod and the National Lutheran Council negotiated with Great Britain concerning the German Lutheran missions in East Africa and sent Pastor A. C. Zeilinger of Prairie du Sac, Wisconsin, to hold the field until it would be returned to the German Lutherans or transferred to other Lutheran bodies.

When the New Guinea field was opened by the Neuendettelsau Missionary Society, it asked Senior-Missionary John Flierl to transfer from Australia. He landed at Finschhafen on July 12, 1886. The Iowa Synod's 1928 statistics reported fifteen mission stations with 18,689 baptized Christians. There were twenty-eight ordained missionaries and twenty lay missionaries working at this former Neuendettelsau mission.

The Rhenish Society chose the Madang District of New Guinea as its field in 1887. After the 1930 merger of the Iowa, Ohio, and Buffalo Synods, the Rhenish Society assigned its Madang field to the newly-formed American Lutheran Church. Working on that field were twelve ordained and eight lay missionaries with 28,605 baptized natives. By then twenty-three sons and daughters of the former Iowa Synod were serving on the mission fields of New Guinea.

The Luther Academy

In 1936 Reu proposed to the Board of Regents that the seminary establish a two-week summer Luther Academy patterned after the *Luther Akademie* at Sondershausen in Germany. Reu wanted a forum at Wartburg Seminary where distinguished theologians and notable intellects from other disciplines could hear one another for breadth of perspective and growth in understanding. Another purpose of the academy was for members of the various Lutheran bodies in America to meet, to be seen, and to be heard, for the lessening of prejudices and the development of friendly relations.

Dr. William Streng, who led the Luther Academy program some years after Reu's death, said, "According to some experts, it may well be said that the American Lutheran Church was spared some of the doctrinal controversies of other church bodies because so many pastors had been alerted to new dimensions in theology through the Luther Academy."

The academy became what was probably the first continuing education program for pastors among Protestant churches in this country. Today this program is carried on by the Luther Academy of the Rockies.

The Iowa Synod and its seminary were noted for their conciliatory spirit. Reu lived that spirit. He taught his students: "No polemics in the pulpit." He warned against poisoning the minds of children by bringing polemics into catechism classes. He denounced polemics directed against other Lutheran synods. He never tired of attending intersynodical meetings in the hope that he might help bring about better understanding.

Reu was particularly anxious to win leaders of the Missouri Synod, which had such a large place in his heart. He said, "*Da ist Bein von unserm Bein und Fleisch von unserm Fleisch* [There is bone of our bone and flesh of our flesh]." He wanted understanding, not at any price, but based on God's Word without additions or detractions. At Reu's death, A. Pilger wrote in the *Kirchliche Zeitschrift's*, "In Dr. Reu the Missouri Synod lost its best though not its only friend in the American Lutheran Church." [144]

John H. Becker wrote of him, "In all humility, which was the finest characteristic of his personality, but with a firm mind, he sought a better understanding, that the church he loved might grow, and the Lord he served might be glorified. Thus lived and worked the Genius of Wartburg Seminary." [145]

Reu was acting president of the seminary from 1938 to 1940. He served as professor, writer, and churchman at Wartburg Theological Seminary forty-four years. He helped prepare six hundred pastors for their ministries.

CHAPTER 28

LIFE IN THE SAINT SEBALD CONGREGATION

The pilgrim people of the Saint Sebald colony believed that teaching belongs with preaching. In 1853 they brought Loehe's parish teachers seminary from Michigan to Dubuque where it became a seminary for training pastors. In 1854, the seminary's new owner, the Iowa Synod, was organized at the Saint Sebald parsonage located in a clearing in the church's eighty-acre forest. In 1857 the Iowa Synod moved the seminary from Dubuque to a farm a mile west of the St. Sebald church.

In that forest clearing, Saint Sebald conducted an elementary school for parish children from farm homes on the nearby prairie or scattered in forest clearings in the south quarter of Clayton County. Pastor Johannes Deindoerfer and his successors taught children the disciplines of the public school in a setting of Christian faith and worship founded on Luther's Small Catechism and biblical history. The Saint Sebald pastors taught mornings and afternoons five days a week in addition to their pastoral duties.

The church's eighty-acre forest had been purchased in keeping with Loehe's original plan, that each colony should buy for its church a tract of land to serve as a *Pfarrgut* (pastor's good) to help support the pastor. For the first one hundred years, the Saint Sebald forest served only to supply firewood for the heaters and stoves of the parsonage, the school, and the church. Later, as lumber prices soared, the parish was able to provide considerable sums of money from the sale of oak and walnut logs.

In 1857, when the seminary arrived in the colony, Saint Sebald became the seminary church. The seminary students did their practice teaching serving as catechists at the Saint Sebald school under the supervision of the Saint Sebald pastors.

With seminary President Georg Grossmann as their pastor and with the seminary staff and students seated among them on Sundays following Loehe's *Agenda,* the liturgical life of the Saint Sebald congregation was enlivened and enriched. During Deindoerfer's pastorate, Saint Sebald had celebrated the Eucharist seven to nine times a year. In 1862 Grossmann recorded twenty-two Communion services with 641 people partaking. Two winter Sundays with only seven and five at the altar no doubt reflected either blizzard conditions or epidemic sickness. The high point that year was *Gruendonnerstag,* Green (or Maundy) Thursday, with forty-six people communing. Fifty-one children were born to the colony in the seven years since the congregation started. The log parsonage-church must have been packed on such occasions. As the parish grew, additions were made to the building.

Under the pastorates of Deindoerfer, Grossmann, and their successors through 1918, all who wished to commune were required to come to the parsonage for private confession on the Saturdays preceding the Eucharist. All communions were registered in the church records. Grossmann listed himself in the Communion records as G.G. and his wife Nanny as N.G. Sigmund and George Fritschel were recorded as Professor S. F and G. F. All others were listed by their last names, preceded by an initial if more than one family bore that name. Wives were listed under their husbands' names as, for instance, "Frau Schmidt." The personal names of married women were not given.

Not only children of Saint Sebald studied at the parish school. Students from surrounding areas that did not have a school enrolled and boarded with families of the Saint Sebald congregation. The products of this school were faithful Christians who read and prayed daily in family devotions. They helped organize other churches in the area, including congregations in Strawberry Point, Arlington, Aurora, Clayton Center, Littleport, Elkport, West Union, and Eldorado.

Deindoerfer, who had served as the colony pastor in Michigan, continued as Saint Sebald's first pastor from 1853 to 1856, when he accepted a call to Madison, Wisconsin. While at Saint Sebald, he also began work in West Union and Eldorado. Later he worked in Ohio as a pastor and as president of the Eastern District of the Iowa Synod. From 1878 to 1904, he edited the synod's *Kirchenblatt* (church paper). From 1893 to 1904 he succeeded Grossmann as president of the Iowa Synod. He died May 14, 1907, at the age of seventy-eight.

When Deindoerfer left Saint Sebald, he was replaced by Daniel Dietz, sent by Loehe from Neuendettelsau. A year later, in 1857,

Grossmann arrived with the seminary from Dubuque. Dietz then took Grossmann's place as pastor of Saint John in Dubuque. Grossmann became Saint Sebald's pastor along with his duties as seminary president. He served the congregation as pastor until 1872. In 1874 he left with the seminary when it moved to Mendota.

After the seminary facility at Saint Sebald was built, with both Fritschel brothers on the faculty, Grossmann gradually withdrew from teaching at the seminary to focus on the Saint Sebald congregation. But because he also served as president of the rapidly growing Iowa Synod, he had more work than he could do well. This created dissatisfaction in the parish, and Saint Sebald asked the Iowa Synod to replace Grossmann as its president. The synod refused to do this, but appropriated funds to hire a parish school teacher for Saint Sebald.

This assistance arrived in 1859 when Wilhelm Loehe sent four deaconesses to help the young Iowa Synod. One served Saint John in Dubuque, another served as matron of the seminary at Saint Sebald, a third worked in Des Moines, and the fourth was stationed in the Saint Sebald congregation. [144] Probably because they were "merely women," none of their names are recorded in the history of the Iowa Synod or in Saint Sebald histories.

The congregation called Pastor Jakob Baumbach as Grossmann's pastoral assistant in 1868. Born at Hessen-Darmstadt, Germany, and sent by Loehe, Baumbach (January 6, 1817–July 27, 1879) had just arrived with his wife Elisa (March 11, 1817–January 16, 1872). He served Saint Sebald with Grossmann from 1868 to 1872. Then he left to develop the congregations in West Union and Eldorado. He died at Eldorado at age sixty-two. Both he and Elisa are buried at Saint Sebald.

In 1872, J.A. List became Saint Sebald's pastor and served until 1875. During that time he organized a pattern of thorough church records that his successors followed. Records had been poorly kept after Deindoerfer left in 1856. No confirmations were recorded from 1861 to 1871.

Until 1867, the Saint Sebald congregation worshiped in the parsonage-church built by Amman and Deindoerfer. It stood just east of the present parsonage, and the church bell hung from a black oak tree. During the Civil War the bell cracked. It was sent east to be repaired but it was never returned.

The present church building was erected in 1867. The congregation changed its plans for its new church from stone construction to frame, back to stone, and finally built a frame structure costing $3,400. It had no steeple, no bell, and no basement. The walls were unpainted plaster. The window panes were clear glass. The benches were handmade and uncomfortable. The altar was made from a large dry-goods box.

Wilhelm Loehe inscribed a pulpit Bible and sent it to Saint Sebald for use in its new church. Today this Bible is preserved in the archives of the Evangelical Lutheran Church in America at Wartburg Theological Seminary in Dubuque.

The Saint Sebald Cemetery

The first few burials were made in a vale just south of the present church. After a few years, a cemetery was platted at its present location and those bodies were moved to it. Johannes and Anna Weege Jr. had lost four children in the 1850s. It is probable that one or more of them were first buried in the valley. When their bodies were moved into the cemetery, the reburials were done with their feet toward the north, and the rest of the Weege family were laid to rest with the same wrong orientation, the only family in the cemetery whose bodies were placed this way.

The first section of the cemetery (the south half) was partially bounded on the north by a ravine that deepened as it ran eastward into the forest. As available lots in the south half were depleted, lots were taken north of the ravine, beginning next to the church and then row by row toward the east.

For the first ninety years, excess earth from the graves after burials was formed into mounds on which flowers were planted. Because grave vaults were not provided to enclose the casket, it took but a few years for a wooden casket to decay and collapse under the weight of the earth above it. Thus the grave mounds eventually disappeared.

The grave mounds made cemetery mowing and weeding difficult and tedious. In the 1940s, vaults came into use. Existing grave mounds were scraped away and this earth was used to fill the ravine that ran through the cemetery.

Pastor G. H. Fuehr made an exceptional notation concerning the burial of Henry Rogees who died on Christmas 1906: "Day laborer in St. Sebald area. *Was not a member.* (Emphasis added.) There was no funeral or burial service. Was buried in northeast corner outside cemetery fence." This attempt to exclude an unbeliever was probably made in vain. In recent years Rogees's grave was lost and forgotten. When the cemetery expanded eastward, it may have inadvertently enclosed this grave.

Cemetery exclusions included members of the Order of Freemasons. Whether this rule would still be enforced in today's mellower society has not been tested. To date the rule appears never to have been transgressed.

The Devastations of Infectious Diseases

The practice of vaccinating children against measles and other diseases was still seventy-five years in the future. Consequently, there was great risk of children's deaths from epidemics.

Scarlet fever struck during many winters. In 1876 the epidemic was most severe. Twenty-three children were baptized in the colony that winter and fifteen children were buried. Scarlet fever took three children of Christoph and Henrietta Kutschat on January 7, 8, and 9 and three children of John Adam and Maria Dorothea Huebsch on February 28, March 5, and March 7. Friederich and Katherina Allenstein lost one the last day of 1875 and one January 15, 1876.

Diphtheria was a killer in the fall of 1891. The August Eichlers lost two children on October 2 and 10, the Friederich Baumgaertners lost one October 13, the Conrad Andreaes lost one October 18, and the Karl Baumgaertners lost two children on December 18 and 19.

Tuberculosis took the lives of many adults. Lacking proper hygiene, quarantine, or antibiotics, when one member of a family was attacked by tuberculosis, others were often infected as well. Four members of the John Steltzenmueller family between the ages of nineteen and forty-nine died of "t.b." in the years from 1893 to 1899. The Adam Neuenkirks lost a fifteen-year-old in 1897 and a 23-year-old in 1902. The Rudolf Hermanns lost a twenty-nine-year-old in 1904 and one aged 32 in 1911.

Five deaths are listed under typhoid fever in the late 1900s, another disease preventable with proper hygiene. Wells were often shallow and easily contaminated by animal wastes that accumulated in nearby manure piles.

Families often included ten to fifteen children. Diseases spread within the family in part because of crowded conditions and in part because good hygiene was not part of the culture. A common drinking cup hung by the pump at the well and a water pail with a common drinking dipper stood by the sink in the kitchen. Sharing a drinking cup was so American that the advice in school hygiene textbooks was not that each person have his or her own cup but that one should place both lips inside the common cup when drinking so as not to have the rim of the cup between one's lips.

Prenatal care and midwifery was such that many mothers died during childbirth and many children were stillborn. The cemetery records note nineteen children who were stillborn. It is probable that other stillborn children were buried without record being made of their deaths. Six women are recorded as having died during childbirth.

Funeral and Mourning Practices

Death visited the colony frequently, not only because the birth process imperiled both mother and child, but because medicines were primitive. Pastor Georg Heinrich Fuehr, who served Saint Sebald forty-three years, was a trained homeopathic physician. But vaccines and antibiotics were nearly a century away. Most winters there were many homes where a black bow or wreath on the door announced that the family was in mourning.

Nurtured in the resurrection faith and surrounded by Christians who shared their grief, the survivors normally bore their sorrow with quiet strength. Death had assaulted their family, but Christ had taken away its sting with his resurrection. When death came, it was not necessary to look for a Bible and to search for what God might say. Most families gathered around the table for morning and evening devotions as naturally as they assembled for bodily food. When death came, one passage was familiar to their minds and hearts: "The Lord gave, and the Lord has taken away; blessed be the name of the Lord" (Job 1:21b).

For many years, morticians and embalmers were not involved in the funeral preparations. Family and friends did what was required. Women washed and clothed the body of the deceased. A family member or a friend prepared a pine coffin, often a small box made to nestle a child.

Prior to the funeral, the body of the deceased was never left alone. One or more friends or relatives sat at "wake" with the corpse through the night or nights between death and the funeral. Food was supplied by friends or relatives for the watchers and for the grieving family.

On the day of the funeral, the pastor and congregation assembled at the home of the bereaved for a brief preparation consisting of Scripture, meditation, and prayer. A hymn was sometimes sung from memory.

A funeral cortege then assembled led by the pastor with his horse and buggy. The coffin was borne on a wagon followed by other wagons, horse-drawn buggies, and surreys. In winter snows, the coffin was carried to the church on a bobsled followed by more sleds and sleighs. Then a full service of worship (*Gottes-dienst*) was conducted by the pastor with hymns led by Cantor Johannes Weege.

The grave had been dug by friends from the congregation (as is still done at Saint Sebald today). There was no vault and no tent. After the worship service, pall bearers led by the pastor carried the coffin at the head of a procession from the church to the grave. They placed the coffin on boards laid across the open grave.

At the close of the burial rite, bearers suspended the coffin on ropes or leather straps slung under it. The boards across the grave were removed, and the coffin was lowered into the earth as a hymn was sung from memory. Later when English had come into use, the hymn often sung at the grave was, "O Where Is the Home of the Soul to Be Found?"

Many took a turn at dropping a symbolic shovelful of earth onto the coffin. All stayed by the grave to sing or watch as men with hand shovels finished filling the grave.

Tragedies That Shook the Colony

1. On July 21, 1898, two Saint Sebald families lost husbands and fathers in a tragic accident that is still retold from generation to generation in the Volga area. James Crane of Volga wrote in his diary, "George Schuchmann and John Schuchmann killed tonight. Their engine went through the bridge at Volga City with them."

The Schuchmann brothers, Georg Phillipp Gottlob, thirty-seven, and Johannes Carl Gottlieb George, thirty-one, came into Volga City that evening with a steam engine, a water tank, and a thresher they had just purchased from Stemmer and Dittmer of Elkader. They left Elkader about 1:30 P.M. with their new outfit and reached the covered bridge on the Volga River at Volga at about 7:30 P.M.

At a coroner's inquest after the accident, George Tinkham, a witness, gave this testimony:

"I was coming toward the bridge about 7:30 P.M. that evening and met George Schuchmann standing near his traction engine about three hundred feet from the bridge. I shook hands with him and said, 'You are not going to cross that bridge with your engine? I would advise you not to do so as I do not believe it to be safe.' George said, 'I believe I will try it.' John Schuchmann, a brother of George, was on the bridge inspecting it before this, and when he returned he said he did not believe it to be safe.

"George went and looked at the bridge. [According to tradition, after he returned, he said, 'In the name of God we'll go.'] The separator was detached and John and George Schuchmann got on the engine and started on the bridge. They went about twenty-five feet without planks, then stopped. And then they started to run the engine across the bridge by hand, turning the fly wheel. When they started to run it by hand, George asked me to get on and steer it for them. I got on and we moved the engine about two spans length when George told me to get off and they would turn the steam on.

"George and John got on the engine and ran it until the front end of the engine was close to the end of the bridge. I was standing about the middle of the bridge when the rear end of the engine went through, tipping over backwards, taking the planks and timbers with it, and burying George and John under the rear end.

"They had planks on their water tank for use in crossing bridges, but did not use them at all."

Another brother Carl Albert Friedrich (known as Fred) Schuchmann, who had come along as water hauler, was walking alongside the engine as it broke through the bridge. He jumped, grabbed hold of a rod on the side of the bridge's cover, and saved his life.

Georg Phillipp Gottlob's's death bereaved his wife Magdalena (nee Eder) and their six children. Johannes left behind his wife Elizabeth (nee Wuest) and three children. Both families were left with practically no money or property. Both brothers had been members of the Order of Modern Woodmen, carrying life insurance policies of three thousand dollars and two thousand dollars. But shortly before they died, Pastor G. H. Fuehr, faithfully following the practice of the Iowa

Synod, had counseled them to give up their membership in this non-Christian lodge. Their families were left dependent on relatives and friends in the colony.

2. Georg Michael Weger was born November 21, 1832, in Schlauersbach, Bavaria. In April 1866, on the day he was naturalized as a U.S. citizen, he received license to marry Kunigunda Roth (born April 11, 1839, at Petersaurach, Bavaria). They waited many years for a child. After fourteen years they were blessed with Maria Kunigunda on April 9, 1880. But the mother Kunigunda died on the day of the birth.

On March 15, 1881, Michael married Carolina Nee Griesinger Alllenstein, who had lost her husband to tuberculosis and alcoholism. Two children had been born to that union.

On November 15, 1883, Michael Weger was killed. The *Brushcreek* (today's Arlington) *News* printed the following story:

"KILLED BY A RUN AWAY last Thursday afternoon, Michael Weger, a respectable German whose home was about five miles east of here. In company with his step-daughter Mary Allenstein, [Michael] was returning home from Strawberry Point. They were near the railroad crossing, at the Gilchrist place, when the afternoon freight train came up behind them and frightened the horses so that they became unmanageable and broke into a run. The team had run about 15 rods when the tongue dropped down and caught in the ground, raising the wagon up, throwing the occupants quite a distance, the man's head striking on the frozen ground, breaking his skull and killing him instantly. The girl had a collar bone broken, and was otherwise so badly injured that it is feared she will not recover.

"A. O. Kingsley [Strawberry Point industrialist] was near when the accident happened and was instantly at their side. Finding the man dead, he first procured assistance and removed the girl to Charles Little's. He then had the unfortunate body of the man removed to his home."

Michael's daughter Maria did not die.

Michael Weger's nephew George Weger came to work the bereaved family's farm. Though he was thirteen years younger than the twice widowed Caroline, George married her fourteen months after the accident. By this union, George gained a farm and six daughters—four by Caroline's first marriage and two by her second. George and Caroline were further blessed with a son and a daughter.

Rituals Celebrated in Homes

Normally, children were baptized two or three weeks after birth. In winter, rather than expose a new-born to severe weather and other people's germs, the pastor was often asked to drive to the child's home in his "cutter" (a one-horse sleigh) for the baptism. This practice continued even in the 1920s, because automobiles were usually so helpless in winter temperatures and on winter roads that many farmers mounted their cars' axles on blocks during winter to relieve pressure on delicate tires.

Marriage rites were usually conducted at the bride's home or at the future home of the bride and groom. Church parlors or reception halls did not exist. Wedding celebrations often included a barn dance accompanied by a lone fiddler. Some guests came from distances of twenty miles or more by horse-drawn vehicles and stayed the night. Even Saint Sebald colonists who had cows at home waiting to be milked stayed into the early morning hours, dancing and consuming quantities of beer and wine.

Of daily importance was the rite of family devotions, usually conducted at the breakfast table and at bed time. John Frederick Starck's *Daily Hand-book In Good and Evil Days* in the standard German text of 1776 was in popular use. A product of German pietism with a scope less than catholic, it contained meditations for each day of the week and prayers for morning and evening devotions. It was translated into English by Joseph Stump and published by the Burlington, Iowa, Germany Literary Board in 1904.

There was no common practice as to which parent served as priest or priestess in the home. In the writer's home his father, a great-grandson of Karl Amman, conducted devotions until he left for assisted care at age 79. When the writer reached age four, his father put aside German devotions and chose an English Bible and English prayer books for morning and evening worship. When the writer and his bride returned from their honeymoon, the bride's mother sat them down in her kitchen and read for them a German prayer that lasted all of five minutes. The roots of the faith that sustained the colony were nourished above all in its homes.

The Saint Sebald Schools

During the colony's early years, the parochial school and the confirmation classes were taught in the parsonage-church. In 1879 a one-room school was built to house these classes. All classes were conducted in German. The school was enlarged in 1903 with the addition of a kitchenette and wood-storage space. The dimensions of the entire building were about 32 x 26 feet.

The enlarged school building had an entry hall at the south. To the left of the hall was the kitchenette. To the right, open to the hall, was the wood storage area. Wood was needed for the kitchen stove and for the unjacketed pot-bellied heater that stood left of center in the school area. A long smoke pipe ran along the ceiling to a chimney opposite the door.

The first desks were a sloping wall ledge that served for writing and as an arm rest. The pupils sat on homemade benches. Later, factory-manufactured desks with seats for the pupils to face forward were installed. They were thirty-six inches wide, designed to accommodate two pupils each, some of whom were young adults. The desks were arranged in two rows the length of the room, with a center aisle and two side aisles.

Chalkboards and maps were at the north end with storage cabinets in the corners. The pastor sat front and center on a round-backed chair at a small table desk.

The county erected a public school, known to colonists as "the English school," 150 yards southeast of the parsonage on land deeded by the church as a gift to the township January 7, 1862. The deed was signed by Charles (Karl) G. Amman and G. M. Eder, church trustees. This public school was completely surrounded by forest. Its enrollment consisted almost entirely of colony children who learned their first English in its classes. Colonists including the writer's mother, Helena Baumgaertner, whose farm home adjoined the church parcel on the south, attended the German parish school and the English public school in alternate years.

The German parish school closed in 1918 when its teacher, Pastor Georg Heinrich Fuehr, retired from the parish. The school building continued to be used for Sunday school. Outside the public school hours, it served a German school with classes in reading German print, in writing the now obsolete German script and conversational German, and the confirmation classes. The German school and confirmation classes were conducted by the pastor on Saturdays and Sundays during the school year and on weekdays during the summer. The school building also served as the fellowship hall for congregational potluck dinners.

When the *Frauenverein* (Ladies Fellowship) was organized (see below), the ladies often conducted their meetings at the school. At about the same time, the Luther League youth group came into being and met there on Sunday evenings.

The Publishing Business

Not only were the roots of the Iowa Synod's Wartburg College and Wartburg Theological Seminary at Saint Sebald, so were those of its Wartburg Publishing House. In 1873 the Iowa Synod moved a small book store to Saint Sebald. The store had been started two years earlier in Iowa City by a Pastor Hoerlein as a private venture that he turned over to the synod just before his death. Now Pastor Johannes A. List continued the business while serving as pastor at Saint Sebald. In 1875 when List was called to Mendota, Illinois, he took the synod book store with him.

About 1886 the book store and a publishing business were combined in Waverly as "Wartburg Publishing House." Paulus List, son of Pastor J. A. List, became its manager. In the early 1900s, Paulus List moved the firm to Chicago. Wartburg Publishing House printed the Iowa Synod version of the General Council's *Kirchenbuch* (Church Book) at Chicago in 1915. It published many other books, among which were the *Wartburg Liederbuch* (Songbook) for Sunday schools by Pastor C.A. Harrer, the *Wartburg Hymnal*, Johann Michael Reu's seminary texts (*Homiletics et al.*), parish school texts, and teachers' helps such as *Biblische Geschichte fuer Schule und Haus* (and its English Version *Biblical History for School and Home*) and *How I Tell*. It also published such periodicals as the *Kirchliche Zeitschrift* (Church Magazine), *Das Kirchenblatt* (The Church Paper), *The Lutheran Herald*, *Das Judenblatt* (*The Youth Paper*), *Die Missions Stunde* (The Missions Hour), *The Missionary*, and an almanac in both English and German.

As a result of the merger of the Iowa, Ohio, and Buffalo Synods in 1930, the Wartburg Publishing House eventually combined with Ohio's "Lutheran Book Concern" in Columbus. But books came from the press bearing the Wartburg Publishing House trademark as late as 1943. By 1947 the new combination was called the Wartburg Press.

The Kleinleins and the Kleinlein Hollow

Five years after the colony was founded, Johann Peter Kleinlein (who had financed the relocation of the seminary to Saint Sebald; see chapter 16) added a vital center of supplies for the colony by building a flour mill, a cheese factory and a brewery in what came to be known as "Kleinlein's Hollow," a mile east of the Saint Sebald church.

Peter, born September 12, 1827, and Johannes Leonhard Kleinlein, born January 11, 1839, at Grossreuth, near Nuremberg, Bavaria, were the sons of Johann Leonhard and Barbara Kleinlein. Their mother Barbara was born June 6, 1806, at Hefen near Fuerth in Bavaria.

On April 10, 1854, at Neuendettelsau, Bavaria, where he probably consulted with Pastor Wilhelm Loehe, Peter Kleinlein, his mother, and his brother Johannes joined a group of migrants that included Sigmund Fritschel, George Prottengeier, Michael Schueller, and Michael Steltzenmueller (see chapter 13). The Kleinleins and the Steltzenmuellers headed directly for Saint Sebald. The others wound up there later.

The Kleinlein brothers and their mother arrived at Dubuque with Michael Schueller's party of migrants on July 11, 1854. From there they made their way to Saint Sebald.

Peter Kleinlein, according to a story in the *Sunday Cedar Rapids Gazette* of May 1, 1949, came to Saint Sebald with a bag ringing with gold coins. Peter could have bought all the land then occupied by the Saint Sebald colony. But he was looking only for water and the power that running water offers. He went into a steep valley southeast of the colony and bought land that included two tributary valleys with springs of water. Their joint flow was to merge in a mill race that would run to the "Hollow" where he planned to build his industries and his home.

Beginning in 1859, Peter and his brother built a mill, a cheese factory, and a brewery, and three frame residences for his family and staff, including the *braumeister* (brewmaster) Friederich K. Zeuch.

The Kleinlein Mill

The limestone for the mill was quarried from the hill west of the hollow. My great-grandfather Conrad Hock was hired as chief stonecutter. The stones were slid from the hillside quarry on a temporary bridge to the slowly rising walls of the mill below. The low end of the bridge was gradually raised as the walls of the mill were built. Finally, when the third floor was under construction, the bridge ran an almost level course about one hundred feet across open space to the mill.

In an astounding engineering feat, Peter constructed the mile-long mill race (or sluice) that carried water from the southeast spring around a long hill to a dammed up millpond filled with water from the west spring. From the pond the sluice carried water in an abundant flow along the west hillside. The location of the mill race is still apparent from earth formations below the west hillside road. The mill race levees end at an eighteen-inch iron pipe that carried the water with a sixty-five horse-power force to the mill wheel.

On their voyage to America, the Kleinleins had made friends with George Prottengeier and so were aware of Prottengeier's training as a miller in Bavaria. Prottengeier had settled on a farm at Saint Sebald to be near his sister Margaretha and her husband Sigmund Fritschel at Wartburg Seminary. But in 1859 Peter Kleinlein persuaded him to turn the farm over to his parents and take over the operation of the newly erected mill.

The mill ground white and buckwheat flour until World War I when the rationing of wheat and a lack of substitutes for wheat flour forced the mill to close. After the war the mill was reopened for a short time to grind animal feed.

In about 1880, Georg Prottengeier's second son Hermann Georg completed his apprenticeship and succeeded his father as the miller. In the early 1900s, Will Bowers took over direction of the milling operations until it closed.

On the south slope of the hollow just below where the mill race carried water from the south spring, the Kleinleins built their brewery from the same quarry that supplied limestone for the mill. The brewery entrance was sheltered by an arched tunnel where teams and wagons unloaded the ingredients from which the beer was brewed and where kegs and barrels of beer were shipped out on other wagons. This arched entrance was another masterpiece of engineering. To store beer at the proper temperature, stone vaulted cellars were built into the hillsides, traces of which are visible today.

On December 20, 1879, the chief brewer Friederich Zeuch was killed by a bursting barrel of beer. Friederich was one of five Zeuch brothers who migrated from Kassel, Hanover, Germany. A grandson, also named Friederich, in an August 17, 1964, letter to Julie Lux Thompson of Hopkinton, August 17, 1964, called himself an atheist. But "my grandfather Frederick Zeuch and my great uncle John (Pastor Johannes) Deindoerfer were great friends." In spite of Friederich Zeuch's friendship with Saint Sebald's founding pastor, Pastor G. H. Fuehr apparently refused to conduct a funeral for this Brewer who was also a professed atheist. His grave stone can be seen in the Saint Sebald cemetery. But his death is unlisted in the church records.

In 1854, the year after Pastor Johannes Deindoerfer and Karl Amman opened the colony at Saint Sebald, Deindoerfer's brother George and his wife Sabina came to Saint Sebald to farm. According to Zeuch's grandson's letter, his parents were one of the daughters of George and Sabina Deindoerfer and a son of Friederich Zeuch.

At the foot of the eastern hill where a road led from the valley to the present Highway 13, the Kleinleins built their cheese factory with stone from the same quarry that supplied the mill and brewery. Here, along with the standard cheeses, they made a smelly Limburger that was a Saint Sebald favorite. The cheese was stored for aging in stone-arched caves built into the slope nearby. The remains of these caves are easily found today.

Peter Kleinlein's brother Johannes (John) became head of the Kleinlein industries some time before Peter died on December 18, 1897. Peter, John, and John's wife Anna were all buried at Saint Sebald. John died October 17, 1904, Anna October 17, 1912.

When John Kleinlein retired, the industries were operated by his son Johannes Leonhard Gottlob, who was succeeded by his sons Anton (Tony) Friedrich and Christian (Chris) George.

The one-room Kleinlein School, Cass No. 10, where the writer studied for eight years and taught for two years was built on the western hill overlooking the hollow. At the height of its operations, the Kleinlein Hollow had everything but a general store.

A public road led west from the hollow through what is today the Roger Knehans farm to the Saint Sebald colony. For many years, much of the colony's commerce was directed along that road to the Kleinlein Hollow.

Another road ran the opposite way up the eastern slope carrying flour, cheese, and beer to Strawberry Point and other communities in Cass, Cox Creek, and Lodomillo Townships and as far as Delaware County. Alma Bowers Hock Krenach remembers an experience Tony Kleinlein had when he drove a beer wagon to Dyersville. Some men in Dyersville overpowered him and stole his entire load of beer barrels. The thieves were easily identified. The priest in this Roman Catholic city, grieving over the offense his fellow townsmen had given, raised a collection to reimburse the Kleinlein losses.

Kleinlein beer dispensaries became places where the German and English communities fellowshiped both in the Kleinlein Hollow and in Strawberry Point. On festivals such as Independence Day, John Kleinlein served celebrants at a Strawberry Point side-walk "cafe" on the west side of Elkader Street.

The Builders

The brothers Henry, Chris, John, and Charles Frederick (modern spelling), sons of Otto and Anna Friederich at Saint Sebald, formed a carpenter team in the 1880s. The houses they built had a uniform design that can still be recognized throughout the Strawberry Point area. These two-story houses were twenty-four feet square, with four rooms, a full basement and a 24 x 24 foot attic. The roof sloped four ways from a central eight feet square flat surface surrounding a chimney built through the center of the house.

A Frederick barn a-biulding

Simple 8 x 10 foot porches with a roof and two slender posts graced the house on two sides. A woodshed addition and open porch serviced the kitchen. A rain-water cistern was built in the basement to supply soft water to a pump in the kitchen. This constituted the house's only plumbing. A soon-to-be well-worn path led from the kitchen to an outdoor "biffy."

In addition to these dwellings, many barns and other out-buildings were erected by the Frederick brothers. Barn raisings were occasions for community-shared labor and celebrating with lunch and beer. The empty hay loft of a new barn was usually inaugurated with an evening barn dance.

The Village Blacksmith

Edward Friederich Samuel Donath was born at Saint Sebald in 1870 and shod horses for the Saint Sebalders at his shops in Osborne, Mederville, and Strawberry Point from 1890 until 1946 when farm tractors and autombiles had made Belgian, Clydesdale, and Percheron horses obsolete. Into his 80s he forged plow shares, wagon wheel rims, and a variety of tools. In 1950, reminiscing for a *Cedar Rapids Gazette* reporter, he recalled, "At least we get paid something for what we do now. I can remember when we used to shoe a horse for fifteen cents—reset the shoe, that is. If a *new* shoe was wanted, we got forty cents.

"But I wish they'd come and get the work they leave here [and pay for it]. I tell the farmers that they'd be pretty hard put if they had to milk their cows all year and wait until the end of the year to get their money. But they bring work here in the fall and forget about it until they have need for it in the spring. Meantime, my time and money is all tied up in that piece of work."

There were five blacksmiths in Strawberry Point when Ed Donuth opened his shop. At the end of his career, he was the only smith left and was taking in work from fifty miles away.

The Threshers

The reaper and grain separator (thresher) became common equipment in the late 1800s. The threshers, pulled and powered by huge steam engines, were major investments. Most farming communities shared the cost and labor by forming "threshing rings." It was inevitable that farmers of the Saint Sebald colony formed a threshing ring of their own. Their first engine was a large steam unit. In the 1920s and 1930s they used a heavy Rumely "oil pull" engine fueled by a curious mixture of kerosene and water. The Rumely was operated by Martin Baumgaertner. The grain separator was in the care of Friedrich (Fred) Kramer. In the late 1930s the Rumley was replaced by a 15-30 McCormick-Deering tractor.

An "Oil Pull" Rumely Tractor

In the early years, the threshing ring was so large that farmers often had to wait several weeks after the grain was cut for the threshers to arrive. Often a long spell of rainy weather caused sheaves stored in small "shocks" on the ground to deteriorate. So many farmers stored the sheaves in rain-proofed stacks until the threshers came. The stacks were perhaps twenty feet tall with near-verticle sides from which bundles of grain could be easily tossed onto the intake conveyor of the threshing machine.

To feed the threshing crews, the women of the colony also shared help. Supplying a large crew of hungry threshers with an adequate supply of fried chicken and apple pie was a challenge even for a skilled kitchen crew.

Colony Life in Human Color

Karolina Baumgaertner (the writer's great-aunt) was born at Kaszemeken, East Prussia, April 30, 1852, and came to Saint Sebald in 1872, where she waited tables at Wartburg Seminary. On April 6, 1874, Karolina married seminary student Rudolph von Veltheim. Born in

Braunschweig, Germany, on January 20, 1839, Rudolph was the youngest of three sons of the Baron von Veltheim. It was common for noblemens' sons who had no hope of inheriting the title and the estate to study a profession. Von Veltheim may have contacted Wilhem Loehe at Neuendettelsau, who then directed him to the Saint Sebald seminary.

But when he married, Rudolph gave up his studies and built a home by a spring on the farm now occupied by the James Baumgartner family (2004). They had four children born at Saint Sebald and baptized by Pastor G. H. Fuehr.

1. Anna Maria Dorothea, born September 20, 1877.
2. Bertha Helena, born December 1, 1879.
3. Emilie Karolina Wilhelmina Katherina, born August 17, 1881.
4. Wilhelm Karl Ludolf, born November 7, 1884.

Little Wilhelm's birth caused excitement and joy when word of it reached the elder von Veltheims at their Braunschweig estate. Neither of Rudolph's brothers had produced a male heir. They asked Rudolph to bring his family to Germany. Baby Wilhelm was to inherit three castles, thousands of acres of land, and a great town mansion (today a museum shown in many books).

First, it was necessary for Rudolph and Karolina to consult Attorney B. W. Newberry in Strawberry Point, who drew an affidavit affirming that Wilhelm was indeed Rudolph's legitimate son.

Then, before settling on little Wilhelm's inheritance, Rudolph moved his family to Berlin so that peasant-born Karolina could learn the "social graces." Then they took over Bartensleben, the largest castle of the Veltheim estate. Wilhelm was given private tutors to train him in French, German, manners, music, dancing, and military tactics.

When Wilhelm died in 1972, a niece living in Saint Louis procured a bag of soil from his birthplace at Saint Sebald, carried it to the funeral at Bartensleben, and added it to Wilhelm's grave near where his mother Karolina Baumgaertner von Veltheim lay. She had died September 12, 1938.

Hermann Baumgaertner and Anna Niedermeyer were married on August 20, 1873, at Saint Sebald by Pastor Johannes A. List. They were blessed with fourteen children. In January 1967 their grandson A. G. Baumgaertner wrote concerning them:

> "Some of their experiences and even their difficulties were always recited by them with great humor: The wild dogs [timber wolves?] that broke into the spring house and

made off with a fresh supply of meat. The trading with Indians for venison...Very young sons August, Charles and Martin lying on their tummies on the floor of the log cabin, peering down the hatch into the cellar at the brand new (open) barrel of molasses just purchased. Despite warnings from Grandma, Uncle Charles went end over end into the molasses below. Grandma pulled him out by his collar but his boots remained in the molasses below.

"The Austrians hired to clear land of timber and their ability to do a "waltzer" with full steins of beer on top of their heads and quite a few steins of beer inside of them."

When Hermann died on May 8, 1927, his obituary described the circumstances under which "the deceased and his wife started housekeeping. Five acres were bought at that time and afterwards cleared of brush and trees. Being a man who never went into debt, he added to his farm as he earned money, until many acres were owned. Practically all of it had to be cleared. Today no better land can be found in all of Iowa."

Johann von Riemath, an upper-class German in Labowischken, East Prussia, was disowned by his family because in about 1850 he had married their milkmaid Wilhelmina (Minnie) Rebaschus. They had nine children. Lacking proletarian skills, Johann was killed in a saw mill accident about 1880.

The first three fatherless children August, Wilhelm, and Augusta Riemath came to Saint Sebald in 1881. Wilhemina remarried at age fifty. She and her new husband Ernest Horn, age thirty-eight, also decided to go to America with her children John, Carl, Anna, and Helena.

Wilhelmina's other two daughters stayed in Germany. Daughter Theresa was ill, so daughter Karolina stayed to take care of her. This saved their lives. The rest of the family drowned on the steamship *Cimbria*.

On Sunday, January 21, 1883, the *New York Times* ran this story on the front page: "The Hamburg American Line steamer Cimbria, which left Hamburg on the 17th inst. for New York came into collision with the British steamer Sultan on Friday morning, off Borkum, an island of Prussia, in the North Sea, 26 miles northwest of Emden. The Cimbria quickly sank." The next day the *Times* front page carried "THE LIST OF THE MISSING" which included "Ernst Horn. Wilhelmme (sic) Horn. Johann Riemath. Carl Riemath. Anna Riemath. Helene Riemath."

Also: "LOST IN THE NORTH SEA—OVER THREE HUNDRED PER-SONS GO DOWN WITH THE CIMBRIA—VESSEL SUNK ABOUT 2 O'CLOCK IN THE MORNING—NO TIME FOR LOWERING BOATS— THE PASSENGERS GIVEN LIFE BELTS—A LIST OF 364 MISSING PER-SONS—THE CAPTAIN AND FIRST OFFICER PROBABLY DROWNED"....

"The Cimbria left Hamburg on Thursday with 380 passengers and a crew numbering 110."

"Mr. J. F. H. Meyer, agent for the ship line, 'thought it very strange that the Sultan did not remain on the scene and at least make an attempt to rescue some of the Cimbria's people.'"

One life boat came to shore with 39 persons. How many were rescued in other life boats was not reported. One sadly pictures Wilhelmina Riemath trying to save her two-year-old daughter Helena in the 15 minutes that the ship was afloat after the collision.

The Forty-three-Year Fuehr Pastorate

George Heinrich Fuehr was installed as Saint Sebald's pastor in August 1875. He came from a nine-year pastorate at Berea, Ohio. His forty-three years at Saint Sebald was the longest term any pastor served this congregation.

Fuehr was pastor, teacher, missionary, postmaster, builder, physician, and pharmacist. Between the Kleinlein industries and the skills of Pastor Fuehr, the Saint Sebald colony was almost as self-sufficient as a small town.

In fact the Saint Sebald colony with its industries, college, and seminary became recognized by the U.S. government when a post office was established in the original parsonage-church with Pastor Fuehr as postmaster. Area residents had their mail addressed to Saint Sebald and called for it at the parsonage. Saint Sebald histories indicate that this post office began and ended with G. H. Fuehr's pastorate, 1875–1918.

In 1876, a year after Fuehr arrived at Saint Sebald, he persuaded the congregation to build a barn to shelter his teams of horses. The log parsonage-church was no longer in good condition. So, two years later, in 1878, his flock agreed to erect the present parsonage. The following year, 1879, the parish school house was built, and the parsonage-church, no longer needed as a school, was torn down. The pastor's hard-working teams of driving horses needed better shelter;

in 1899 the congregation built a larger barn that stood until 1948 when it was sold and torn down.

Pastor Fuehr had been trained as a homeopathic physician. He served the colony as its medical doctor and pharmacist. He dispensed chiefly well-known remedies that today would be called nonprescription drugs as well as some of today's prescription drugs. The prescription drugs most in use in the colony were aconite and belladonna (or kahliphos). Aconite's active ingredient is monkshood, diluted to one part per trillion, and taken for anxiety and for colds. Belladonna alkaloids and barbituates are a combination of medicines used to relieve cramping and spasms of the stomach, intestines, and bladder or to decrease the amount of acid formed in the stomach. Considering the state of medical progress in the late 1800s, Fuehr's practice was likely not only as advanced as that of other physicians in the county, he probably did less harm than most.

Pastor G. H. Fuehr

The story of Karl and Maria Baumgaertner's first son Johannes Gottlieb August Hermann Baumgaertner (mercifully called "Hans") reported by his daughter Magdalene Akre is one instance of Pastor Fuehr's combined pastoral and medical ministries and of the life and piety at Saint Sebald in the 1800s.

Hans was born September 27, 1878, and was carried six hundred yards through the forest a week later to be baptized by Pastor Fuehr. As was the custom, the first son was given the names of both grandparents and both sponsors.

In December 1891, diphtheria struck the Karl Baumgaertner family. Their baby Wilhelmina died December 18 at the age of nine months. The next day four-year-old Sophia died. Then thirteen-year-old Hans became deathly ill. His mother Maria, like Samuel's mother Hannah, made a solemn vow that if God through the ministrations of Pastor Fuehr would spare the life of her Hans, she would give her son to the service of the Lord. Pastor Fuehr manually cleared the choking membrane from Hans's throat. He then kept breathing his own breath into Hans's chest until the crisis passed.

The next year Hans was confirmed. In those days, before labor-saving machinery was available, a boy at the age of fourteen (and at that time Karl's and Maria's *only* son) was a valuable asset on a farm. But Maria remembered her promise made during Hans's illness, and Karl consented to the sacrificial loss of his son's help. Karl took his son to Clinton, Iowa, and enrolled him in the Wartburg Academy in the preparatory course for the ministry. Ten years later, on July 6, 1902, after studies at Wartburg College and Wartburg Seminary, Hans Baumgaertner was ordained at his first pastorate at Memphis, Illinois, thirty miles from Saint Louis.

In 1911 he organized the first Iowa Synod congregation in Colorado among German Russian immigrants at Fort Collins. His daughter Magdalene Akre describes a unique event in her father's Colorado ministry: a midnight debate Hans had with famous Judge Ben Lindsay of the Juvenile Court in Denver, Colorado. Judge Lindsay was pushing a bill through the legislature for the abolition of child labor. "[M]y father decided someone had to throw a wrench in the works, for if the bill passed, our German Russians would not be allowed to have the help of their children under age sixteen in the sugar beet fields....Dad pointed out that it was ridiculous to compare the work of the children in the sugar beet fields—where they moved along the rows and picked out the seedlings required to make room for the mature beets in the bracing, sparkling clear air of Colorado—with the coal miner's children in the cold damp pits of Wales where children never felt the warmth of the sun or breathed any fresh air through their coal dust laden noses and throats. The debate went on for several hours and was written up in *The Denver Post*. It stirred so much feeling among the listeners and readers that the bill to abolish the labor of the immigrant children in the sugar beet fields was defeated."

In 1924, Pastor Baumgaertner accepted a call to Immanuel Lutheran Church at George, Iowa, where he served through World War II. He died December 14, 1948.

Pastor Fuehr retired in 1918. He died November 21, 1920, and his body was laid to rest in the Saint Sebald cemetery. His wife Philipina died December 23, 1928, and was laid next to her husband.

The Care of the Aged

The first son born to the pioneers was expected upon his marriage to take over the family farm. Often an addition was built on the parents' house to accommodate the newlyweds. The young couple was expected in turn to care for the parents until they died.

The senior couple continued to assist with the field work, the garden, the chickens and other chores as long as they were able. When they became enfeebled, there were usually grandchildren available to attend them.

Where this pattern was not workable, relatives and friends in the colony gave the aged hospitality in their own homes. Konrad and Barbara Prottengeier lived on a small acreage at Saint Sebald. When Barbara died on March 27, 1878, the Georg and Anna Wuest family moved in with Konrad. In 1881 when Anna Wuest died, Konrad made his home with his daughter and son-in-law, Albert and Anna Andreae, on their farm. He lived there nineteen years until his death on February 8, 1900. He had lived through all of the nineteenth century but three years.

It was through the dedicated Christian labors of deaconesses that professional family support services, hospice work, and health care centers as resources of care for the aged were pioneered in Loehe's Neuendettelsau. About sixty years later, in 1940, the Strawberry Point Lutheran Home, one of the earliest nursing homes in northeast Iowa, was organized under the leadership of the Saint Sebald colony and its pastor Paul Eilers.

This, too, was a pioneering effort, since only in recent times when a majority of women became employed outside the home did professional care for the aged come into general acceptance in the United States.

The Saint Sebald Ghost

Stories of the "Saint Sebald ghost" began to accumulate about 1879. They centered in the George Schuchmann family home, built by Karl Amman 200 paces from the church. The following is substantially the version told by the writer's grandmother Christina (nee Schuchmann) Hock:

When Christina was a girl of twelve, strange noises began to disturb her home. Loud rustlings and howls in the chimney were so severe that her father George fired his gun up the stack. But this brought no relief.

Some nights, when Christina and her sisters went upstairs to bed, invisible hands would grab their legs and hold them immobile. When their father responded to their screams and came to their rescue, he rapped on those invisible hands with a cane, but those hands would not release their victims. Only when he prayed the Lord's Prayer did the "ghost" let go.

The ghost worked more than the night shift. At the Saint Sebald parish day school three hundred feet away, it bothered the children as they went about their school work.

The *Brush Creek* (now Arlington, Iowa) *News* carried this item Friday, April 9, 1980, (contributed by Ruth Hillson to *Volga City, Iowa*, a history published by the Clayton County Genealogical Society): [147]

"As most of my neighbors express it, 'The devil is attending school at the German preacher's [Pastor G. H. Fuehr's] and agreeable to his satanic nature is bent on mischief.' . . .

"About the 1st of March trouble commenced in the German school at this place, books were written in, torn and otherwise mutilated. The mischief was laid on two large boys and they were punished, but still denied having anything to do with it. Finally things grew worse and the boys were expelled from school.

"This seemed to make matters a deal worse, for besides the continual writing in and tearing of the books, children were bitten and scratched, and the whole school put into a perfect fright. The Preacher concluded to sit with the children and see if the 'spirit' or whatever it might be would touch him, and while he was sitting on one side of a little girl and Mr. [George] Schuchmann on the other, she dodged her head and screamed as if in great pain, and blood was freely flowing from her ear, and upon examination, marks of teeth was (sic) plainly discernable.

"Being fully convinced that it was the work of spirits, Miss Schuchmann wrote on a slate, 'Are you a condemned spirit?' The...answer, 'I am,' instantly appeared, cut into the slate as with a sharp instrument. All who were watching declare that there was no pencil or other instrument near the slate nor could it have been done with visible hands. Other demonstrations equally incomprehensible have occurred."

Christina Schuchmann told her children essentially the same account. The words on the slate were in German: *"Bist du ein verfluchten Geist von Helle?"* (Are you a cursed spirit from hell?) Answer on the slate, *"Ja!"* (Yes!)

Schuchmann family remembrances included the difficulties a student from the Saint Sebald seminary had teaching the parish day school.

Children complained that something was molesting them and dared the student to sit where they were seated. When he accepted their challenge, the seat rose in the air with him.

On one occasion, Pastor G. H. Fuehr was said to have heard a loud commotion in the church building. As he entered the front door to check on the noise, he saw a figure dressed in black standing at the altar. As Fuehr watched, this figure plunged a sharp instrument into the missal [altar book] and disappeared. Legend says that Fuehr preserved in his home that missal with a triangular shaped hole through every page.

Celia Andreae submitted an article to *Volga City, IA* [1148] in which Pastor Fuehr reports that one Sunday he felt a tugging on the back of his robe while he was in the pulpit preaching. He kept on preaching without looking back. The "ghost" was said to have climbed trees near the parsonage at night in attempts to frighten Pastor Fuehr.

While attending the parish school, Celia Andreae's aunt Maria was reported to have come in from recess to find her slate scratched from top to bottom as though clawed, with shavings left on the desk. Having been told by her mother not to say anything if she saw something unusual, she wiped off the shavings and returned to her studies.

Mrs. George Otdoerfer (the writer's grandmother-in-law) told the family legend of George Otdoerfer's sister Amelia Pebler. As a child in the parish school, Amelia found a knife driven through every page of one of her books. The family called this a "hexebuch" (witch's book).

The Saint Sebald legend placed responsibility for the origin of the ghost on one of the colony youths. (Respect for truth and love for neighbor requires that the writer not name the youth given in his family's story, since folk legends such as this contain more superstition than truth.) This lad was said to have mail-ordered a copy of the *Sixth and Seventh Books Of Moses,* a work dealing with the occult. With this guidance he conjured the "ghost" into making its appearances.

An Andreae family legend has it that Conrad Andreae II, Celia's uncle, while in his early twenties, found in the mail box a mail-order package addressed to him that he had not ordered. Just then a young man arrived and claimed the package. He explained that it was a book on black magic that he wished to keep secret from his family. Shortly after that supernatural events began to occur at Saint Sebald. [149]

Christoph Andreae told the writer's father of the final events concerning the ghost that took place years later when the "sorcerer" died. Christoph was among the men who kept wake with the body. They noticed that the book on the occult was lying on the dead man's breast. They removed it and laid it on the table. Soon they found it back on the dead man's breast. This procedure was repeated. They took the book out to the shop and clamped it tightly in the vise. When they returned to the house, the book was back in the coffin. The conjurer was buried with it. (See *Volga City, IA* for a slightly different version of the closing scene.)

The Steeple

In the fiftieth anniversary year of Saint Sebald, 1903, the congregation added a steeple to the church. The steeple towers nearly one hundred feet into the sky and carries a clear-toned sixteen hundred pound bell.

Frieda Zwanziger remembered that it was built by the congregation's George Kruessel and a Mr. Erke of Lamont. The cost of the steeple was $824. The bell was purchased for $440.

Dollars lost much of their value in the next ninety-three years. In 1996 Saint Sebald surrounded the steeple base with 324 square feet of additional construction to enclose the front steps and to provide an elevator. The cost was more than $100,000.

That fiftieth anniversary year the school was enlarged with the addition of a woodshed. The church, the school, and the parsonage were all repainted. Cost for labor and materials was $589.75.

Colony pioneer George Schuchmann I, Amman's son-in-law, whose farm adjoined the church, fervently opposed the steeple addition. When it was built, he and his wife moved to live with their daughter in Oelwein and transferred their membership to Zion Church. But when George I died the following year, Anna Ammann, his widow, returned to the Saint Sebald colony that she had helped found. George's family buried him in the Saint Sebald cemetery where a grave marker attests to the ministries he and Anna performed as founders of Saint Sebald..

In 1913 the Saint Sebald congregation sold the south twenty acres of its eighty-acre tract to Karl Baumgaertner. The deed reads,

Know All Men by These Presents:

That we the Trustees of the Ev. Luth. St. Sebald Church of Cass and Sperry Townships in Clayton County, Iowa, in consideration of the sum of Five Hundred Dollars paid in hand by Charles Baumgartner of Clayton County and State of Iowa, do hereby SELL and CONVEY unto the said Charles Baumgartner the following described premises situated in the County of Clayton and State of Iowa to-wit:

The South One Half (½) of the North East Quarter of the South West Quarter of Section Thirty Four (34) in Township Ninety Two (92) North of Range Six (6) West of the Fifth Principal Meridian,

And we covenant with the said Charles Baumgartner that we hold said premises by good and perfect title; that we have good right and lawful authority to sell and convey the same; that they are free and clear of all liens and encumbrances whatsoever,

And we covenant to warrant and defend the said premises against the lawful claims of all persons whomsoever,

And the grantors aforesaid hereby relinquish all contingent rights, including dower or homestead which they have in and to such premises.

Signed this 5th day of April A.D. 1913 [by] Conrad Andreae, George H. Otdoerfer, August Bartels.

Parish Education after Pastor Fuehr

After the parish dayschool closed, the school building continued to serve as a center for Sunday school, vacation Bible school, and confirmation classes.

In 1930-31, when the writer was enrolled in confirmation studies, a summer school taught by Pastor E. Rudolph Melchert served children in grades 1-8. This school operated Monday through Friday, from 9 A.M. to noon, the first four weeks after public schools closed for the summer.

All grades practiced reading German and writing the German script that was in use before modern Germans adopted the English alphabet. The text books were a German primer called the *Vuebel* (pronounced "fee-bel"), *Biblische Geschichte* (Bible History), and *An Explanation of Dr. Martin Luther's Small Catechism by Dr. M. Reu*. A three-foot ruler served as the disciplinary tool.

Classes met together in the one large school room. Wide seats and desks, seating two pupils each, were still in use. Students in grades

7-8 focused on Bible history and the catechism. The lower grades were taught German language skills and Bible history. All classes memorized hymns and poetry both in German and English.

The pupils' accomplishments were demonstrated at a congregational picnic on the school and parsonage grounds at the close of the summer school. After the picnic and before the five-gallon ice cream container was opened, the children sang songs and recited their Christian "pieces," mostly in German. The writer, who came from a home where German had not been taught to the children, recited German poems and hymns with acceptable diction but with little comprehension. Seventy years later he can still sing *"Alle Voe- gel Sind Schon Da"* (All the birds are here already).

After the four-week vacation Bible school closed, the confirmation class (grades 7-8 or older) continued to meet through the rest of the summer, Monday-Friday, 9 A.M. to noon. When public schools opened in September, confirmation studies continued on Saturdays, 9 A.M. to noon. The pastor's teaching burden never let up.

At recess time, the vacation church school scattered to play—often in the forest or in the cemetery. Boys loved to climb saplings and swing out, letting the sapling serve as a spring, lowering the lad (he hoped) for a comfortable drop to the ground. When the boy misgauged the flexibility of the tree, and found himself hanging ten feet above the earth, he expected his buddies to grasp his feet and pull him lower for a less hazardous drop. Occasionally at that moment the school bell rang; his mocking companions headed for the school, leaving the lad hanging in the air, forced to fend for himself.

In the cemetery a few feet west of the school grandparents and great (or even great-great) grandparents and other relatives slept. Children were aware of their family roots as they studied and played.

The Church Furnishings

The Saint Sebald church building underwent continuous renovations and improvements. For many years the people sat on uncomfortable straight-backed pews formed by parishioners from plain lumber. When the mill-manufactured pews currently in use were installed is not known.

There is also no record as to the origin of the present altar or when it replaced the original dry-goods box, but the temporary altar was probably in use but a short time.

The pulpit was built by John Georg Wuest, a cabinet-maker who arrived before 1864. It was therefore built early in the life of the congregation. Leo Wuest and Minetta Donath, in their contribution to the "Prottengeier-Koeberle Family Tree," claimed that "Grandpa (John George Wuest) made the altar, pulpit, and the baptismal font of the Saint Sebald church." But other histories credit Wuest with only the pulpit. The woodwork of the font resembles the work done by the maker of the pulpit. But the altar appears to have been created by a more professionally skilled craftsman.

The pulpit where the pastor stood "six feet above contradiction" was placed high against the wall in the southeast corner and was reached by a stair and door from the sacristy. In 1941 that doorway was walled in and a picture of Jesus the Good Shepherd has occupied that wall space since. The pulpit was lowered to its present level eighteen inches above the floor and is now reached from the chancel.

The Colony Begins to Americanize

In 1919 Pastor Leon Gehret succeeded Fuehr. The German language parish school closed. Perhaps Gehret was unwilling to commit such a large share of his time to daily classes. But more likely the anti-German climate in the United States caused by World War I made the parish less inclined to use the German tongue for other than confirmation classes and worship.

Emil Melchert (whose grandfather E. R. Melchert served as pastor of Saint Sebald from 1926 to 1935) described an experience his father Pastor Gerhard E. Melchert suffered at the hands of anti-German bigots in 1917 one Sunday after preaching a German sermon in a town in southern Illinois. As Melchert walked through the town four men accosted him with guns and pitch forks. After tying his hands, they put a rope around his neck and led him to the town bridge. They tied one end of the rope to the bridge wall, forced him to stand on the wall, and then offered him the privilege of "some last words."

Afterward Melchert remembered only that he tried in some way to confess his faith in Jesus Christ as he addressed his captors for about ten minutes. Finally one of the men said, "I'm not going to waste my time with this guy any longer," and walked away. The rest followed. With relief, Melchert climbed down from the wall and untied the rope.

But the people of Saint Sebald would not give up entirely the use of German in confirmation classes, meetings, and worship. For this the colony would need another fifteen years of cultural change. In 1919 most of the colonists who were above age sixty spoke very little English. Male heads of households learned only enough English to do business in the nearby towns. At home only German was spoken.

That meant that the only place that colony children could learn English was in the public schools. This was an additional benefit of giving up the parish school that they had attended in alternate years. Attending the public school full time did much to Americanize the young.

Some who served in the military found the colony too confining when the war was over. A World War I song asked, "How will you keep them down on the farm, after they've seen Paree?" At Saint Sebald, veterans and other young men and women began to leave the colony for employment in Waterloo and Dubuque. Some ventured as far as Detroit and elsewhere. Wherever they went, they helped organize or strengthen Lutheran congregations with their gospel witness. When Fred Hock and Helena Baumgaertner married, they settled in Waterloo. They were two of eleven charter members who organized Trinity Lutheran Church, which in twelve years became the flagship Lutheran parish of Waterloo.

Freed from teaching the parish school, the Saint Sebald pastors were better able to minister to the colony's first generation, who were aging and whose American-born children were entering their fifties.

These children had been the "baby-boomers" of the 1870s and 1880s. Only thirty-seven children were baptized in the 1850s, sixty-eight were baptized in the 1860s. But two hundred forty-five babies were baptized in the 1870s and two hundred ten in the 1880s. As the colonizing generation passed its child-bearing years, many young people left because farm land had become scarce and expensive; the birth-rate fell. Only one hundred sixty-three children were born in the 1890s, one hundred fifteen in the 1900s, and sixty-six in the 1910s

As second and third generations left shortly after the age of maturity, the size of confirmation classes declined from twenty-three in 1878 to two in 1912.

The Frauenverein

During Gehret's two-year pastorate, the "Frauenverein [women's society] of the Ev. Luth. St. Sebaldus Congregation, St. Sebald, Iowa," was organized on May 18, 1919. On February 7, 1935, the ladies began to conduct their meetings in English, and they became known as the Ladies Aid Society.

A constitution was written stating that the "purpose of the society (*Verein*) is to cultivate and promote the social life among us and others in a truly Christian spirit, as well as to be active in works of Christian charity within our congregation, synod and the Kingdom of God in general."

This constitution, which governed during the fifteen years of the *Verein,* also stated that "the pastor of the congregation usually presides at the meetings." In 1935 the Ladies Aid version limited the pastor's presiding to the "devotional part of the meeting."

Minutes of the first meeting in translation from German:

Minutes [*Protokol* of the organizing meeting on May 18, 1919.

The meeting was conducted by the pastor of our congregation and was opened with song and prayer.

There were 18 ladies present from our St. Sebaldus congregation. They resolved to form a women's society [*Frauenverein*] The constitution [*Statuten*] will be worked out and placed before the next meeting.

The ladies agreed to meet on the second Thursday of each month beginning at 2:00 P.M. The place of meeting will be the congregation's school house or the home of one of the members, depending on what the society determines. For the hospitality that is needed, members will serve in alphabetical order. In the event that a problem prevents a member from serving, the next person in the alphabet will take her place. In connection with the hospitality, each member shall bring a freewill offering for her food.

The first officers elected by majority vote:
President: Frau (Mrs.) Julia Baumgaertner
Vice president: Fraeulein (Miss) Esther Andreae
Secretary: Frau (Mrs.) Clara Gleason"

Twenty-one members attended the second meeting. After that attendance varied from 4 in the cold months to an average of about twelve.

The pastor's wife was often recorded under her customary title in the minutes, *protokol.* The membership list for 1934 names her

"Frau-pastor Melchert" (Mrs. Pastor Melchert). In the culture of the colony, she was usually addressed simply as "Frau-pastor."

The Ladies Aid operated under that name at least through 1952. Then it became a chapter of the synodwide Women's Missionary Federation until the 1958 merger of the American Lutheran Church, the Evangelical Lutheran Church, and the United Evangelical Lutheran Church into The American Lutheran Church. The women of the merged church were appropriately named The American Lutheran Church Women. In 1988 with the merger of The American Lutheran Church, the Lutheran Church in America, and the Association of Evangelical Lutheran Churches into the Evangelical Lutheran Church in America, the women again adopted the churchwide name: Women of the Evangelical Lutheran Church in America. With both mergers. the St. Sebald ladies became a chapter under the churchwide name.

Whatever its title, the women's auxiliary at Saint Sebald was dedicated to study, service, and witness to the gospel of Jesus Christ.

Once their society was established few details of the congregation's work took place without the organized support and assistance of the Saint Sebald women. Pastor Fuehr and his predecessors had also been dependent on the women's support. Especially when Wartburg Seminary students and confirmation students from the prairie needed hospitality in order to teach or study at St. Sebald, the women opened their homes and their tables without direction.

The Historic Tracker Pipe Organ

Gehret was followed in 1921 by Pastor W. F. Knappe who served until 1926. Pastor E. Rudolph Melchert served from 1926 until 1935.

In 1928, Saint Sebald celebrated its seventy-fifth anniversary. In honor of the occasion, it dedicated a used pipe organ built by the Hinners Organ Company of Pekin, Illinois, closed since 1942. The early history of this organ is not known. But Robert A. Hinners, grandson of the company's founder John L. Hinners, estimated that it was built by his father Arthur around the year 1914. The Hinners company had no records of who had traded the organ in on a larger instrument.

Saint Sebald records show that it purchased "a used No. 6 pipe organ for $785, prepaid to Strawberry Point." It was "a used organ which had been taken back to the factory, rebuilt, sold to us, and guaranteed to be as good as new."

The instrument is a tracker action (mechanical action) pipe organ, reputed to be the most trouble-free and longest lasting. Each key is connected to the air valve of the pipe with a piece of wood or wire (or both) called a tracker.

In 1966 David Harold Andreae, in the essay "St. Sebald's Historic and High Quality Pipe Organ," from which this history of the organ is condensed, wrote, "As these beautiful old Hinners tracker organs become fewer, our old Hinners will become more valuable than it is now. Even today organists from as far away as Waverly and Dubuque who have heard our organ come to play it because of its beautiful tone, and because it is just plain fun to play."

The metal pipes were made by Anton Gottfried. The gold pipes are only adornment. The Hinners catalog stated, "The full scale Pedalklavier of 27 keys is the same as in the largest of organs, but since the notes above the lower octave are never or only rarely used for church service, we omit them as a needless expenditure."

When the organ was installed in 1928, no electricity was available to activate the organ blower. Wind pressure was created by a hand pump lever. The energy for this labor was usually supplied by a youth who was annually paid twenty dollars for his services. After 1944 the blower operated with an electric motor.

The Language Question

Lutheran congregations formed in Revolutionary War times adopted English in the nineteenth century. The Ministerium of Pennsylvania produced an English liturgy for its congregations in 1860. But most Midwestern Lutherans of German or Scandinavian heritage did not arrive in America until the last two-thirds of the nineteenth century. They worshiped in their European tongues well into the 1930s.

World War I stimulated prejudice against immigrant use of the German tongue on the street or in public worship. This moved the leaders of all Lutheran synods to hasten the introduction of English into worship and Christian education.

In 1918 the Wartburg Publishing House published its *Wartburg Hymnal*, an English service book and hymnal that included the *Common Service*. This service had been produced in 1888 by the eastern Lutheran church consortiums known as the General Synod and the General Council along with the United Synod in the South to provide a common English liturgy for the Lutheran church bodies in America with their various European backgrounds. The editor, O. Hardwig, expressed in its preface the opinion that "[m]any congregations will introduce English services at this time."

For most of its history the Saint Sebald German colony had worshiped in the German language using Loehe's *Agenda* (liturgy book). From the time of its publication in 1915, the colony used the Iowa Synod's *Kirchenbuch* liturgies from which the pastor chanted and the people sang the liturgical responses. The pastor sang the threefold prayer from the ancient Greek liturgies, *"Kyrie Eleison, Christe Eleison, Kyrie Eleison"* (Lord, have mercy; Christ, have mercy; Lord, have mercy). The people responded, *"Herr, erbarm Dich unser; Christe, erbarm Dich unser; Herr, erbarm Dich unser"* (Lord, have mercy upon us; Christ, have mercy upon us; Lord, have mercy upon us).

Saint Sebalders had a tradition of closing their German worship services with a single-verse hymn:

Unsern Ausgang segne Gott (God, bless our going forth)
Usern Eingang gleichermaszen (Likewise our entrance)
Segne unser taeglich Brot (Bless our daily bread)
Segne unser Thun und Lassen (Bless our deeds and omissions)
Segne uns mit selgem Sterben (Bless us with a peaceful death)
Und mach uns zu Himmelserben (And cause us to inherit heaven)

About 1930, led by Pastor E. Rudolph Melchert, the congregation began using an English service from the *Wartburg Hymnal* one Sunday per month.

In 1936, Pastor Paul Eilers, a new graduate from the seminary, who was trained in English and had a limited knowledge of German, accepted Saint Sebald's call. By this time, Saint Sebalders had reduced German worship to one Sunday each month. Pastor Eilers gallantly conducted that German service and preached with his "bookish" German for some months. This led the congregation to meet and consider dropping German. At that meeting an elderly lady said, "I'd rather have a German sermon when it's a good one. But if it ain't a good one, I'd just as soon have English." The motion to adopt full time use of English was approved.

Saint Sebald accepted English much more graciously than its 1854 partner in organizing the Iowa Synod, Saint John of Dubuque. Herbert M. Prottengeier wrote in *the Prottengeier-Koeberle Family Tree, 1964)*, "In 1906 Dad was called to be associate pastor at Saint Johns church at Dubuque, specifically to introduce the English language....It wasn't long before the resistance of some of the older German parents...turned the congregation into two hostile camps. It was a regular civil war which spilled over into the civil courts. I can still see the name PROTTENGEIER in 3-inch, red type, spread across the headlines of one local Catholic-owned paper, happily panning the Lutherans."

Gemixte Pickles

Dropping German at worship did not eliminate its use in the colony homes and in social dialog. But after eighty-five years away from Germany and with German no longer preached and taught, the quality of the German tongue that was spoken declined.

As its children learned and used English in the public school, the colony developed a blend of German and English that observers labelled "gemixte pickles" (a mixture of pickles). Samples: *Sprech* (speak) became *Schwetz. Das ist a schoene barn* (That is a nice barn). *Sie war ganz aufgedopt* (She was all doped up medically). *Wenn* du *net weisst, dann weiss ich auch ennehow net* (If *you* don't know, then I sure don't know). *Du hast witter net corcht!* (*Du hast wieder nicht gehoert*, which translates, you didn't listen again!).

If someone was invited as a dinner guest at a future date, an expression of hearty acceptance might be, "Ja, and I'll fry (*freu*—delight) myself till then." Sympathy to someone's pain was expressed with, *"Dass ist ganz arch!"* (That is very hard!) A frequent question after "Hello" was *"Wass machsts du?"* (What have you been doing?)

As English conquered the community more and more, senior colonists used colloquial German even as they urged parents to preserve German usage in the colony: *Lern die Kinder Deitch!* (Teach the children Deutsch, German). The quality of German in use by the community testified to how appropriate this concern for the language had become.

Colonists who became fully bilingual enjoyed humorous exchanges and word plays based on German-English combinations: "Is it true that your son is attending college?" "Yes, he wants to become a professor. But so far he's just a *Brot-fresser* (a bread-eater)."

Gemixte Finances

The pastor was called to Saint Sebald at an agreed upon salary, supplemented by gifts such as chickens, geese, half a butchered hog, sacks of potatoes or apples, canned vegetables or fruit, and bottles of wine. These gifts of produce were common in Midwestern Lutheran parishes.

In the 1940s Pastor Walter E. Diemer served a Minnesota parish where such gifts were the custom. One Sunday in early winter, a farmer told Mrs. Diemer, "We'll butcher a hog one of these days so you will have some meat to eat fresh, and some you can keep frozen outside in a wooden box." Frau-pastor Diemer anticipated this windfall with much pleasure. But weeks went by with no sign of the hog at the parsonage. So she suggested that Pastor Diemer inquire of the farmer's son, when he appeared for his confirmation class, as to when they might expect the promised pork. Which the pastor did. And the boy answered, "Oh, that hog got well!" [150]

The Saint Sebald parish operated without a budget. Expenses other than the pastor's salary were insignificant. The cash portion of the pastor's salary was collected by the treasurer through personal contacts with the heads of families as he chanced to meet them at church services. Families usually paid this salary contribution in lump sums, often after selling a load of hogs at the market. Since this support was consequently sporadic, during slumps in the economy the pastor's salary was often delayed or paid only in part. Salary defaults became acute for Pastor E. R. Melchert in the early 1930s as the Great Depression moved into its depths.

Pastor Melchert retired from the ministry in 1935. Pastor Paul Eilers accepted Saint Sebald's call in 1936. Pastor Eilers had graduated from Wartburg Seminary in 1934. During the depression, like other professional and skilled persons, many pastors were unemployed (or in church jargon, "without call"). Eilers had waited two years for his first pastoral call.

Unable to pay agreed-upon salaries to their own pastors, the parishes of the recently-organized American Lutheran Church were unable to send enough "benevolent" funds to enable synod headquarters to pay the salaries of home and foreign missionaries. The church became less able to expand its ministries into communities begging for pastors to come and organize new congregations, and less able to finance the number of missionaries needed for the beachheads it had established in New Guinea and India. Executive positions at ALC headquarters and professorships at the colleges and seminaries also went unfilled.

Staffs were pared to the bone and worse at the church's headquarters, in the mission fields, and at its educational and charitable institutions. But the ALC still found its income falling short of expenses by more than half. Having no knowledge of how long the Great Depression would continue, the American Lutheran Church was unwilling to go into debt.

Instead, the ALC adopted in 1933 what was called a "pay-as-you-receive" policy. Income from parishes was used first to pay *fixed* expenses (utilities and interest on debts) at headquarters and at all institutions and mission fields. The remaining income was equally apportioned among all pastors and employees dependent on these gifts. Each month all salaries were totalled. All institutions of the church were forbidden to incur a deficit.

At Saint Luke Lutheran Church in Saint Paul, Minnesota, a subsidized mission congregation, the writer's predecessor in his worst month received $3.59 in salary from the Board of American Missions. Medical costs for the birth of this pastor's first two children were paid by Ramsey County as part of its burden for families on "relief."

The Walls of Zion Come Down

While the depression delayed his first pastoral call, Paul Eilers had to tread water as a salesman in a shoe store in Cedar Rapids. In 1936 he arrived at Saint Sebald with the promise of an annual salary of seven hundred dollars.

All previous pastors at Saint Sebald had preached and taught the gospel to people nurtured in a German culture in a German colony. Eilers was at home in the American culture and skilled at communicating the Christian faith to people with no Lutheran heritage. His evangelical outreach broke through cultural walls that had isolated Saint Sebalders from their neighbors for eighty-five years. Shepherded by this young pastor, dozens of children, young singles, and families entered the church.

On March 10, 1938, Eilers baptized three adults. On July 7, 1939, he baptized six adults. On May 5, 1940, he baptized nine adults.

Primitive Utilities and Patriarchal Sexism

Until 1937 two large wood-burning stoves divided the pews into four sections. Smoke pipes from the wood stoves rose to and passed along a high ceiling toward the chancel and the chimney. The pipes provided much radiation surface adding to the heat that came from the stoves.

The stoves each had surrounding shields to channel the heat upward and to protect worshipers seated on the front pews of the rear section from discomfort—particularly Karl Baumgaertner, who sat in that pew next to the center aisle and led the singing. (He had done this ever since the Kantor Johannes Weege died.)

Children beyond infancy were seated in the pew sections in front of the stoves, boys on the left and girls on the right. Adults, behind the stoves, were similarly separated: men on the left, ladies and infants on the right. A mother caring for infants received no help from the father, since it was culturally unacceptable for the sexes to sit together at a worship service. This separation provided a measure of privacy to young mothers who commonly nursed their babies during the service.

The German colonists considered it indecent when visitors from the American culture joined the Saint Sebalders at worship and chose to sit together as a family with the sexes mixed. The sexes were segregated also when they rode in a horse-drawn, two-seated, surrey: men and boys on the front seat, ladies and girls at the rear. This segregation continued to govern seating when surreys were replaced by automobiles. Here it was not a question of decency, but of male rights to the front seat. These priorities were also followed at the Holy Communion: men and boys first.

At Christmas a large locally-cut evergreen tree was placed near the pulpit and decorated with garlands, ornaments, and live candles. Deacons sat next to the tree with a bucket of water and a small mop to damp out any candle that burned too close to a branch.

In addition to the candlelight, the church was lighted by three large kerosene lamps that were spaced down the center aisle and by three smaller kerosene wall lamps on each side of the sanctuary.

Other than on Christmas Eve, there was seldom an evening service before the days of electric lights. Lenten services were conducted during Wednesday morning hours.

The Church Facilities Become More Inviting

Shortly after Eilers came, Saint Sebald began a program of improvements to its church building made possible by a bequest from Mrs. Kunigunda Otdoerfer Koehler.

In a remodeling project, the high ceiling with its pressed metal surface was hidden by NuWood applied to the ceiling and to the walls. New doors were hung. New carpeting was purchased for the chancel. New paraments were acquired for the altar and pulpit. The church was given a new roof. The church and school were painted and wired for electricity. The first service using electric lights were used was Christmas Eve 1943.

World War II had begun. In 1943 Eilers was called to the army chaplaincy. Pastor Howard E. Hahn succeeded him as pastor at Saint Sebald, serving from 1943 to 1948. Hahn was followed by Pastor Robert E. Glaser 1948-1950. In October 1950 William A. Gebhard was installed.

Beginning with Robert Glaser's pastorate, Saint Sebald assisted in the founding of Saint Paul Lutheran Church at Volga and continues to share its pastor with this congregation. During William Gebhard's pastorate, the Saint Paul congregation erected its church building.

Preparations for the one hundredth anniversary of the founding of Saint Sebald began in 1951. That year water and sewer pipes were laid to serve the church and parsonage. Early in 1952 the church building was raised eighteen inches, and excavation was done for a basement with new foundations and block walls. An oil-burning furnace was installed. A kitchen and two restrooms were constructed. Asphalt tile was laid in the sanctuary to cover the old wooden floor. The entire project cost little more than $10,000. Many hours of labor were contributed by the congregation.

As centennial gifts, member Alex Schmidt made wood candlesticks, a cross, and a missal stand for the altar. Later he added the communion rail and a credence shelf.

Pastor Gebhard was followed in 1954 by Pastors Herman Cronrath (1954–1960), Albert J. Bringle (1961–1963), Roger L. Buhr (1963–1967), Andrew S. Olsen (1967–1969), Terry S. Johnson (1970–1974), Palmer E. Sevig (1974–1979), Steven C. Fobian (1979–1983), Albert L. Hock, interim pastor (1983–1984, 1992, 1999–2001), Charles M. Smith (1984–1992), Jerome G. Godson (1992–1999), and Linda L. Reichstadter 2001 to the present.

There have been five sons of the Saint Sebald congregation ordained to the ministry of the gospel: Johann Burkhart (about 1871), Johannes Gottlieb Baumgaertner (1902), Albert Llewellyn Hock (1945), Otto Alfred Zwanziger (1955), and David Harold Andreae (1969).

During the summer of 1980, Pastor Steven Fobian led the Saint Sebalders in another renovation of the church building funded by a bequest from the estate of Martha McCarron. The ceiling was lowered, the wood trim was replaced, and the pews were refinished. They installed a new oak balcony railing, new lighting, bronze entrance doors, and carpeting over the entire floor (including the balcony) and the outdoor platform and steps.

In 1984 the parsonage was renovated at a cost of $12,500. In 1993 a new fence was built around the cemetery.

In 1996, during the pastorate of Jerome G. Godson, elevator access for handicapped people was provided by a $100,000 addition to the tower end of the church. Funds for the addition were provided in part through the sale of logs from the fifty-acre forest that still surrounds the church, but chiefly by the sale of PepsiCo stock appreciated in value from a bequest made twenty years previously by Carl Wuest.

On the church lawn southwest of the building, a historical marker was erected in 1952 by the Historical Committee of the Iowa District of the American Lutheran Church. The plaque reads: "On this site St. Sebald Ev. Lutheran Church was established in 1853. In its original parsonage-church, the Ev. Lutheran Synod of Iowa was founded August 24, 1854. Wartburg Seminary was located two miles southwest on Seminary Hill, 1857-1874."

EPILOGUE

What of the doctrine of the ministry that was under debate for seventy-five years between the Missouri Synod and the founders of the St. Sebald colony, Wartburg College and Seminary, and the Iowa Synod? As stated in the Forward, this question has never been resolved—not in today's Lutheran Church—Missouri Synod, not in the Evangelical Lutheran Church in America or among Lutherans elsewhere. Within the major Lutheran bodies themselves opinions vary along a continuum than runs between high church authority and lay pastorates.

In his encyclical *Ut Unum Sint*, Pope John Paul II has invited the "separated brethren" to offer suggestions to the Roman Catholic Church for a revision of the papacy that might remove whatever barriers they see in this office that keep them from healing the breach of the sixteenth century. This is a wan hope to set before us Lutherans who cannot find unity among ourselves on the questions concerning pastoral authority. But some do wonder if Lutherans may eventually be able to settle with Roman Catholics the problems they find in today's papal office and at last find a magisterium under which to face unresolved doctrinal and moral questions that threaten new schisms in the Church throughout the world.

APPENDICES

APPENDIX I.

Frankenhilf Families Who Stayed in Michigan

When the Frankenhilf congregation was separated from the colonists who moved to Iowa, the families who stayed in the original colony were named Bauer, Heinrich Dahl, Carl Glave, P. Gress, Michael Gruber, A. Heinlein, Katherina Hofmann, Michael Huber, Kamm, Paulus Popp, J. Schwab, M. Schwab, Michael Schwarz, Lerich Sippel, and Johannes Lerich Trump. They continued the Saint Michael's Evangelical Lutheran Church that had been organized in the spring of 1853. Today its address is Richville, Michigan. In February 1854, they called Pastor H. Dicke of Amelith, Michigan, to serve them every third Sunday and every Wednesday. They hired Karl Gottlob Amman's cousin Michael Schwarz to teach their children reading, writing and arithmetic during the winter months. The children's parents helped Schwarz on his farm in payment for his services. Michael Huber was appointed cantor to lead the singing, replacing Johannes Weege Sr., who was now carrying on this ministry at Saint Sebald. Their first full-time pastor was installed April 1, 1862.

APPENDIX II.

Families of the Saint Sebald Colony in 1855

The title of this list in the *Kirchen Buch* (Church Records) is *Familienverzeichnis* (Family Register): Carl Gottlob Amman; Johannes Weege Sr.; Johann Huebsch; Johannes Wegmann; Andreas Hueblein; Johann Georg Deindoerfer; Johannes Weege Jr.; Michael Leske; Gottfried Niedermeyer; Gottlieb Niedermeyer; Johann Michael Stelzenmueller; Georg Strickstock; Johann Huebner; August Draeger.

APPENDIX III.

In 1979 the writer chaired a Twin Cities committee of Lutheran pastors that broke ecumenical ground by inviting Archbishop John Roach of the Archdiocese of Saint Paul to preach at a Lutheran-Catholic All Saints celebration at Central Lutheran Church, Minneapolis. Before the invitation was issued, the writer wrote to the heads of the three major Lutheran jurisdictions in Minnesota asking them to endorse this event. The American Lutheran Church and Lutheran Church in America bishops enthusiastically gave their support. But the Rev. Dr. O. H. Cloeter, president of Minnesota District South of the Lutheran Church—Missouri Synod, sent a letter refusing endorsement. He could not support such a "union service."

When the writer saw the name "Cloeter" signed to this missive, he telephoned the Missouri district president to ask, "Could Ottomar E. Cloeter, who was pastor of Holy Cross Lutheran Church in Saginaw in 1853, have been one of your relatives?" "Yes," he replied. "He was my great-great grandfather." The writer found irony in the refusal he had received from the great-great grandson of the pastor who 126 years earlier had earnestly invited the writer's great-great grandparents to leave the Lutheran colonies of Michigan.

Wilhelm Loehe had always kept high on his list of priorities for the Saginaw colonies that the colonies should give witness to the gospel among the Ojibways (Chippewas) of Michigan. As reported in chapter 1 (see **Indian Missions— Loehe's Dream**), for a few years, the handful of Lutherans in the Saginaw colonies did fruitful work among the Ojibways who remained in their area. But as increasing numbers of whites invaded their Michigan homeland, the Ojibways had kept moving westward into northern Minnesota, from which they crowded the Dakotas (Sioux) southward out of the forests onto the Western plains. This had created an ongoing conflict between the Ojibways and the Sioux. In 1821 the U.S. government built Fort Snelling at the confluence of the Minnesota and Mississippi rivers to maintain separation between these warring Native American nations.

Among all the leaders of the Saginaw colonies, none had a greater heart for the Native Americans than Loehe missionary Pr. Ottomar Cloeter. But soon the last of the Ojibways moved beyond his outreach. In 1856 Cloeter left his pastorate at Holy Cross in Saginaw and followed them to northern Minnesota.

He established a mission post at Lake Mille Lacs where the Ojibway have a reservation today. He lived and taught among them until 1858 when he was forced out of the area by a native skirmish from which he barely escaped with his life. His mission station was laid waste. After the Civil War, he served as a missionary to the Indians at Crow Wing, Minnesota. In 1868 Cloeter moved southeast of Saint Paul to rural Afton, Minnesota, where he gathered German immigrant farmers into what became Saint Peter Church, a congregation of the Missouri Synod. He worked there until his death March 17, 1897. He is buried in the St. Peter Cemetery.

APPENDIX IV.

Saint Sebald Home Processing and Cooking

Some understanding of the way of life in the "settlement," as the settlers usually termed their colony, can be caught from their food processing and cooking. Although the settlers came from various German provinces, the recipes and methods brought from each section soon became the common property of all.

These recipes are from the writer's mother's handwritten cookbook. They are representative of much of the cooking that the granddaughters of Johannes Weege Jr. were taught or learned from other colonists, and with which they cooked for their families. The most basic cookbook was stored in their minds. From it they sorted out menus for the next meals while they weeded huge gardens, fed setting hens and baby chicks along with large flocks of laying hens and roosters, by hand helped milk herds of dairy cows night and morning, by hand sewed children's clothing and underwear, laundered with a washboard, mended clothing for the whole family, nursed babies and children with childhood diseases, kept a house and yard, canned hundreds of quarts of fruits and vegetables, processed fresh-killed hogs and cattle, and fermented quantities of home brew and sauerkraut.

Very little of the food supply of those in the settlement was purchased in a store. There were home recipes involved in much of their everyday life. These are representative samples.

Baking

For a family of seven, a housewife baked six large loaves of bread twice a week. On Saturdays she made several pans of cinnamon rolls and coffee cake and often doughnuts, all made from her basic bread dough.

When these ran low and it was not yet the designated day to bake bread, she made **Baking Powder Biscuits**

2 cups flour   2 heaping tsp baking powder
2 tsp lard   ½ tsp salt
Enough milk to make a dough.

This was also the recipe for dumplings cooked with a stew, or anything else that modern cooks create from Bisquick.

Our Springerle (Anise cookies)

6 eggs   3 cups sugar

Stir 1 hour the yolks and sugar. Add 3½ cups flour. Beat whites and stir well together. Add ½ tsp anise seed and as much soda as can be held on point of knife. Baking powder can be substituted. Mix as other cookies. Roll and cut with cookie cutters into Christmas symbols. Let lie over night. Bake next morning. [Ed: Keep in tight container. They dry easily and get hard.]

Georg Weger's Lebkuchen (molasses cookies)

2 cups molasses   ½ c sugar   ¼ cup shortening
3 cups flour   ½ cup nuts   1 tsp cinnamon
½ tsp cloves   1 heaping tsp soda
Grated rind of 1 lemon (or citron)

Heat molasses. Add shortening, spices, and nuts. Stir in flour. When cool, add soda dissolved in a little hot water.

Rhubarb Custard Pie (Sabina Druecker)

Fill an unbaked pie crust level full with raw cut rhubarb. Sprinkle about 1 tsp flour mixed with ½ cup sugar over the rhubarb.

Make a custard by mixing 1/3 cup sugar with 1 tsp cornstarch and adding 2 egg yolks with enough milk to fill the pie. Pour the custard over the rhubarb. Bake in 400 degree over 50-60 minutes.

Use the egg whites for meringue. Add 2 tsp cold water and 2 tsp sugar to whites before beating. Apply and brown in oven.

Braun Pfeffernuesse

2 quarts flour   1 scant pint syrup   1 scant cup sugar
3/4 cups melted butter or lard   tbsp soda in a little milk
2 eggs   ½ tsp cloves   1 tbsp cinnamon

Heat syrup on the stove and add to the rest. Mix well. Knead on bread board. Roll finger thick. Cut in little round forms. Bake slowly.

Spice Cake

1½ cup sugar   1 cup lard   3 eggs Salt
1 cup sour milk with 1 tsp soda
3 cups flour   1 tsp each of cloves, cinnamon, nutmeg
1 tsp lemon flavoring   1 cup raisins   1 cup nuts

Add your beaten egg whites separately at the end.

Other Staples

Potato Noodles

Mix 2-3 eggs with 4 cups mashed potatoes salted to taste. Add 2 cups flour, or as much as it takes to be able to roll finger size noodles 3-5 inches long with flour-covered hands. Lay in baking pan on a bed of pork cracklings or crisp bacon crumbs. Bake one-half hour to set noodles. Pour milk over noodles ¼ inch deep or more. Continue to bake another 1½ hours and keep basting noodles with more milk, but end up with pan baked dry. Noodles should be firm and well-browned. [Ed: They taste even better when leftovers are reheated.]

Kartoffel Kloesse (raw potato dumplings)

Grate potatoes. Squeeze juice out by placing in a cloth and squeezing until quite dry. 3-4 eggs. Couple of handfuls of browned sugar crumbs or cubes. Flour enough to hold up—not too stiff. Will be quite soft when made into 1½ inch balls. Drop in slowly boiling water. Cook one-half hour. Serve with meat and brown gravy. Good with pork roast.

Hosen Bindchen (pants strings)

Make egg noodles ¾ inch wide. Fry until brown in a slow pan. Serve with honey or syrup, or eat unsweetened as a substitute for potatoes.

Preserving Food

Sauerkraut in Jars

Fill fruit jars with chopped cabbage. Add 1 teaspoon salt to each jar. Fill jars with hot water. Cover and set away.

Dill Pickles in Stone Crocks

Place on bottom a layer of grape and cherry leaves and a generous amount of dill. Next a layer of middle sized pickles. Repeat layers till jar is full. Take 8 parts water and 1 part salt. Boil, cool, pour into crock until contents are covered. Put a weighted board on cucumbers. After three days, pour off liquid and boil it once more. Cool. Pour back on. Let stand until sour.

Mustard Pickles

Fill 2-quart jar half full vinegar. Add 2 tbsp salt, 4 tbsp sugar, 1 tbsp mustard. Drop in pickles until full.

Curing Meat

Hilda's Meat Brine (Mrs. Georg Nodurft's)

For curing meat.

For each 100 lbs. of meat, take 10 lbs. salt, 3 lbs. brown sugar, 3 tbsp salt petre, water to cover meat. Boil and cool over night.

To Can Sausage in Casings

Put sausages in fruit jars. Add to jars brine made of 1 cup salt and 1 cup sugar to 1 gallon of water. Don't fill jars quite full. Cook 1 hour or more. Brine is enough for 12-14 quarts.

Smoked Salt Brine Cure

Add 4½ gallons hot water to 9-10 lbs. smoked salt. Cool overnight at outdoor temperature. Pour over your meat in a ten-gallon crock. During the next eight weeks, remove the pieces once in a while and shift them around. Hang up and let drip dry. Finish drying in a warm room till a nice brown.

Preparing Meat

Liver Sausage

This item was produced at hog-butchering time. The liver of the animal was eaten first, and one of the ways of getting variety while this quantity of liver was being consumed was this sausage.

Take equal parts of cooked pork and cooked liver. Grind and season it with salt, pepper, and little cloves or allspice, if you like it. Steam in a pan with a little water.

Baked Ham Slice

Cut a slice 3 inches thick from the center of ham. Trim, leaving some fat. Rub both sides with a mix of 2 teaspoons dry mustard and 3 teaspoons sugar. Put in drip pan and cover ham with 1 quart of milk. Bake slowly 2½ hours. Baste often and keep adding enough milk so ham stays covered.

For the Household

Soap

Butchering took place in the winter to take advantage of nature's freezer, a large wooden box placed outside the house where fresh meat could be kept and enjoyed, in contrast to preserved meats such as smoked hams and canned pork and beef that were consumed in warm weather, when the only source of fresh meat was to kill a chicken.

After butchering hogs, there were mounds of pork fat to render into lard, leaving a succulent by product called "cracklings, the residue left when the melted lard was poured from the kettle. Cracklings were necessary ingredients for some tasty dishes, especially potato noodles. But much could not be eaten by reason of its volume.

The uneaten cracklings were collected through the winter as the chief contribution to a batch of soap, cooked at the end of the butchering season in early spring, usually in the big iron kettle used to scald the hair off freshly killed hogs.

To 60 lbs. of scraps (cracklings), we take 2½ (14-quart) pails of rain water [there were no water softeners] and add 20 cans of lye. Cook about one to 1½ hours until grainy and beginning to thicken. If it threatens to boil over, add more water.

Tried taking 21 cans of lye to 80 lbs. of grease and got real good soap.

The soap rose to the top of the kettle, forming a layer four or five inches thick. This was cut with a knife into bars weighing about one-half pound each.

To Remove Old Paint and Varnish

Boil 1 quart laundry starch thick like cream. Add 4 tbsp lye. Brush on wood and leave a few minutes. Scrape with putty knife. Rinse with ½ cup vinegar and 1/3 cup water.

Water Softener for Washing Clothes

1 can lye, 10 cent bottle of ammonia in 3 gallons of water. Use one half cup for each batch of clothes.

Beer

5½ gallons water   4 ½ cups sugar
1 can of malt (about 2 quarts in size)

Add your malt to about 1 gallon of water and bring to a boil, stirring often.

Pour the malt mix into the rest of the water in the crock and add the sugar and 1½ cakes compressed yeast dissolved in a little warm water. Let beer stand a couple of days or until through fermenting. Skim every day. Bottle and cap. Makes 2 dozen quarts.

For the Animals

Feed for Laying Hens

A little calcium carbonate sprinkled on top of chicken mash for a few days will harden eggs' shells so hens won't break them.

Horse Colic

2 tbsp ginger   1 tbsp soda   1 quart water.

Push in horse's mouth in quart beer bottle. Repeat every half hour.

APPENDIX V.

Constitution of the
Evangelical Lutheran Congregation of Frankenhilf

Translated by Hertha and Philip Wood; edited by Albert L. Hock

I. Concerning the Confessional Teachings

1. We profess the Lutheran Book of Concord of 1580 and all the confessional articles contained therein. In addition, we obligate ourselves to the Lutheran Church. We pledge to it our selves, our congregation and school, and our ministers and teachers without reservation.

2. Our pastors and school teachers vow to teach according to the Book of Concord of 1580 in all its articles of Christian doctrine and ethics. They do this because of their convictions that the Concord in all its articles truly teaches God's Word. This conviction is professed in the pastors' ordination vows and at their installation. This commitment is also made by the school teachers and cantors.

3. Our pastors and school teachers preach and teach in German without exception. German is and will remain the language we are required to use. Our school teachers are obligated to this as well.

II. Concerning the Calling of Pastors and Teachers

4. If our pastorate becomes vacant, we will appeal through our church leaders to the ministerium (president or bishop and staff) of a Lutheran Synod to nominate a pastor for interim service or, depending on circumstances, to the nearest Lutheran parish, requesting it to share its pastor with us.

5. If, when the pastorate is vacant, the congregation has confidence in some candidate or pastor known to them, it may ask that this person be nominated for call to our parish and trust that these wishes will if possible be taken into consideration.

6. If the congregation has no choices to express, the ministerium will propose to the congregation a man who is confessionally true and appropriate for this congregation. In the final case, the elders and other leaders of the congregation will choose among the proposed candidates and issue a call. In the first case, the congregation will listen to the ministerium should they have wishes to express or wish to nominate a godly man.

[Margin note by Pastor Johannes Deindoerfer: "This paragraph shall not make the call procedure a matter of controversy. Church governance procedures are not dogma."]

7. The pastoral call will be sent by the president of the synod with the cosignature of the church council through the officer charged with this task.

8. At the installation the person who has been called must give assurance of his subscription to the confessions of the Church before the assembled congregation.

9. The installation occurs whenever possible in the assembled congregation.

10. The document for calling and ordaining of the pastor will require subscription to the confessions of the Church over the pastor's signature.

11. If the congregation has more than one pastor, the same process for call shall be adhered to for each pastoral position, with the additional requirement that both pastors be in agreement concerning the office of the ministry.

12. When a church or school staff position is vacant, the pastor(s) of the congregation are authorized to select, call and install a godly man, subject to the considerations or express wishes of the congregation and the qualifications required for that office.

III. Concerning the Dismissal of Pastors and Teachers

13. The congregation cannot unseat or remove a pastor or other servant of the church without consultation with the ministerium.

14. In such cases the ministerium will immediately conduct an investigation into the worthiness and diligence of the accused and into whether he has performed his duties according to the standards expected of pastors.

15. Inasmuch as the congregation and its children may endure great damage from an unworthy and unfaithful pastor without complaint, the ministerium is obliged to conduct unrequested visitations in the congregation. If a servant of the church is found to be at fault, he is to be confronted through the steps for admonition according to Matthew 18, and if application of these steps to the unrepentant servant of the church is unavailing, the ministerium is obliged to dismiss him immediately from his office.

16. Should the congregation not be in agreement with this judgment of the ministerium, it may appeal the decision to another ministerium of the true faith. The church servant will remain suspended from his office until the subsequent decision

17. When proceeding to remove members of the church staff or teachers of the school, the pastor of the congregation will follow the basic rules just described for the presiding and visiting ministerium.

IV. Concerning the Salaries of Church Servants

18. The income from the Pfarrgute [land dedicated for support of the clergy] plus all the perquisites and rights of the pastorate belong to the pastor from the day of his installation in the position. Income from the Pfarrgute may also be used for the salaries of other church staff and parish school teachers.

19. During a pastoral vacancy income from the Pfarrgute may be directed to founding a pastors' widows and orphans fund in the congregation. The ministerium will see to it that this fund is properly administered and at the vacancy of the parish will immediately appoint a reliable member of the congregation and a neighboring pastor to this task and place the strongest importance on correct accounting of this fund.

20. Perquisites received during a vacancy will belong to the interim staff whom the congregation will compensate for travel costs and food at rates commonly expected in the region.

21. Funds budgeted for lower church or school staff positions that are unspent during vacancies belong to the general treasury of the church but may also be paid to appointed substitutes by decision of the ministerium.

22. Perquisites will be received only to pay what is due for rites that benefit a single person or such appropriate services as are provided. In regard to this the congregation is to be taught so as to avoid the delusion that the beneficiaries of these rites and services are paying for the grace of God.

23. Perquisites are to be paid based on guidelines set by the pastor and congregation for all the church staff.

24. The congregation will help the pastors and school teachers with moving costs and labor in so far as it is able.

V. Concerning the Kirchengute
(land dedicated to the support of the church)

25. Settlers will set aside at least a dollar from every 2,000 gulden that remain after payment of their travel costs for the purchases of the Pfarrgute and the Kirchengute.

26. The poorest should be permitted, instead of setting aside money, to clear as much land for the Kirchengute or the Pfarrgute as is necessary to reach a monetary equivalent of at least two days labor.

27. If possible, the Kirchengute [church land] should be an undivided tract.

28. The Sunday offering in the Klingelbeutel [bell sack—a sack on the end of a pole] is designated for local expenses (not benevolence).

29. Income from the Kirchengute [church land] will be used to make up any deficit in the free-will offerings needed to pay current expenses. These expenses include the cost of caring for the church, God's Acre, parsonage upkeep and utilities, the cemetery, the sacristy, and the school house.

30. Any surplus from the Kirchengute and Pfarrgute will be available for the poor in the congregation.

31. The Kirchengute will be under the custody of the pastor.

32. The church's funds and its properties will be supervised by men elected for this purpose. The pastor will chair a group of godly and capable men to constitute the church council.

33. Anyone who is lukewarm or who is not above reproach in his conduct will not be nominated by the pastor as his assistant or to the church council.

34. An even number of men will be elected to the church council so that the pastor's vote may break any ties.

35. Auditing of the church records shall be done by the ministerium.

VI. Concerning the Pfarrgute

36. Half of the money set aside by the settlers (see item 25 concerning the Kirchengute land) will used to purchase the Pfarrgute (land dedicated for the support of the clergy). The Pfarrgute can be expanded through free-will transfer of land and capital, through legacies and gifts.

37. The Pfarrgute will be administered by the pastor, since he is the chief beneficiary of its income.

VII. Concerning Visitations

38. The ministerium (president or bishop and staff of the synod) will conduct a visitation in the congregation annually.

39. The visitor will examine the governance of the Kirchengute and the Pffarrgute, the church records, Communion registrations, the teaching and conduct of the pastor and other church servants and school teachers, the church services and liturgies, the cleanliness and appointments of the sanctuary, in short, everything concerning the church's life and conduct.

40. During the visitation order and propriety should be observed, any steps of admonition should be conducted, and excommunications should be resolved.

VIII. Concerning Excommunication and Public Absolution

41. Open and unrepentant sinners will be excommunicated (that is, excluded from the congregation) if they remain unrepentant after the first, second and third admonistions.

42. The third degree of admonition occurs in an open meeting of the pastor and congregation. Matthew 18.

43. An excommunication is declared by the pastor in the midst of the congregation.

44. In every case of excommunication the pastors may take the steps of excommunication and absolution in consultation with the next neighboring congregation (seeking its support to uphold the ban).

45. A person who has been excommunicated may not hold membership in any congregation or any church position.

46. A person who has been excommunicated may be present at the worship service through the sermon, but not at the celebration of the sacraments. He may not serve as sponsor at a baptism or as a witness at a church wedding. Should he die while under the ban, he may not receive a church burial.

47. Ecommuncation ends with the express contrition of the excommunicated person, an open request for forgiveness, and an open absolution from the lips of the pastor.

IX. Concerning Marital Matters

48. No member of our congregation may conclude a mixed marriage.

49. No one may marry a person forbidden under Leviticus 18 and 20. We do not extend, however, this prohibition to analogous legal degrees of relationship that do not include relationships by birth.

50. We do not give any validity to secret engagements agreed to without the prior knowledge of parents and guardians.

51. We expect the children of all marriages celebrated in this congregation to be brought up in the Christian faith as it is confessed by the Lutheran Church.

52. This congregation teaches that there is only one ground for divorce, namely, adultery.

53. We do not grant membership in this congregation to persons who have been divorced unless they demonstrate open and sincere repentance and seek, if possible,

to undo this mistake.

54. Divorced persons whose separation is the result of their faulty behavior may not remarry.

55. It is the responsibility of any man who tempts a virgin to fornication to offer to take her for his wife. Exodus 22:16, Deuteronomy 22:28-29.

X. Concerning the Order of Church Servces

56. Our church services are conducted according to the order in J. K. Wilhelm Loehe's *Agenda*.

57. Emergency Baptisms may be conducted by midwives in extreme cases. Where possible, the pastor will be called to perform this sacrament. If neither of these can be reached, a Christian man of integrity may baptize.

58. All persons making private confession should call on their confessor one or two days before receiving the Sacrament of Holy Communion.

59. It is left to each person according to his or her needs to choose general or private confession.

60. Our pastor enjoys the Sacred Supper with us and receives it from his own hand. Absolution or other blessings that he needs as one

who is commissioned to care for souls are communicated to him by his confessor orally or, if necessary, in writing.

61. We do not offer the Holy Communion to strangers with the exception of last rites (Communion of the Sick).

62. We host marriages and funerals.

63. With prior notification and supervision of our pastors, members of our congregation may gather whenever they wish to sing, read and pray.

64. On Sunday we voluntarily abstain from all worldly work that is not required by necessity and love.

XI. Concerning the School

65. Parents encourage the teaching and care of their children and will do what is necessary to support this work.

66. Parents will be assisted by the school in their efforts to teach and care for their children.

XII. Concerning Admission into the Congregation

67. If someone wishes to be accepted into our congregation, he or she should notify our pastor. The order for admission occurs in the open meeting of our pastor and congregation.

68. Unless there are prior tests and probationary periods, only those persons may be admitted who can supply satisfactory witness concerning their confession of faith and their behavior from a recognized Lutheran, that is, a right-believing, soul-caring person or a person known to us as a confessionally true Christian, irreproachable in his or her behavior.

If the Lord Jesus should wish us to exclude an open and unrepentant sinner from our congregation, then refusal of admission would serve as a warning to the sinner of his or her need to repent.

69. Any applicants who cannot bring the afore-mentioned witness or who are not known to us well enough as confessionally true and irreproachable in their behavior as serious Christians will be examined concerning their confession and past behavior.

70. If it is determined by this examination that the person who is requesting admission is in accord with us concerning faith and confession and has adequately demonstrated this, it will be recommended that he or she be given a period of time for proof of earnestness of

confession and behavior under the supervision of the congregation. By this he or she will have opportunity to learn to know exactly the church and its services. We will also learn by this time, so far as normal people can determine it, if he or she is truly serious in confession and behavior. If one should appear to be lax and indifferent, or even an open and unrepentant sinner, we cannot admit this person until he or she proves otherwise.

71. It it comes to light during this examination, however, that the person requesting membership does not yet have a proper understanding of what is true or false belief but has a proper hunger for truth and church community, our pastor is ready to take him or her into a special time of catechesis. The period of catechesis will be concurrent with his or her probationary period.

72. The probationary period cannot as a rule be less than six weeks.

Signed:

J. Deindoerfer, Pffar.   C. Glave

Carl Gottlob Amman   j. G. Kamm

Michael Schwarz   L. Sippel

Heinrich Dahl   J. Schwab

Paulus Popp   Georg Bauer

BIBLIOGRAPHY

1. "Wilhelm Loehe and Wartburg Theological Seminary, 1972 the 100th Anniversary of His Death," lecture by Gerhard Ottersberg.
2. *George M. Grossmann, Wartburg's Founder and First President,* by J. W. Lynes and Pastor Sigmund H. Sandrock.
3. *The Brothers Fritschel,* by Gerhard Ottersberg, published by Wartburg College.
4. *Wartburg College 1852-1952,* by Gerhard Ottersberg, Waverly Publishing Co., 1952.
5. *Protokol Buch* (minutes book) *der Evang. Luth. Gemeinde zu St. Sebald, Iowa, 1865-1926.*
6. *Kirchenbuch* (church book) *die Evang. Luth. Gemeinde, St. Sebald, 1855-1874.*
7. *Kirchenbuch fuer die Predigplatze bei St. Sebald, 1891-1915.*
8. *Tauf* (Baptism) *Register fuer die Pfarei St. Sebald, Iowa, 1872-1941.*
9. *Confirmanden* (confirmation) *Register fuer die Pfarei St. Sebald, Iowa, 1872-1971.*
10. *Trau* (marriage) *Register fuer die Pfarei St. Sebald, Iowa, 1872-1971.*
11. *Sterb* (death) *Register fuer die Pfarei St. Sebald, Iowa, 1872-1985.*
12. *Protokol Buch des Frauenvereins* (minutes of the Ladies Society) *der Ev. Luth. St. Sebaldus Gemeinde, St. Sebald, Iowa,* volumes 1919-1932, 1934-1940, 1941-1952.
13. *Wartburg Kalendar der Ev. Luth. Synode von Iowa und andern Staaten fuer das Jahr unseres Herrn 1920,* Wartburg Publishing House, Chicago.
14. Saint Sebald Cemetery Records.
15. *Our Centennial,* St. Sebald Lutheran Church, 1953.
17. *The Origin of St. Sebald,* by Roger L. Buhr 1967.
18. *Aus den Tagen der Vaeter* (In the Days of the Fathers) *Stories of the Beginnings of the Iowa Synod,* by George J. Fritschel. Translated from the German language by Herbert M. Prottengeier.
19. *Quellen und Documente* (Sources and Documents), George J. Fritschel.
20. *Geschichte der Iowa Synode* by Johannes Deindoerfer, Wartburg Publishing House.
21. "St. Sebald's Historic and High Quality Pipe Organ," essay by David Harold Andreae.
22. *So I Send You, A Bi-Centennial Event Commemorating Wartburg Seminary at Seminary Hill,* Commemoration Committee of Clayton County Area Ministry, September 12, 1976, Griffith Press, Inc., Elkader, Iowa.

23. *Frankenhilf, 150 Years of Heritage,* 1851-2001, St. Michael's Lutheran Church, Richville, Michigan.

24. *125th Year Wartburg Seminary Calendar 1979.*

25. *History of Clayton County, Iowa, Schools and Sperry Township Schools* by Clayton County Genealogical Society, Elkader, Iowa, 1988.

26. *1854-1929 A Missionary Synod with a Mission,* by G. J. Zeilinger, Wartburg Publishing House, Chicago, 1929.

27. *History of the Lutheran Church in America,* by J. L. Neve, 1934, Willard D. Allbeck.

28. *The Encyclopedia of the Lutheran Church,* three volumes, edited by Julius Bodensieck, Augsburg Publishing House.

29. *Lutheran Cyclopedia,* edited by Erwin L. Lueker, Concordia Publishing House, Saint Louis, 1954.

30. "The Gospel and the Crisis of Authority," essay by Carl E. Braaten, *dialog* 31 (Fall 1992): 302-310.

31. "Law and Gospel: Essential Proprium or Embarrassing Peculiarity?" essay by Richard J. Niebanck, *Lutheran Forum* 29, no. 4 (1995): 45.

32. "Evangelical Authority," essay by Paul R. Hinlicky, *Lutheran Forum* 27, no. 4 (1993): 58-62.

33. "Wilhelm Loehe and the Rediscovery of the Sacrament of the Altar in Nineteenth Century Lutheranism," essay by Russell John Briese, *Lutheran Forum* 30, no. 2: 31-34.

34. "Thinking About History: The Missouri Compromise," essay by Mary Todd, *Lutheran Forum* (Christmas 1997): 43-46.

35. "While We're At It," columns by Richard John Neuhaus, *FIRST THINGS,* no. 58 (December 1995): 74, and no. 59 (January 1996): 74 and 75.

36. *The Golden Threads* I (1983), II (1984), III (1986), by William G. Weger, Central Publishing Company, Inc., Indianapolis.

37. *1800-1968 Mauer Schmidt Eppler* by Verne Mauer, Dubuque, Iowa.

38. *History of the Ojibway People* by William W. Warren, Minnesota Historical Society Press, Saint Paul, 1984.

39. *The Nodurft—Nodorft Family Tree* 40.

40. *Prottengeier-Koeberle Family Tree* by Herbert M. Prottengeier, Flint, Michigan, 1964.

41. *Family History of the Schuchmann Family 1939 and Updates.*

42. *Family History of Carl Baumgartner of Goldap, East Prussia, Including Austrian Ancestors Exiled from Salzburg Province in 1732 and Maria Helena Weege of St. Sebald, Iowa,* by Magdalyn Baumgaertner Akre, published by the author at Deer Hill—Hoodsport, Washington, 1983-1993.

43. *Kirchenordnung der evangel. lutherisch. Gemeinde Frankenhilf.*

44. *Concordia Historical Institute Quarterly* XLV, no. 2 (May 1972).

45. "Wilhelm Loehe and the Missouri Synod" by James L. Schaaf, *Concordia Historical Institute Quarterly* XLV, no. 2 (May 1972): 53-67.

46. "The Ecclesial Vision of Wilhelm Loehe" by David C. Radke, *Lutheran Forum,* Una Sancta (Fall 1999): 29-33.

47. *Life Together at Wartburg Theological Seminary,* by William H. Weiblen, Union Hoermann Press, Dubuque, Iowa.

48. *Kirchliche Zeitschrift 1876-1943, Reu Memorial Number.*

49 *Tomahawk and Cross, Lutheran Missionaries among the Northern Plains Tribes 1858-1866*, by Gerhard M. Schmutterer, Pine Hill Press, Freeman, South Dakota.

50. *Don't Eat Yourself Full—There's Pie Back Yet*, by Albert L. Hock.

51. *Wartburg Luther League* (of Strawberry Point) *Cook Book*, Arlington Printing Co., Arlington, Iowa, 1923.

52. *The Book of Concord*, translated and edited by Theodore G. Tappert, Fortress Press.

53. *Ebenezer*, edited by Professor William Hermann Theodore Dau, a review of the work of the Missouri Synod 1847-1922, Concordia Publishing House, Saint Louis, 1922.

54. *The Church of the Lutheran Reformation*, by Conrad Bergendoff, Concordia Publishing House, Saint Louis, 1967.

55. *My Past and Day Book*—1866, Maria Hoeger, Archives of The American Lutheran Church.

56. *The Lutheran Church in Papua New Guinea 1886-1986*, edited by Herwig Wagner and Hermann Reiner, Lutheran Publishing House, Adelaide

ENDNOTES

Foreword and Appreciation

1. Translated by Delvin E. Ressel in *Una Sancta* X, no. 2 (1951), from *Gesammelte Werke* 3, reprinted in *Lutheran Forum (UNA SANCTA)*, (Fall 1997), p. 12.

2. Johannes Konrad Wilhelm Loehe, *Kirchliche Mittheilungen aus und Ueber Nord-Amerika* XI (1853), col. 92.

1. The Apostle to America

3. "The Ecclesial Mission of Wilhelm Loehe," David Ratke, *Lutheran Forum*, Una Sancta (fall issue), 1999.

4. *Lutheran Cyclopedia*. (Concordia Publishing House, 1954) p. 589.

5. *A Missionary Synod with a Mission* (Chicago:Wartburg Publishing House), p. 8, published in 1929 as a memoir for the 75th anniversary of the Iowa Synod.

6. Russell John Briese, "Wilhelm Loehe and the Rediscovery of the Sacrament of the Altar in Nineteenth Century Lutheranism, *Lutheran Forum* 2, (May 1996) : 31.

7. *Aus den Tagen Der Vaeter (In the Days of the Forefathers)*, 186-187. Manuscript of translation by Herbert M. Prottengeier.

8. *Die Noth der deutschen Lutheraner in NordAmerika* as translated in *Moving Frontiers*, Carl S. Meyer ed.

9. Quoted by James L. Schaaf in the *Concordia Historical Institute Quarterly* XLV, 2 (May 1972): 57-58, from Loehe to Ernst, February 3, 1845, Loehe Archives 585.

10. Metzger had been a missionary in Africa and had married an African. Schmid remarked that Germans could not ever understand how Americans treated Negroes.

2. Establishing a Seminary and a Synod in America

11. *Lutheran Forum*, Christmas 1997, p. 44.

12. *Ebenezer*, 146, a collection of historical essays written for the seventy-fifth anniversary of the Missouri Synod, edited by William Hermann Theodore Dau, professor at Concordia Seminary, Saint Louis, and editor of *Lutheran Witness*.

13. Quoted by Schaaf , p. 60, Loehe to L.A. Petri, December 16, 1847, Loehe Archives 6594a.

14. Ibid., Loehe to Walther, September 8, 1847, Loehe Archives 7302.

15. *Ebenezer*, p. 164.

16. *dialog* 7 (spring 1998), 140.

17. Some of the more liberal elements of Ohio reacted to this development by separating into the Wittenberg Synod (1847) and the first and second and third English Districts that successively formed synods and joined the liberal General Synod. Their complaints included Ohio's lack of zeal in adopting English, acceptance of lodge members, and openness to fellowship with non-Lutheran bodies.

18. This institution was sometimes called Missouri's "practical seminary" as distinct from the academic/traditional/theological seminary at Saint Louis. The purpose of the "practical" school was to train more mature men with an abbreviated course of study.

19. "The Predestination Controversy," *Ebenezer*, p. 407.

20. *The Apology of the Augsburg Confession*, Article XIII, "The Number and Use of the Sacraments."

21. Karl H. Wyneken, *Concordia Historical Institute Quarterly* XLV, no. 2 (May 1972): 76.

22. Ibid., 77

3. Frankenhilf

23. Amman to family, June 16, 1850. Archives of the Evangelical Lutheran Church in America, Wartburg Theological Seminary, Dubuque, Iowa.

4. The Beginnings of Wartburg Seminary and Wartburg College

5. The Frankenhilf Colony Takes Root

24. Gerhard Ottersberg. *Wartburg College 1852-1952* (Waverly, IA: Waverly Publishing Co., 1952), p. 15.

6. The Doctrine Of The Ministry

25. Richard John Neuhaus, *Pro Ecclesia* V, no. 1: 45.

26. John Hannah, *Forum Letters* 25, no. 9, (February 1992): 3.

27. Jaroslav Pelikan has recently entered the Orthodox Church.

28. An example of the trauma suffered by some pastors was Pr. Chr. B. Hochstetter, an assistant to Grabau, who served on Buffalo's team in the debate with Missouri. During the 1866 colloquium between Buffalo and Missouri, Hochstetter changed sides and then led the secession of pastors from Buffalo to Missouri.

29. Grabau very early transferred some of his congregations in Michigan and Ohio to the Michigan Synod. Some of these later joined the Ohio Synod, but most affiliated with the Wisconsin Synod.

7. What Is The Preaching Office?

8. Frankenhilf's Future—with Loehe or Synod?

30. Fritschel, Aus den Tagen der Vaeter, p. 13ff.

31. Ibid., 23ff.

9. The Tension Grows

32. In 1855 Wyneken wrote, "There is fire in the congregations, at least among those directly stirred up and stimulated. In the congregations pastors preached what is said about the pastoral call as part of the counsel of God, as well as about counter teachings. The quarrel itself was handled in the frequent congregational meetings.

At home and in the chamber, it was the subject of conversation. They brought it before the Lord with sobbing and pleading. Naturally the Franken colonies, because of their relation to Pastor Loehe are particularly interested. When he asserts that the question is still an open one for him and therefore he would not stand in opposition to us, one might ask him first, 'If you have not decided about the matter, why do you act as if it were settled, while at the same time you require of us who have long ago made our decision, that we should act as though it were not decided?'" *Aus den Tagen der Vaeter, 34.*

33. The writer is a descendant of Karl Gottlob Amman and of Johannes Weege Jr. See Appendix IV, page

34. A bit of ecclesiastical confusion existed on the part of both Cloeter and Grossmann in this matter because church practices that are followed today had not yet been clarified. Today, the fact that Cloeter assumed authority to place Grossmann under discipline would indicate that Grossmann was a member of Holy Cross Church and by virtue of that membership also a member of the Missouri Synod. At that time, in spite of its congregationalism, the Missouri Synod's clergy seem to be independent of the congregations.

35. Fritschel, *Aus den Tagen der Vaeter,* p. 37 ff.

36. Ibid., p. 39ff.

37. Ibid., p. 39.

38. If Walther agreed with this, he perhaps later modified his position when he wrote, "We do not mean to indicate that we are among those who believe that their understanding requires no development or correction. It is rather our serious endeavor to make progress in the recognition of the truth, and with the help of God, to free ourselves more and more from the errors which still cling to us....People thought that after withdrawing from the left there was no possibility of erring in the other direction. Thus it came to pass that no one departed further from true Lutheranism than those who wanted to be the strictest Lutherans." (Undocumented quote by Marie Meyer in the *Lutheran Forum* (Spring 1997): 41.)

39. Fritschel, *Aus den Tagen der Vaeter,* 41.

10. The Frankenhilf Schism

40. Ibid., p.42 ff.

41. J. L. Neve, *History of the Lutheran Church in America* (Willard D. Allbeck. 1934), p. 203.

42. *Proceedings of the Missouri Synod 1932,* pp. 154-155.

43. Loehe, *Kirchliche Mittheilungen aus den Ueber Nordaamerika* XI (1853), col.92.

44. Loehe to Petri, January 21, 1954, Loehe Archives 6603a.

45. C. F.W. Walther, *Der Lutheraner* VIII (February 17, 1852).

46. James L. Schaff, *Concordia Historical Quarterly* XLV, no. 2 (May 1972): 66.

47. Fritschel, *Aus den Tagen der Vaeter,* p. 112, "The untruth of the statement that Deindoerfer ran away is entirely refuted by the minutes [see chapter 10, The Frankenhilf Schism]. The correction of the distortions is printed in *Quellen un Dokumente,* pages 163-169."

11. The Pilgrimage to Iowa

12. The Planting Of Saint Sebald

48. G. J. Zeilinger, *A Missionary Synod with a Mission* (Chicago: Wartburg Publishing House 1929), preface.

13. The Seminary Begins Again

14. The Founding of the Iowa Synod

49. Peter Kleinlein was a passenger who Fritschel had pastored on the voyage from Germany and on the trip to Dubuque. A wealthy man, he was about to establish the Kleinlein industries at the Saint Sebald colony [see chapter 29].

50. Zeilinger, *A Missionary Synod,* p. 6.

51. Herbert M. Prottengeier appended this comment to his translation of George Fritschel's *Aus den Tagen der Vaeter.* "At the time of the founding of the Iowa Synod, there had arisen in the General Synod in the east what Dr. F. Bente calls 'a Lutheranism greatly modified by American puritanism and American Methodism.' Dr. A. R. Wentz, another well-known historian, said, 'Their main contention was that the Lutheran Church can have a national development on American soil only by adjusting itself to its environment. By this they meant that the Lutheran Church in America must make wide concessions to the revivalistic and puritanic spirit of surrounding denominations.' According to the *Lutheran Cyclopedia of 1899,* 'They [the General Synod] rejected all Symbolical Books [Lutheran Confessions] except the Augsburg Confession.'" (p. 63)

15. The New Synod in Mission

52. Fritschel, *Aus den Tagen der Vaeter,* pp. 142-148.

53. Ibid., pp. 153-160.

54. *Quellen un Documente,* 224.

55. Ibid., 223.

56. William H. Weiblen, *Life Together at Wartburg Theological Seminary* (Dubuque, IA: Union Hoermann Press, 1990), p. 9

57. Fritschel, *Aus den Tagen der Vaeter,* pp. 162-172.

58. Ibid., pp. 172-176.

16. The Seminary Rejoins the Colony

59. Ibid., pp. 176-183

17. Life at the Wartburg

60. Ibid., pp. 183-189.

61. Zeilinger, *A Missionary Synod,* p. 30.

62. Ibid., p. 49.

63. Ibid., pp. 30-31.

18. The Missions to the Indians

64. Gerhard M. Schmutterer and Charles P. Lutz, *Church Roots—Mission Martyr on the Western Frontier* (Minneapolis: Augsburg Publishing House, 1985), p. 132.

65. Ibid., p. 134.

66. Ibid., pp. 134-135.

67. Ibid., p. 137.

68. Ibid., p. 137.

69. Zeilinger, *A Missionary Synod,* p. 38.

70. Schmutter and Lutz, *Church Roots,* pp. 140-141.

71. After the seminary was moved from Saint Sebald and the property was sold to Ludvig Schmidt, one of the Fritschel homes became the Ludvig Schmidt home.

72. Carl Schmidt (grandson of Andreas Schmidt, who worked the seminary farm, and son of Ludvig Schmidt, who purchased the farm when the seminary was moved to Mendota) remembers that as a child he often found lead type from the printery that rain washed out of the earth.

19. Iowa-Missouri Colloquy Number One

73. Johannes Deindoerfer, *Geschichte der Iowa Synode* (Chicago: Wartburg Publishing House), p. 128.

20. Wartburg College at Galena

74. Gerhardt Ottersburg, *Wartburg College, 1852-1952: A Centennial History* (Waverly Publishing Co., 1952), pp. 30-31

75. Ibid., p. 34.

76. Ibid., p. 31.

77. Ibid., p. 31.

78. Ibid., p. 33.

79. Ibid., p. 33.

80. Ibid., p. 34.

81. Ibid., p. 34-35.

82. Ibid., p. 35.

21. Wartburg Seminary Moves to Mendota

83. For seventeen years, the Strawberry Point community, which was still without a high school, had been virtually untouched by the presence of the Wartburg educational institutions that were teaching on high school, college, and postgraduate levels only five miles away. The wall that separated the Wartburg "castle" from the community was its German language instruction. No graduates of Clayton County public schools ever enrolled at this institution of higher learning while it was located there. But after Wartburg College and Wartburg Seminary moved away from Saint Sebald and adopted English, four youths from the Saint Sebald congregation prepared in their classrooms for the ministry of the gospel and dozens more for other careers.

84. Iowa's view became generally accepted in other Lutheran synods and eventually by many in the Missouri Synod, some of whom broke away in the 1970s and joined the Evangelical Lutheran Church in America in 1988.

85. *The Encyclopedia of the Lutheran Church* I (Minneapolis: Augsburg Publishing House), p. 45.

86. Deindoerfer, *Geschichte der Iowa Synode*.

87. Zeilinger, *A Missionary Synod*, p. 44; Deindoerfer, *Geschichte der Iowa Synode*, pp. 132-148.

88. Zeilinger, *A Missionary Synod*, p. 48.

89. Deindoerfer, *Geschichte der Iowa Synode*, p. 219.

90. *Ebenezer*, p. 166.

91. Ibid., p. 169.

92. J. L. Neve, *History of the Lutheran Church in America* (The Lutheran Literary Board, Willard D. Albeck, 1934), p. 202.

22. Iowa and the Eastern Synods

23. The Predestination Controversy

93. Neve, *History of the Lutheran Church in America,* p. 207

94. Report of Missouri's Western District, 1877.

95. Neve, *History of the Lutheran Church in America,* p. 208.

96. Deindoerfer, *Geschichte der Iowa Synode.*

97. *Ebenezer,* pp. 172-173.

24. The Merger of the Iowa, Ohio and Buffalo Synods

98. Minutes of the Ohio and Iowa Synods.

25. The College(s) at Mendota, Andrew, Clinton, and Waverly

99. Ottersberg, *Wartburg College 1852–1952,* p. 39.

100. Ibid.

101. Ibid.

102. Ibid., p. 41.

103. Ibid., p. 43.

104. Ibid., p. 44.

105. Ibid.

106. Ibid., p. 45.

107. Ibid., p. 45-46

108. Ibid., p. 46.

109. Ibid., p. 48.

110. Ibid., p. 46.

111. Ibid., p. 49.

112. Ibid.

113. Ibid., p. 49-50.

114. Ibid., p. 50.

115. Ibid.

116. Ibid., p. 51.

117. Ibid.

118. Ibid., p. 52.

119. Ibid.

120. Ibid., p. 53.

121. Ibid., p. 54.

122. Ibid.

123. Ibid.

124. Ibid., p. 55.

125. Ibid., p. 56.

126. Ibid., p. 57.

127. Ibid.

128. Ibid., p. 59.

129. Ibid., p. 75.

130. Ibid., p. 77.

131. Ibid., p. 77-78.

132. Ibid., p. 77.

133. Ibid., p. 78-79.

134. Ibid., p. 79.

26. Wartburg Theological Seminary Moves Back to Dubuque

137. Weiblen, *Life Together at Wartburg Theological Seminary*, pp. 16-17.

138. Ibid., p. 17.

139. Ibid., pp. 21-23.

140. Ibid., p. 18.

141. Ibid., p. 30.

27. Era of the Rev. Dr. Johann Michael Reu

142 John H. Becker, "The Genius of Wartburg Seminary," *Kirchliche Zeitschrift*, Reu Memorial Number: 63.

143. A. Pilger, *Kirchlische Zeitschrift*, Reu Memorial Number: 24.

144. Ibid., p. 40.

145. Becker, *Kirchliche Zeitschrift*: 68).

28. Life in the Saint Sebald

146. Zeilinger, *A Missionary Synod*, p. 97.

147. *Volga City, IA* (Clayton County Genealogical Society), p. 485.

148. Ibid., p. 184.

149. Ibid.

150. As told by Pr. Diemer's nephew Pr. Theo H. Judt.